The Cotswolds

WITH OXFORD
& STRATFORD-UPON-AVON

About the author

Damian Hall is a freelance outdoor journalist who grew up in the hilly mill town of Nailsworth. He went to school in Stroud and Gloucester, and as a student sold ice creams on Minchinhampton Common. But he didn't think much to the Cotswolds when young because they didn't have any good football teams and Radiohead never played there.

He went travelling and lived in a much hotter country long enough to earn a passport. Yet when time came to settle down the hillbilly came back to the Cotswolds, where he now lives with his wife, daughter, a small soft spot for Forest Green Rovers and a large gooey spot for blustery walks along the glorious limestone Edge.

He contributes regularly to *Country Walking* and *Outdoor Fitness*, and his books include *Walking In The Cotswolds*, *Somerset Coast Path* and the official *Pennine Way* National Trail guide.

Anyone interested in guided walks should get in touch via www.damianhall.info.

Published by AA Publishing (a trading name of AA Media Limited, whose registered office is Fanum House, Basing View, Basingstoke, Hampshire RG21 4EA; registered number 06112600) © AA Media Limited 2014

Maps contain data from openstreetmap.org © OpenStreetMap contributors Ordnance Survey data © Crown copyright and database right 2014.

A CIP catalogue record for this book is available from the British Library.

ISBN: 978-0-7495-7595-3
ISBN (SS): 978-0-7495-7631-8

Cartography provided by the Mapping Services Department of AA Publishing

Printed and bound in the UK by Butler, Tanner & Dennis

A05140

Visit AA Publishing at theAA.com/shop

AA

THE AA GUIDE TO

The Cotswolds

WITH OXFORD
& STRATFORD-UPON-AVON

WE KNOW BRITAIN

CONTENTS

▶ Finding your way

Use the maps below together with the atlas section and the town plans throughout the guide to explore the Cotswolds. The A–Z section lists the best of the region, followed by recommended attractions, activities and places to eat or drink. The Places Nearby section then lists other points of interest within a short travelling distance to help you explore a little further.

Many of the restaurants that we've included carry an AA Rosette rating, which recognises cooking at different levels nationwide, from the very best in the local area to the very best in the UK. Pubs have been selected for their great atmosphere and good food. You can find more Rosette-rated places to eat at theAA.com.

We're guessing you probably have your accommodation sorted already, but for those who like to play it by ear, we've recommended a few campsites to help you out (see page 56). Caravan and campsites carry the AA's Pennant rating, with the very best receiving the coveted gold Pennant award. If your tastes run more to luxury then theAA.com also lists AA-rated hotels and B&Bs.

INTRODUCTION

You'll like the Cotswolds. Almost everyone does. If the region was an animal, it would be a plump, fluffy cat, purring contentedly by a pub fireplace. Despite the Cotswolds being the UK's second largest protected landscape (after the Lake District) and the largest Area of Outstanding Natural Beauty in England and Wales, so much of it feels cosy, comfortable, contented and just sort of... right.

There's something implicitly reassuring and irresistibly pleasing about the unapologetic idyll of syrupy villages tucked into lush curvy combes. Influential 20th-century novelist J B Priestley called the region 'the most English of all our countrysides'. A visit to the Cotswolds is likely to leave you feeling that everything is comfortingly right with the world (although you may feel the need to go to the gym after over-indulging on all that lip-smackingly fantastic nosh. Ignore it).

Most people come to the Cotswolds to experience the chocolate-box pretty villages: the centuries-old churches, cute cottages and dry-stone walls made of that oolitic limestone that glows so warmly in the sunshine, especially on a late winter afternoon. And there are plenty of places to taste all that – both with and without the crowds. As a rule of thumb, if it begins with B it's probably very handsome but very popular.

However, if you concentrate only on that idea of the Cotswolds, you're missing out on what really makes the region special. Sure, rush around the manor houses, consume an infinite number of cream teas and 'accidentally' push other tourists into the river in order to take unobscured photos of Bourton-on-the-Water's five bridges. All that's well known and still worth experiencing. But make sure you leave time for what day-tours from London don't capture about the Cotswolds. The region's lesser-known corners offer a different sort of pleasure, should you make the effort to seek them out (see 10 Hidden Gems, page 67).

By that we means the soaring views from the dramatic limestone Cotswold Edge that unravel for over 60 miles, into the moody mountains of Wales; the ruins of Roman villas with their extensive, intricate mosaics; all that fresh, healthy, locally produced, organic food enlivening the farmers' markets and local restaurants alike; ancient beech woodlands ablaze in autumn, or carpets of snowdrops in winter and bluebells in spring; thriving arts and crafts such as silversmithery and glass-making, folk music and storytelling; theatrically-situated hill-forts – the Cotswolds alone has 35 of them – Jurassic grasslands splashed with wildflowers, vivid orchids and flickering butterflies; that sense of timelessness found in villages that have remained much the same for centuries; real ale in cosy pubs; leisurely wanders in handsome historical towns and cities such as Oxford, Cheltenham, Cirencester and Stratford-upon-Avon; extraordinary abbeys, cathedrals and 'wool' churches; enigmatic stone circles, Neolithic long barrows, round barrows, castles, shams, follies, manor houses and stately homes with blooming kaleidoscopic gardens that turn you into Alice in Wonderland; and the region's many ghost stories (or are they stories?). And let's not forget the Cotswolds' brilliant, idiosyncratic festivals, some of which include sports outrageously overlooked-by-the-Olympics: chasing a cheese down a vertiginous hill, river football and, naturally, welly wanging.

The people here have a quirky sense of humour. But compellingly original events such as these say something vital about the Cotswolds – something that doesn't tend to make it into the tourist brochures. The region has a distinctive spirit that can be traced through the centuries. It's an ethos of seeing things through, of working hard to get things right, that plays out in a venerable craft tradition.

The skill of dry-stone walling, for example, has been kept alive in the Cotswolds for at least 5,500 years. The same technique found in the area's Neolithic long barrows is still practised (and taught: see cotswoldsruralskills.org.uk) in the Cotswolds today. The region keeps its crafts alive in an era when so many other useful rural and wilderness skills have been lost to us.

When the Cotswolds' centuries-old wool industry finally declined, cloth production took its place – a genuine homespun – pun intended – industry based on local skills, ingenuity and an understanding of the natural world. Artist and social theorist William Morris moved the base of his Arts and Crafts Movement here in the 19th century, and that same philosophy is still flourishing today. It's no coincidence that the wonderful resurgence of farmers' markets is so strong here too, along with folk arts and other traditional aspects of British culture, such as storytelling. (And, yes, that includes Morris dancing, for better or worse). Crucially all this is a celebration of local people supporting each other, of the old-fashioned concept of community lost elsewhere in the country, without it ever getting too *League Of Gentleman*.

The Cotswolds isn't just a backdrop for tourist photos and faux-celebrity photoshoots. It's a real place, with real people, doing real things. And hopefully you'll see, enjoy and contribute to that too.

There's no firm agreement on the exact boundaries of the Cotswolds, but for this book we're reaching out to Oxford in the east, Gloucester in the west, Stratford-upon-Avon in the north and stopping just outside Bath in the south.

◀ Bliss Tweed Mill (previous page) ▼ Arlington Row, Bibury

TOP ATTRACTIONS

▲ Anne Hathaway's Cottage & Shakespeare's Birthplace

Shakespeare's wife once lived in a pretty thatched cottage on the very edge of Stratford (see page 204), and it stayed in the Hathaway family until the 19th century. Much of the original family furniture remains. About a mile and a half away is the house where the world's most famous playwright was born and grew up (see page 203). You might see a live performance in the back garden.

▼ Royal Shakespeare Company

Stratford's Royal Shakespeare Company (see page 207) is probably the best classical theatre company in the world. Since its foundation in 1879 pretty much every serious British actor has trod the boards in an RSC production. It's not just Shakespeare either; works by O'Neill, Hugo, Stoppard and more have been seen. You can book a tour round the theatres or do your best to get a ticket to a production; both worth thinking about ahead of time, obviously.

◀ Hidcote Manor Garden

Hidcote (see page 135) was created in the early 20th century, and is home to plants that were collected by the owner Lawrence Johnson from the Alps, Kenya, South Africa and others. There are plenty of varieties from the UK as well, so you'll get a comforting but disconcerting feeling of familiarity and the exotic.

▶ Cotswold Wildlife Park and Gardens

160 acres of landscaped zoological park, surrounding a Gothic-style manor house, with more than 260 different animal species (see page 81). Lions, leopards, white rhinos, red pandas, sloths, lemurs and giraffes are among the fun fauna in residence. If all the animal activity gets too much, there are also gardens with floral displays all year round.

◀ Pitt Rivers Museum

Don't miss eccentric, eclectic Pitt Rivers Museum (see page 168). Essentially one big room full of display cases, most artefacts have hand-written labels and are of an amazing range of both subject and ethnic origin. The shrunken heads are infamous, but there are also toys, canoes, religious items, weapons and even a witch in a bottle.

◄ Blenheim Palace

Blenheim (see page 250) is best known as the birthplace of oil-painting, cigar-chomping hero of WWII, Sir Winston Churchill, but its history goes back to the early 18th century. The Palace itself is frankly, huge, with an amazing interior and 2,000 acres of grounds, partly landscaped by 'Capability' Brown. Expect to spend the day, but still not see it all.

► Birdland

Not to be confused with the New York City jazz club of the same name, this is an actual land of actual birds (see page 74), home to the only group of king penguins in England. There are also flamingos, pelicans, penguins, cranes, storks, cassowaries, waterfowl, over 50 aviaries of parrots, falcons, pheasants, hornbills, touracos, pigeons, ibis and many more.

◄ Ashmolean Museum

Opened in 1683, the Ashmolean (see page 167) is the oldest museum in the country. It contains important art pieces and artefacts, from Ancient Greece to the 20th century. It's a perfect balance between the academic, the engaging and the entertaining – you'll find yourself getting educated without even noticing.

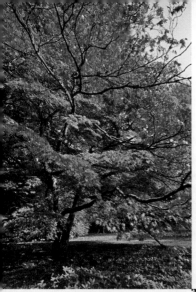

◄ Westonbirt Arboretum

If there's somewhere more spectacular to see autumn colours, not just the Cotswolds but in Britain, we'd sure like to know about it. An astonishing collection of some of the oldest, biggest, rarest and most magnificent trees in the world (see page 220). A sure-fire crowd-pleaser at any time of year.

► Cotswold Motoring Museum & Toy Collection

As well as its collection of vintage and classic cars and various motoring curiosities (see page 73), this is also the home of Brum, star of his own BBC TV show. The museum hosts a variety of exhibitions, so there should be something to keep everyone entertained.

◄ Sudeley Castle

Visited by Elizabeth I, Henry VIII and Anne Boleyn, home to Catherine Parr and refuge to Charles I during the Civil War, there's no shortage of historical heavyweights attached to Sudeley (see page 217). Today you can enjoy a fascinating wander round the rooms and get a glimpse of how the Tudor half lived. The grounds are impressive too.

HISTORY OF THE COTSWOLDS

In the admittedly fairly unlikely scenario that you're being threatened with nasty consequences unless you can sum up the history of the Cotswolds in one word, the word to remember is 'wool'.

Those honey-coloured villages may make you think progress is something that happens somewhere else, but the Cotswolds have played host to great industries, great cities and great wars. Great people have come from here too: war-winning prime ministers, famous poets, playwrights and writers. In fact considering how much history has happened in these hills and valleys, they've no right whatsoever to still look this damned good.

The first Cotswolders were Mesolithic nomads who hunted and gathered some 10,000 years ago in what was then a heavily wooded region. Around 4000 BC, Neolithic (or New Stone Age) man began to farm. Neolithic Cotswolders cleared much of the primeval forest to make room for their animals and crops. They also left us their long barrows – huge, mysterious tombs, such as Belas Knap, near Winchcombe, and Nympsfield Long Barrow, near Nailsworth.

Bronze Age residents (2000–650 BC) redecorated the place, building round barrows and stone circles such as the supposedly

◀ Footpath at Uley Bury

magical circle at Rollright in the northeast Cotswolds. It's nigh-on impossible to count the same number of Rollright Stones twice in a row, which might lead you to think that the stones pop up and down behind your back through concealed trapdoors just to torment you. They also started building farming terraces called strip lynchets, and liked them so much they continued on until the early medieval period. You can see the remains of these around the region today.

The Iron Age (800 BC to Roman occupation) saw waves of Celts settle in what would become the United Kingdom. The newcomers built some 35 hill-forts in the Cotswolds, most notably at Uley Bury (the most theatrically positioned), Painswick Beacon (the most dramatic), Crickley Hill (which has the most history) and Haresfield Beacon. During this period Cotswolders preferred to live on the hilltops, but in all other times the area's people built their settlements below the escarpment, in the valleys and combes (presumably because it's a bit less windy when you're nestled into a hillside).

Romans built Cirencester, Gloucester and Bath, the 182-mile Fosse Way (which travels right through the Cotswolds, running from Exeter to Lincoln – one section is now the A429), and lavish, mosaic-floored villas such as Chedworth and Great Witcombe. Cirencester, or rather *Corinium*, became the second largest city in Britain and a centre of a new trade: wool. The Romans discovered that while the well-drained Cotswolds hills, with their thin top-soil, were passable (if unspectacular) for crop-growing, they provided excellent pasture for woolly things. Thus began the region's legacy of large-scale sheep farming.

When the Romans all ran off home, the Saxons – for the nitpicky, the name covers several Germanic tribes – jumped in, and the Dark Ages ensued. The Saxons made little Winchcombe the capital of the not-inconsiderable kingdom of Mercia, and it's likely the phrase 'Cot's Wold' comes from this period. At the time, sheep were grazed in large 'cots' or enclosures on the wolds, around what's now Cutsdean in the north Cotswolds. A literal Anglo-Saxon translation of Cotswolds gives us 'sheep-hills', while a direct contemporary German translation yields 'high wooded land' (the hill tops were more wooded then). Competing theories suggest chieftains and gods named Cot or Cod.

The Normans arrived, a little aggressively it must be said, in 1066. William the Conqueror made Gloucester his base for a time, bringing further prosperity to the Cotswolds. The Normans built churches and carried out their epic Domesday Book survey. According to the Book, the area was heavily cultivated for the most part, but the west side was still very wooded – and, allegedly, in the entirety of the Cotswolds there was just one wall, which seems unlikely.

The Normans took the area's wool industry to a new level, clearing more land for grazing and putting the industry largely in church hands. Woolly things soon outnumbered (human) Cotswolders four to one. The Cotswold Lion sheep – big and hornless, with a white face and long, heavy fleece – emerged as the dominant breed. Their descendants can be seen at Cotswold Farm Park (see page 133), near Guiting Power.

By the Middle Ages, the Cotswolds was one big grazing pasture. Wool wasn't just making the region rich, it was making the country rich. Wool exports accounted for more than half England's wealth, and half the nation's wool came from the Cotswolds. This increased income helped create a new middle class, and their money was often ploughed into building glamorous manor houses and so-called wool churches, such as the handsome examples in Winchcombe, Cirencester, Burford, Northleach and – the best of the bunch – Chipping Campden. Indeed, most of the Cotswolds' best-looking buildings owe their existence to this period of prosperity.

High taxes and competition from Spain forced a decline in the wool trade in the second half of the 15th century. It looked like the end of the Cotswolds' prosperity. But the region had another trick up its sleeve (pun intended).

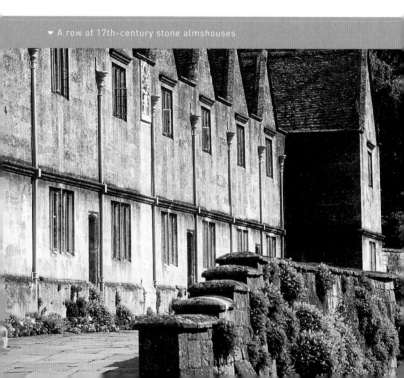

▼ A row of 17th-century stone almshouses

Starting in Temple Guiting way back in around 1185, the act of weaving, spinning and wool-cloth making had been spreading slowly throughout the region, initially as a cottage industry, before catching on and becoming a genuine industrial trade. By the end of the 16th century, cloth had replaced wool as the region's big earner. The Cotswolds sent finished cloth to India, Europe and the New World. By the 1700s, the Five Valleys around Stroud – Frome, Slad, Nailsworth, Painswick and Toadsmoor – teemed with water-powered mills. As many as 150 mills worked to dye fabric with the region's distinctive colours, Stroudwater Scarlet and Uley Blue. The long-lasting hues were derived from natural river salts, and gave British military uniforms their vividness.

The cute rows of terraced cottages you'll want to take photos of in Bibury, one of the most handsome Cotswolds villages, started out as cramped workers' cottages. It's rather ironic that they're now quite coveted. 17th-century politician Sir Baptist Hicks started out as a clothier from Chipping Campden. He paid for the market hall you can still see if you visit the town, and went on to be lord mayor of London. Today you can best revisit this era in the Golden Valley (so named after the wealth the mills there created), near Stroud.

Greater social and aesthetic change came to the Cotswolds in the form of the Enclosure Acts. Between 1700 and 1840, rich land owners cordoned off large tracts of land that had traditionally

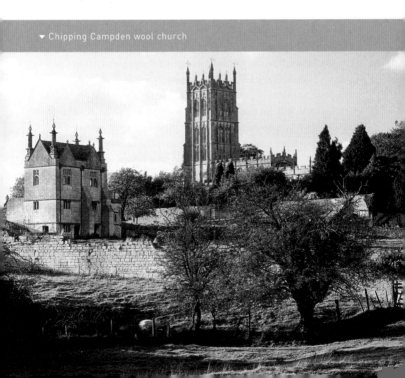

▼ Chipping Campden wool church

▲ The Cotswold Way, Painswick Beacon

been held in common. This privatising land grab deprived local people of their ancestral rights to graze animals and collect wood freely, and the resulting strife in part created Britain's modern working class. The Acts brought the region most of its signature drystone walls, often in the form of new boundary markers – though the technique dated back to the Stone Age, when the same style of construction was used for long barrows. Today the 4,000 miles of walls in the Cotswolds are roughly equivalent in length to the Great Wall of China.

The Cotswolds' lack of coal meant that the regions' cloth mills were eventually out-manoeuvred by their Yorkshire rivals, who could use steam-powered trains to get their product to ships faster. Thankfully for the Cotswolds' scenic beauty – although not its 19th century economy – the region never saw full-scale industrial overdevelopment. The long period of poverty that began in the 1850s ironically ensured an economic future for the Cotswolds as a tourist destination. Villages fell into a state of picturesque antiquarian decay. The region experienced genuine suffering, causing industrial action and mass migration to the New World (New South Wales, Australia has its own miniature Stroud and Gloucester).

There were still exciting times ahead for the region, albeit on a smaller scale. In the 1890s William Morris and his followers made Chipping Campden a thriving centre for the Arts and Crafts Movement. An antidote to industrialisation, this artistic and social vision included a strong strain of utopian neo-medievalism and an implicit call for a return to nature. Morris moved his family –

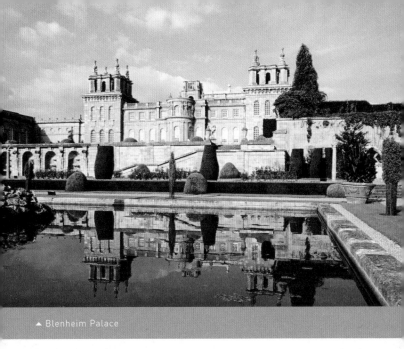

▲ Blenheim Palace

including his wife's lover – to Kelmscott Manor. Writers and artists followed, and Arts and Crafts buildings can still be seen in Campden, Painswick and Sapperton. Morris was also very active in preserving older buildings, especially those classic wool churches.

Beyond Morris' enduring legacy, the Cotswolds has had a disproportionately large impact on Britain's history and culture. Winston Churchill was born and brought up at Blenheim Palace (see page 250), in the Oxfordshire Cotswolds. William Shakespeare too is often claimed for the region. Many other writers and poets were from the Cotswolds, moved there or were inspired by the time they spent in the region. These include Laurie Lee (see page 35), Jane Austen, *Peter Pan* author J M Barrie, *Thomas The Tank Engine* author Rev Wilbert Vere Awdry, John Betjeman, J B Priestley, Edward Elgar, T S Eliot, Alexander Pope, W H Davies, Beatrix Potter, Charles Paget Wade and J K Rowling (who stole the name Dursley for her Harry Potter books).

Thanks to advanced farming methods, today some four-fifths of the Cotswolds are agricultural land. There are still sheep about, and some limestone quarries are subtly still going. Happily, traditional skills –potters, textile designers, glassmakers, blacksmiths, silversmiths and more – prosper in the area. Along with the Cotswolds' growing reputation as a foodie destination, local farmers' markets are enjoying a massive resurgence. Stroud's market is the nation's largest. Tourism is now by far the region's biggest industry, bringing around £1 billion to the Cotswolds annually.

BACK TO NATURE

Up close the Cotswolds' bubble-wrap hills and curvy valleys may seem like the perfect aesthetic shapes, but the region's underlining geography and geology are as quirky as welly wanging.

Rather than the conventional up-and-down shape that we traditionally consider as 'hills', the region is a large, sloping plateau. The plateau builds slowly from Oxfordshire, so slowly – sneakily even – that you hardly notice the escalation. At the top of the hill-chain, the ground pretty literally plummets from beneath your feet. This is the Cotswold Edge, the Western end of the escarpment. This stark juxtaposition of heaven and earth reveals vast views across the Vales of Evesham, Severn, Berkeley and Gloucester, falling away into the Malverns, and beyond them the moody mountains of Wales.

The Cotswolds may only reach a comparatively modest height of 1,082 feet (330m), but they're part of the country's largest continuous geological feature. The gigantic slab of limestone stretches all the way from Dorset to Yorkshire. The Cotswolds are the rock formation's most prominent part. Rivers have slowly sculpted the landscape over the centuries, creating dry and wet valleys.

▲ The Devil's Chimney, Leckhampton Hill ▲ Uley Bury

The area spanning northeast from Stroud to Chipping Campden is an elevated plateau, or 'high wold'. This windswept landscape feels invigoratingly open, with big skies and deep valleys that sometimes can't be seen until you're tumbling down into them. But around Stroud there are some long, deep, and wide valleys very different from the north wolds in character – the Five Valleys. From Tetbury heading east a gentle 'dip-slope' bridges the transition between the plateau and lowlands terrain. The dramatic Edge softens as you follow it south. The scarp is particularly characterful near Dursley, with its outlier hill Cam Long Down. The view is best enjoyed from Uley Bury hill-fort.

The plateau is made of oolitic limestone. If wool defines the human history of the Cotswolds, this rock defines its physical creation, and therefore most things that have happened here. Almost everything about the Cotswolds – the shape of the terrain, the soil, plants and animals, man's industry, culture and history – is directly linked to the golden stone under these hills.

Oolitic limestone is a compressed mishmash of sediments, including clay, sand and the remains of gazillions of tiny sea creatures that lived 210 to 140 million years ago in the Jurassic period, in the warm tropical seas that once covered the area. The stone is rich with fossils. Ogle a Cotswold cottage up close, and you'll spy hundreds of crushed shells. Unquarried, the rock can resemble tightly packed fish egg. Hence the name – Oolite, or 'egg stone', from òoion, the Hellenic Greek word for egg.

Some 10,000 years ago, around the end of the last Ice Age, pressure from an ice cap to the north caused the giant limestone slab to buckle, forming the Cotswolds as we now know it. The melting snow and ice became rivers and streams, which gradually cut down through the limestone and gave the landscape its pleasingly smooth contours.

The limestone is comparatively soft and easy to shape when first taken from the ground, but it hardens over time. It thus makes an ideal building material. Locals have used this natural resource to build homes, long barrows and other structures since the Bronze Age (2000–650 BC). Indeed some of the walls in ancient long barrows are made according to the same method the Cotswolds' later inhabitants used to build the dry-stone walls the region's known for today.

In Cotswolds villages, the uniformity of the stone often masks the fact a given house might be hundreds of years older or newer than its neighbour. The Cotswolds have their own, timeless aesthetic. Oolitic limestone has a special, lingering glow in sunlight, which is especially pronounced at dusk. Often likened to

▼ Blue flax at Broadway

honey or syrup, the stone seems to preserve and magnifying the sunlight's warm colour. As J B Priestley wrote in his seminal *English Journey* (1934), it is '[a]s if they know the trick of keeping the lost sunlight of centuries glimmering about them.' William Morris noted how Cotswold houses seem almost to grow out of the land underneath them.

The stone's colour varies across the region, tending to be more honey-golden and buttery in the north and a little greyer, more silvery and creamier in the south. Compare for example the colour of Broadway in the north – as golden yellow as it gets – with Painswick – as white as you'll see, albeit only halfway down the Cotswolds.

The limestone's thin topsoil has traditionally prevented the region from being extensively farmed, though modern farming methods have begun to change this. The Cotswolds' grasslands have survived relatively untouched since the Jurassic age. In fact the region has over 50 per cent of the country's unimproved (read: never substantially altered to make it more suitable for farming) Jurassic grassland. The Cotswolds' designation as an Area of Outstanding Natural Beauty (AONB) – one tier below a National Park – recognizes the region's 'rich, diverse and high quality

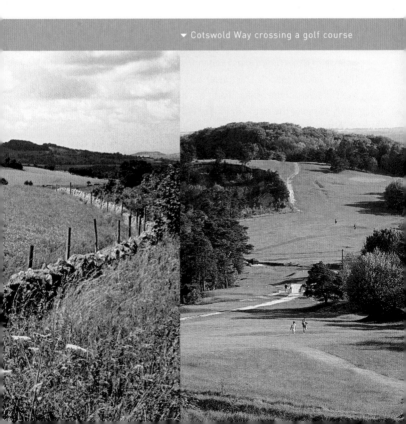

▼ Cotswold Way crossing a golf course

▶ Berkeley Castle

landscape'. The Cotswolds are also home to five European Special Areas of Conservation, three National Nature Reserves and over 80 Sites of Special Scientific Interest.

Orchids can be found growing wild on the grasslands. Green-winged and early purple varieties arrive in late April and May, while common spotted, bee, frog, musk and pyramid crop up in summer, as do the rare and beautiful purple and gold pasque flower and Cotswold pennycress – arguably the region's signature flower. You may also see white oxeye daisies, bird's-foot trefoil, scabious, kidney vetch (which attracts common blue, rare chalkhill blue and Duke of Burgundy butterflies), hoary plantain, rock-rose, salad burnet, and knapweeds. Much of the woodland cover is ancient too, and in autumn, the beech woods along the Edge are ablaze with colour.

The UK has half the world's bluebell population. Bluebells start flowering in the southwest, before fanning out across the country. These flowers often serve as indicators of ancient woodlands. In woods below the Cotswolds scarp in spring, you'll find carpets of bluebells wafting their natural perfume.

In spring and summer, you can see the vivid clash of bright red poppies and the bright yellow rapeseed that makes the local farmland a tourist attraction in its own right. Snowshill's gently swishing fields of lavender may remind you of the vivid colour palette of Crouching Tiger, Hidden Dragon. You'll also likely see the thistle-esque teasel. The flower has a special historical place in the Cotswolds: the spiky heads were used in the manufacture of cloth, to raise the nap – the fuzzy surface – on velvet.

Many local places have taken their names from the landscape, such as Edge, Wotton-under-Edge and Sheepscombe, which wonderfully combines the natural surroundings with the region's traditional industry.

There's also plentiful birdlife, including buzzards, kestrels and sparrowhawks. The meadow pipit, with its puffed chest – often confused with the skylark – is perhaps the Cotswolds' signature bird. Bullfinches and yellowhammers dart between hawthorn and gorse. Migrating ring ouzels and wheaters stop off in spring (look on open hills and golf courses). Chaffinches, as well as skylarks and meadow pipits, stop by in autumn. If your tastes are more mammalian, the Cotswolds offer a chance to glimpse deer, foxes, rabbits, hares, grey squirrels and badgers (if they haven't all been shot). Many locals also believe in the presence of mysterious black cats...

LORE OF THE LAND

The wealth of the Cotswolds lies in much more than its immaculate villages built of warm stone. Ancient burial sites dot the land, and with them come tales of treasure. Near the Longstone is a long barrow, the Gatcombe Tump. Here an old woman from Minchinhampton who was able to charm away ailments, afterwards called Molly Dreamer, dreamed that she would find a long-lost pot of gold. She and her husband dug deep into the barrow. until she had her hand on the pot, and was mouthing 'Come up! Labour in vain!' But as the words passed her lips a spirit appeared and frightened her off.

Near Bisley is a mound dubbed the Money Tump. Local legend holds that a wealthy chief dropped his riches there while fleeing Saxon invaders, and that the site is haunted by headless figures. A Roman general allegedly buried yet more treasure in nearby Golden Coffin Field. Despite many attempts over the centuries, these hidden fortunes have yet to be unearthed.

In this farming country, being in tune with nature was serious business. Taking note of the moon's phases was particularly important, as the guiding saw of the Chipping Campden farmer shows: 'Cut the lambs' tails in the rising moon and a south wind blowing, and never kill a pig when the moon be a-wasting [waning].' Farmers who disobeyed the rule would allegedly find it impossible to make good bacon, because the animal's flesh would not absorb salt properly. Broad Campden farmers also never sowed wheat except 'at the coming up of the moon'. Agricultural productivity also depended on locals' ability to predict the coming of rain. A Wotton-under-Edge rhyme runs: 'When Wotton Hill doth wear a cap [is covered in cloud], /Let Horton Town beware of that.' The sound of Woodchester's bells sent a meteorological message to nearby Rodborough. Damp air conducts sound much better than dry, thus:

Bring out your sou'westers
Say the bells of Woodchester.
All right old thing,
Answers Rodborough, ding ding.

The lore of the stones
Legend relates that two thousand years ago, a king and his army marched through England as far as Little Rollright – an area now on the borders of Oxfordshire and Warwickshire, near Long Compton. Ascending a hill, the army encountered a witch. She called out to the king:

Seven long strides thou shalt take!
If Long Compton thou canst see
King of England thou shalt be.

Disastrously for the king the hill obscured his view, causing the witch to gloat:

As Long Compton thou canst not see
King of England thou shalt not be.
Rise up, stick, and stand still, stone,
For King of England thou shalt be none
Thou and they men hoar stones shall be,
And I myself an eldern [elder] tree.

So here the Rollright Stones stand: the ruler or King Stone, five Whispering Knights and 77 King's Men. In a circle 100 feet across, they wait for the magic spell that will make them human again. In a surprising gesture of solidarity, the witch likewise transformed herself into an elder tree. On Midsummer Eve, local people would cut an elder branch and congregate around the King stone.

As the wound 'bled', some claimed to see the King's 'head' move. Witches and fairies would also gather at the stones at midnight to make merry, and at that time unmarried girls would press their ears to the Whispering Knights, hoping to hear the names of their future husbands.

A pair of holes pierces the Longstone, Gloucestershire's best-known megalith. Locals traditionally believe that at the chime of midnight the Longstone – also called Long John – and its neighbour the Tingle Stone run around the fields near Avening in which they stand. Long John is also said to bleed if pricked with a pin at midnight, and is further renowned for its healing properties. Mothers once passed children through the holes in the stone to prevent or cure rickets, smallpox, whooping cough and other then-fatal illnesses. Young couples would hold hands through the holes to ensure fertility.

Worst women

A tale from the 11th century recounts the exploits of the notorious witch of Berkeley Castle. She kept a tame jackdaw as her familiar, and one day, as the bird chattered to her more loudly than usual, she suddenly turned pale, later to hear that one of her sons and his family had been killed in an accident. Fearing her own impending doom she promptly called for two of her other children – one a monk, the other a nun – and confessed to them that she was a witch. The demonic bargain that had given her her powers ensured that her soul could not be saved, and so they were instructed, upon her death, to wrap her in a stag's skin and to then put the bundle into a stone coffin secured with three iron chains. By this means the witch hoped to cheat the devil out of his due.

The coffin was to remain in the church for three days, but while it lay there devils broke in and cut the chains. As one of the devils dragged the witch

▼ The Rollright stones

from the church, a black horse with iron hooks projecting from its back appeared. The witch was placed on the vicious saddle and pierced through. Her screams could be heard miles away.

Betty Barstoe, buried at the wayside in Betty's Grave,was called a witch for her supposed ability to make farm animals miscarry, prevent butter from solidifying or 'coming' and cream from setting, make gates fall from their hinges, and make people fall ill by dancing in the streets at midnight and spitting pins from her mouth. She was tried and burned, but after she was buried, other witches were said to gather at her grave and work their spells, stopping pedlars and other travellers on route to the market at Fairford. In another twist to the tale, it's said that Betty even left her grave and reappeared, only to be hanged and buried once again. The grave is still covered in flowers in the belief that only this can prevent her resurrection.

Most haunted
Ghosts stalk Cotswold villages in profusion, but though its spookiness seems to have no ill effects on its current residents, the prize for most haunted goes to Prestbury. Chief among the village's ghosts is a horseman who gallops at top speed down the Burgage, a street near Prestbury House, then suddenly screams to a halt. Locals believed the ghost was either a Royalist from Gloucester who was killed by Roundheads with a rope stretched across the road, or a messenger who was bound for Edward IV's camp at Tewkesbury in 1471. Revellers' ghosts come out to play on the grounds of Prestbury House (now a hotel), while a 'Black Abbot' haunts the churchyard, appearing only at Easter. In a cottage in the village, the ghost of a girl can be heard playing the spinet, while a spectral woman sings in a cottage nearby. An old woman in traditional country garb drifts across the fields, meeting the phantom sheep and shepherds that haunt the land.

Painswick also lays claim to extreme ghostliness. Its list of weirdness is long, and includes ghosts searching for buried treasure, black dogs, and creatures like goblins who at dance around a milestone on the Gloucester road. Civil War soldiers and a grey lady also appear. People have heard strange cries and the sound of shuffling feet coming from Chirm Cottage in Kemps Lane. Scariest of all is the phantom coach that can be witnessed at midnight on New Year's Eve on the road from Painswick to Stroud. As the speeding coach crashes, you can hear the sounds of horses, coachmen and screaming passengers plunging to their doom, accompanied by the awesome crack of splintering wood. We can't recommend attempting to catch a glimpse (or hear a shuffle) of these otherworldly phenomena, as so doing may incur a terrible, sometimes even fatal curse...

WALKING IN THE COTSWOLDS

Visiting the Cotswolds and not putting your booted footprints on those lush green hills is like going to Paris and neglecting to see the Eiffel Tower or eat a croissant. This landscape was made for walking. The Cotswolds contain places of satisfying remoteness, authentic wildness and stirring drama. There are theatrically set hill-forts, big views, stone circles, wildflower-splashed ancient grasslands, bluebell-carpeted woodlands, nature reserves and Sites of Special Scientific Interest (SSSIs).

Covering 790 square miles, this is the second largest protected landscape in England, after the Lake District, and the largest Area of Outstanding Natural Beauty in England and Wales. The region's crisscrossed with around 3,000 miles of often well-waymarked public footpaths. In terms of walking, the Cotswolds specialise in two things: the fabulous views from the limestone Edge, and appealingly clandestine valleys for you to get temporarily – and perfectly safely – lost in.

England and Wales have 15 National Trails: government-backed long-distance paths, usually considered to be the most scenic, as well as best waymarked and maintained, routes. One of them is the

◀ Haresfield Beacon (previous page) ▲ Toadsmoor Valley

Cotswold Way, which follows the hill chain as it ripples and bulges. The Way runs 102 miles, from Chipping Campden at the north face of the hill-chain all the way down to Bath at the southern tip. The trail sticks closely to the Edge, giving the walker the best panoramas; right across the Vales of the Severn, Berkeley and Gloucester, the River Severn (the country's longest), to J R R Tolkien's Forest of Dean, the jagged Malverns and the mountains of Wales.

There are many long-distance paths too, such as the Gloucestershire Way, the Oxfordshire Way, the Macmillan Way, the Wysis Way and the Warden's and Windrush Ways, though they don't follow the escarpment like the Cotswold Way does. Not everyone has time to do the whole of the Cotswold Way, which takes most people 5–7 days, but if it's views you want there are plenty of short walks on the Way.

The Edge is higher and more spectacular in the north, and it's no coincidence that that's where you'll find Winchcombe, the unofficial capital of walking in the Cotswolds. The Cotswold, Warden's, Windrush and Gloucestershire Ways all run through the town, as does the 42-mile Winchcombe Way. There are plenty of short walks to be enjoyed here, especially up to Belas Knap and/or Cleeve Common, the highest point in the Cotswolds. 'The town has 'Walkers are Welcome' status,' says WinchcombeWelcomesWalkers.com, 'which means we will endeavour to make your stay and experience memorable.'

Other fantastic bits of the Edge can be easily accessed via short walks from the following places: going from north to south, Chipping Campden, Cheltenham, Broadway, Stanton, Birdlip, Painswick, Wotton-under-Edge, and Bath (not covered in this book). All are well worth visiting in their own right. Places you might not have considered visiting that have easy access to walking on the scarp include Selsley, Uley and Stroud. Leckhampton Hill, Crickley Hill and Cooper's Hill (of cheese rolling fame) are also well worth seeking out. Minchinhampton and Rodborough Commons, and Bredon Hill, aren't on the Cotswold Way, but they also offer the sort of views that will cause you to get very annoyed with yourself if you didn't pack a picnic.

The Cotswolds also know a thing or two about how to produce the perfect valley, and discovering the results is an experience that amounts to almost a separate genre of walking. Nowhere does valleys quite like here: teasingly secretive, often intimate and overgrown, but also deep, wide and long. Some feel like their own little worlds. 'Those green little valleys at once make you feel so oddly remote, miles and miles from anywhere, clean out of the world' wrote J B Priestley in *English Journey*.

The most famous valley in the Cotswolds is of course the Slad Valley, near Stroud, where Laurie Lee both grew up and set his six-million-copy-selling autobiography *Cider With Rosie*. The five valleys around Stroud are the most logical places to go valley-hunting, while Toadsmoor, Miserden and Sapperton are path-less-trodden delights.

As well as views from the Edge and those famous valleys, there are hill-forts (none better than Painswick Beacon and Uley Bury), long barrows (Belas Knap, Nympsfield Long Barrow, Leckhampton Hill) and stone circles (Rollright) to explore. Then there are those Jurassic grasslands, splashed with wildflowers and butterflies from late spring, most notably Cleeve (with around 150 species of herb and grass), Selsley, Minchinhampton and Rodborough, and Haresfield Commons.

There's plenty of woodland walking available too. In fact most Cotswolds walks involve trees. The region's glorious beech woodlands at times cover the steep escarpment. Beech trees aren't everyone's favourite as they can get dark in summer and don't let much else grow beneath them, but in autumn they light up in a gorgeous riot of bronze leaves.

If waterside walks are more to your taste, there are many rivers (the Thames is a Cotswolds river after all) and streams in the Cotswolds, as well as two canals. Other walks will take you past Roman ruins, castles, shams, follies and stately homes.

If you only have a short time in the Cotswolds and want to taste some of those classic villages as well as work up an appetite, the clever thing to do is to pick a route that includes several villages, such as a crowd-pleasing circuit of Stanton, Stanway and Snowshill (of *Bridget Jones's Diary* film fame). Or perhaps you might opt to take in Bourton-on-the-Water, Upper Slaughter, Lower Slaughter and Naunton. Getting some villages involved guarantees you that classic Cotswolds experience: a day out hiking the hills and valleys, topped off with a great feed and a couple of pints of something strange and local before you head to bed in the same handsome and satisfyingly historic establishment.

Walking destinations don't get much more beginner friendly than the Cotswolds. It's not big and wild like the Brecon Beacons or Dartmoor, and you can't get genuinely lost for long – just find a road, and that'll take you back to civilisation soon enough. The more experienced walker might want to head to the Edge. You can get more of a workout there, and really feel like you've earned those big views.

Of course, going for a ramble is also a great way to escape the crowds.

Walking festivals and guiding
Nailsworth (June, nailsworthhealthpartnership.org), **Stroud** (September, stroudvalleysfestivals.co.uk/walking.html), **Dursley** (October, dursleywelcomeswalkers.org.uk), **Horton** (September) and **Winchcombe** (May, winchcombewelcomeswalkers.com) all have walking festivals.

Some companies offer organised walking holidays and luggage-carrying options, include the Pudding Club (01386 438429; puddingclub.com); Contours Walking Holidays (01768 867539; contours.co.uk); and Cotswold Walking Holidays (01242 254353; cotswoldwalks.com).

LAURIE LEE: LOTHARIO, BARFLY, AUTHOR

Laurie Lee, the Cotswold's most famous son, had a complicated relationship with his home region. Born in 1914, Lee grew up in Slad, a village in a valley, not far from Stroud. His mother Annie raised eight children – four of which weren't hers – in a cottage with 'rooks in the chimney, frogs in the cellar and mushrooms in the ceiling'. She perpetually hoped for the return of the children's father, who had abandoned them to live in London with another woman.

Lee left school at 14 and took up an office job in Stroud, but left it to walk to London, with little but a fiddle and an aspiration to be a poet. Seeking adventure, Lee then took passage on a ship and walked through Spain at 19, playing his violin to earn his keep. 'I don't know what idiocies drove me in those days, but they were naïve, innocent idiocies in many ways', he told the BBC in later life. He left Spain in 1936, just as Civil War was breaking out.

Feeling guilty about having left the friends he'd made along the way to face the perils of war, he returned the following year to volunteer for the International Brigade. To re-enter the country, he had to cross the Pyrenees alone in a snowstorm. Lee claimed he was ultimately turned away because of his epilepsy, but not before being imprisoned and sentenced to death on suspicion of being a spy. By his mid 20s, Lee had had all the experiences that would become the material for his trilogy of autobiographies – books that would take him almost the rest of his life to write.

Rather than literature, Lee's passion was poetry, and he had some moderate success with it. He also worked as a journalist, scriptwriter and caption writer, and he made documentary films during World War II. Encouraged by editors and publishers who thought his poems about growing up in Gloucestershire were his best and most original work, Lee finally wrote about his upbringing in Slad in *Cider With Rosie*. Published in 1959 – some 20 years after the events took place – the book brilliantly captures a moment in history, conveying the unique texture of life in post-World War I rural Britain. The arrival of a motorcar in the village signals the end of an era. It's bucolic, nostalgic and funny, but also dark. The book depicts real poverty, an unsolved murder and 'self-slaughter'. It went on to sell six million copies, and become a canon text for English secondary schools.

◀ Slad (previous page) ▼ Laurie Lee

In an entertaining footnote, in *Cider* Lee intimates that a fire at a piano factory was probably an insurance scam. Bentleys, a piano factory in Woodchester (in the Nailsworth Valley, on the other side of Stroud), successfully sued him for libel. His biographer Valerie Grove believes he genuinely didn't know of Bentleys, and might have just as easily called it a boiler factory – which it became in later reprints of the book. The whimsical choice of a piano factory ended up costing Lee a lot of money.

Despite the setback, Lee became financially comfortable and very famous. Yet the success suffocated Lee, and he struggled to find his creative edge. Constantly encouraged to come out with a follow-up book, 10 years later he wrote about his walk through Spain in *As I Walked Out One Midsummer Morning*. The third instalment of autobiography wouldn't be published until 1991. *A Moment Of War* chronicled Lee's involvement in the Spanish Civil War.

Some have doubted the veracity of some of the events described in the last book, which was published over 50 years after the period it recounts. The diaries Lee depended on to construct his narrative

▼ The River Coln

had also been stolen in the interim. Lee believed that 'the only truth is what you remember', although he also sometimes worried about what he called 'the censorship of self' and 'some failure between honesty and nerve'.

Along with poetry and alcohol, women were important in Lee's life, and his love life was complex. For example, his second daughter and his first grandchild were born on the same day, when he was 49. A pre-*Cider With Rosie* affair with the married Lorna Wishart led to the birth to his first child, who he rarely saw. At 36, Lee married Lorna's niece, Katherine, who was 18. According to biographer Valerie Grove, their relationship began when she was 14, after he'd dated both of her older sisters. Lee seemingly didn't put much stock in fidelity, either.

Like his father before him, Lee had tried to escape Slad. The success of *Cider With Rosie* brought him back, and in 1961 he bought a house right next to the legendary Woolpack Inn, his former local. The pub is easily found on the main road (B4070), and today it's filled with photos of the writer. Rose Cottage, where Lee lived (at least on weekends) from 1961 to 1997, is tucked directly behind it – he really couldn't have been any closer. The T-shaped Rosebank (formerly Bank Cottages), Lee's childhood home, is further up the road, along the bank about 20 metres northeast. In 1971 he bought the cricket pitch at nearby Sheepscombe to help ensure its future. Lee clearly loved this green corner of Gloucestershire, but paradoxically it wasn't stimulating enough for him. He spent many years commuting to London, spending the weekends in Slad, and frequently escaping abroad.

Slad was originally called Slade, meaning stream, and although you'd never know it from looking at the place, there were once prosperous cloth mills in the valley. In *Cider With Rosie*, Lee describes Slad Valley as '[n]arrow, steep, and almost entirely cut off... The sides of the valley were rich in pasture and the crests heavily covered with beechwoods.' If you get the chance to visit, you'll likely agree that the description still fits today – though how long it will continue to do so is uncertain, as the valley seems to be constantly under threat from developers. Lee later he told the BBC that '[t]he sun sets down at the end of the valley over the Severn and there's this afterglow which catches those quarries and it just sits there glowing when the light is gone from everywhere else in the valley – it holds the light to the last drop.'

Despite having been a sickly child, Lee lived to 82, passing away in 1997. He's buried in the local churchyard, and his second daughter still lives in Slad, running his estate.

THE COTSWOLDS AT WAR

The Cotswolds may look the epitome of peacefulness, but this quilted landscape has seen some very significant battles and more than its fair share of bloodshed.

The Celts arrived the Cotswolds in the Iron Age (from 500 BC), the beginning of a battle-filled era for the region. The Celts built hill-forts along the Cotswold Edge to protect themselves against attacks from the Severn Valley. Arrowheads and the charred remains of bodies were discovered at Crickley Hill, excavated by Philip O. Dixon between the late 1960s and the early 1990s, and similarly on Bredon Hill the mutilated bodies of 50 men were found – left on the battlefield rather than buried.

The Romans arrived in AD 43. The Dobunni Celtic tribe that dominated the region from the southern Severn Valley to the Mendips was disappointingly quick to strike a deal with them, unlike their neighbours in Wales, the Silures, who violently resisted. When the Romans went home for good, tribal feuds broke out again, and Britain became an easy target for marauding tribes of Angles and Saxons from Denmark and Germany. In the 5th century there's good reason to believe that the Battle of Badon, where the Britons led (according to legend) by none other that certain King Arthur defeated an invading Saxon army, took place close to Bath. The victory led to around 50 years of peace for the region, but the peeved Saxons would be back.

In AD 577, the Cotswolds were invaded from two directions. A large Saxon army marched across the country, approaching from the Thames Valley, while the Angles took control of the region's north-west corner. The Dobunni leaders retreated to Bath, Gloucester and Cirencester, the region's three major cities.

The Saxons launched a surprise attack and seized the hill-fort at Hinton Hill Camp, near Dyrham (north of Bath). The position commanded the Avon Valley and disrupted communications between the three cities. The Britons were still able to team up to attack Hinton Hill, but all three of their kings (Commagil of Gloucester, Condidan of Cirencester and Farinmagil of Bath) were killed, and the Britons were defeated. It was a pivotal moment in British history: the Saxons took charge of the three cities, and in so doing cut the Britons of southwest England off from their fellow Britons in the Midlands. The defeated Celts fled to Wales.

Oddly enough, the final battle in the Wars of the Roses – a bloody feud between the Houses of York and Lancaster, rival claimants to the throne of England – took place in the Cotswolds in 1471. The House of York dealt out a thrashing to their opponents at the Battle of Tewkesbury. Edward, Prince of Wales, was among the 2,000 casualties. He was the only son of Henry VI, and the only heir apparent to the English throne to ever die in battle. His death was instrumental in ending the lengthy conflict.

The Cotswolds were at the centre of the English Civil Wars in the 1640s. Three major battles were fought there, including the War's first and last engagements. Broadly speaking, the populations of the north and west of England were Royalist, while those of the south and east of the country were Parliamentarian. This made the Cotswolds, which sit between these axes, a strong target for conflict. The struggle for power between King Charles I and the Parliamentarians, or Roundheads, finally turned to violence at Warwickshire's tiny Kineton in 1642. Both sides were marching towards London, aiming to take control of the capital, but Charles decided to confront his enemies. He lined his army up along Edgehill, while the Roundheads settled in the valley to the north. The Royalists advanced, but both sides lacked professional military experience. Artillery shells wildly missed their targets and Roundheads fled the scene. By nightfall there was no clear winner, and the next day neither side really fancied continuing on. The result was a dissatisfying stalemate. The Roundheads sped to London to secure the capital, while Charles headed for Oxford, where he'd remain for the next four years.

In 1643 the Royalists attempted to seize Bath, meeting the Roundheads at Lansdown Hill. Heartbreakingly, the forces' two leaders, the Roundheads' Sir William Waller and the Cavaliers' Sir Ralph Hopton, had been childhood friends. Waller used the Edge's natural defence, hiding his artillery behind Celtic earthworks and forcing the Royalists' much larger army to attack uphill. Hopton's cavalry and infantry charges proved futile at first. He was persuaded to have another go and Cornish pikemen made inroads while musketeers sneaked through the woods to attack from the flanks. The Roundheads retreated a short distance, regrouping behind a dry-stone wall. Under darkness they retreated further, and in the morning it looked like a Royalist victory. However the Roundheads had lost barely 30 men, while the Royalists cavalry was decimated and was now too weak to attack Bath itself. Yet another draw.

In 1646 the last major battle of the war took place just north of Stow-on-the-Wold. With the Roundheads on the front foot, they attacked a Royalist army at dawn. The Royalists retreated into Stow itself, where the fighting (or rather the slaughter, according to some historians) continued in the market square until the Roundheads emerged victorious and imprisoned the remaining Cavalier soldiers in the church. There's a Royalist Hotel in Stow-on-the-Wold now, among numerous other lasting reminders of the War in the Cotswolds.

Henry I built a hunting lodge in Woodstock in 1129, along with 7 miles of walls to create a park, which included lions and leopards. The lodge became a palace under Henry's grandson, Henry II, who spent time here with his mistress, Rosamund Clifford. Edward the Black Prince was born here in 1330 and the future Queen Elizabeth I of England was imprisoned here from 1554–58. Woodstock Palace was destroyed during the Civil War.

▼ St Edward's Church door detail, Stow-on-the-Wold

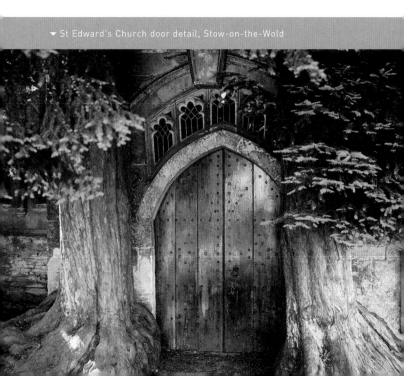

The town of Cirencester endured a lengthy siege, as did Gloucester. Dizzy Malmesbury changed hands seven times, and you can still see bullet marks on its abbey walls. You'll find similar scars on the church towers of Painswick and Winchcombe – the latter are bullet marks left by a Roundhead firing squad that lined Royalist prisoners up against the wall and there shot them dead. The Parliamentary army made the huge breach in Berkeley Castle's western wall. Similarly Sudeley Castle has battle scars – King Charles stayed here. Appropriately, he reputedly also stayed at Stow-on-the-Wold's Kings Arms in 1645. He's even said to have left Moreton-in-Marsh's White Hart without paying his bill, the rapscallion!

Presumably eschewing royally-named establishments, Oliver Cromwell supposedly stayed at Broadway's famous Lygon Arms in 1651 – as did Charles four years later. Charles is said to have disguised himself as a manservant while lying low at Cirencester's The Fleece. The same itinerant royal named Paradise, near Painswick: someone kindly put him up for the night and he decided the place was heavenly.

That was the last direct fighting in the region, though both World Wars would have a big impact. During World War I, open wolds were ploughed for extra food and woods were scavenged for timber. World War II saw numerous airfields built atop the plateaus.

▼ Sudeley Castle

LOCAL SPECIALITIES

There was a time when the Cotswolds' reputation for culinary sophistication might have been summed up by the image of a farmer slumped under a tree with a carrot in one hand and a half empty (or is it half full?) flagon of cider in the other. But that's long out of date.

The change has come about in part due to the amount of Londoners, Royals and celebrities who've purchased second homes in the Cotswolds. Their presence has raised house prices and made it very difficult for locals to buy properties in their own towns and villages, but the big grey cloud's silver lining is that standards in local pubs and restaurants have been raised to award-winning, Michelin star-earning levels. These eateries now equal or better any in the nation.

But that's not just down to Londoners. There's been a country-wide rise in ethical eating, Fairtrade products, organic food and locally sourced produce, but it's been firmly embraced in the Cotswolds. This is still a big farming region, after all – and it's close enough to Devon and Cornwall for fresh seafood to be delivered daily.

Tetbury's Prince Charles has his own organic food range, Duchy Originals, sold in Waitrose, plus a Highgrove farm shop in Tetbury itself. Wherever you go in the Cotswolds, you'll chance upon restaurants serving fresh, locally sourced, ethically made, organic, independent food, along with farm shops and farmers' markets. The Cotswolds have become a gastronomic destination – foodies should look up the Food Tours of the Cotswolds (thecotswoldchef.com) and cookery courses.

MARKETS
Due to the region's history as a centre for the wool and cloth trades, the Cotswolds have a long tradition of markets, as well as many well-prepared market towns. So although the farmers' market phenomenon is fairly recent, it's also a continuation of the region's

traditional practices and values. The best of these markets is Stroud's (Saturdays). The largest in the country, it has featured on numerous television programmes. Other thriving farmers' markets to look for include Cirencester (second and fourth Saturdays of the month), Deddington (Saturdays), Stratford-upon-Avon (first and third Saturdays of the month), Stow-on-the-Wold (second Thursday of the month), Chipping Norton (third Saturday of every month), and Oxford's Covered Market (daily).

Farm shops are another great way to get high-quality produce straight from the source. The better ones include Bisley's Stancombe Beech Farm Shop, Chedworth Farm Shop (cotswoldfarmfayre.com), Daylesford Organic Farm (daylesford.com), The Cotswold Food Store (cotswoldfoodstore. co.uk), Wayside Farm (near Evesham, wayside-farm.co.uk) and The Butts Farm Shop (near Cirencester, buttsfarmrarebreeds.co.uk), but look out for signs as you drive around, and check farmshopping.net. You'll also see roadside signs offering eggs, strawberries and other local produce at sub-supermarket prices.

FOOD
The region's reputation is centred on meats, especially Old Spot pork, Gloucester sausages, boar (from therealboar.co.uk), venison, meatballs (from lovemycow. com), award-winning organic burgers, local lamb, smoked venison, fish from Donnington and Bibury trout farms, and salmon (from uptonsmokery. co.uk). But the Cotswolds' fruit (particularly Blaisdon Red plums), vegetables (especially asparagus), honey, Tewkesbury mustard, ales and beer are also superb. But above all that, the Cotswolds' signature foodstuff is cheese. The region can boast more than 100 varieties, including mild and crumbly Single Gloucester (Godsells Cheese, godsellscheese.com), much rarer than its country-wide cousin Double Gloucester; yummy goats' cheeses (Windrush Valley Dairy); the Camembert-esque St Eadburgha (Gorsehill Abbey,

gorsehillabbey.co.uk) and creamy organic Cotswold Brie (Simon Weaver, simonweaver.net).

Cotswolders also love their puddings. Look out for the Banbury cake (Eccles-esque, currant-filled pastry), a local speciality, and if you're ever near Nailsworth or Stroud, make sure you get up onto Rodborough Common to taste gorgeous, traditional Winstones Ice Cream. This small, family-run company is very popular with locals.

Food festivals to look out for include the excellent two-week-long Stroud Food & Drink Festival (September, stroudvalleysfestivals.co.uk), the Fairford & Lechlade Food & Drink Festival (May, fairfordlechladefoodanddrink. co.uk), the Cheltenham Food Festival (June, garden-events.com), and the Foodies Festival (Oxford, August, foodiesfestival.com).

DRINK

The region specialises in cosy, Cotswold-stone pubs, at their best when there's a fireplace (and that plump, purring cat). There's a good tradition of real ales here, too. Top tipples to look out for include Hook Norton's Hooky (golden bitter), Old Hooky (fruity) and Double Stout (dark, malty); The Patriot Brewery's Bulldog (golden ale) and Nelson (a classic bitter); Cotswold Spring's Codger (dry, crisp, with a hoppy finish), Stunner

(a malty, fruity pale ale) and Rascal (fruity, citrussy wheat beer). Top real ale pubs include The Snowshill Arms, Cheltenham's Royal Oak, Tetbury's The Snooty Fox or Northleach's The Wheatsheaf Inn.

Though the neighbouring counties of Hereford and Somerset have bigger reputations for cider making than the Cotswolds, you'll find some very tasty ciders here too. Start by visiting Coleshill House's Cotswolds Cider Company in Oxfordshire. Barnes & Adams are another local cider-maker, while Jo and Isaac Nixon at Prior's Tipple are artisan cider makers with a passion for creating excellent samples. For more information on Cotswolds beverages (soft and hard), visit cotswoldfinest.com

The wildly popular Frocester Beer Festival (August, dursleylions.com), the South Cotswold Beer Festival (July, bs37.com), the Winter Ales Festival (Tewkesbury, February, tewkesburycamra.org.uk), the Cotswold Beer Festival (Winchcombe, July, gloucestershirecamra.org.uk) and the Hook Norton Festival of Fine Ales (July, hookybeerfest. co.uk) all celebrate the region's contributions to drinking culture.

BEFORE YOU GO

THINGS TO READ

Cider With Rosie is the quintessential Cotswolds text. Laurie Lee beautifully describes a place in Gloucestershire, but also a place in time, capturing a key moment in history just on the cusp of its passing.

Hilarious travelogue writer and former *Times* subeditor Bill Bryson visited the Cotswolds in *Notes from a Small Island*. Radio 4 listeners voted to decide what book best represented Britain, and this won out. Starting from Oxford (after a few troubles with his rental car), Bryson calls in at Woodstock ('I must say I like [it] very much'), Blenheim Palace and Park ('a rural Arcadia', though he wasn't so complimentary about the Pleasure Gardens), Bladon ('nondescript'), Broadway ('absurdly pretty'), Broadway Tower ('sensational'), Snowshill (which seems to briefly please him), Snowshill Manor (which he was greatly intrigued by), Cirencester (where he praises the Corinium Museum's 'outstanding' collection) and finally Winchcombe, rounding off his time in the region with an 'enchanting walk' to see a Roman mosaic on nearby Cole's Hill.

Though William Shakespeare was from the region, the Cotswolds don't crop up often in his revered plays, with the exception being *Richard II*. This play gives us the lines:

> *'I am a stranger here in Gloucestershire,*
> *These high wild hills and rough uneven ways*
> *Draws out our miles, and makes them wearisome'*

Influential novelist J B Priestley visited the Cotswolds for his 1933 travelogue, *English Journey*, and marvelled at the oolitic limestone buildings. He wasn't smitten with Bourton-on-the-Water, but adored nearby Lower and Upper Slaughter. He likened the Cotswolds to a setting from a fairytale and pleaded for them to preserved as they were. 'The beauty of the Cotswolds belongs to England and

England should see that she keeps it.' The region would eventually be granted the protected status of Area of Outstanding Natural beauty. Bredon Hill, a big outlier hill just north of the Cotswolds escarpment, features in plenty of poetry, writing and art. Most famously it is depicted in poem 21 of A E Housman's *A Shropshire Lad*:

> *'In summertime on Bredon*
> *The bells they sound*
> *so clear*
> *Round both the shires*
> *they ring them*
> *In steeples far and near*
> *A happy noise to hear'*

When he was stationed in France during World War I, Gloucester-born poet and musician Ivor Gurney wrote a poignant poem entitled *Crickley Hill*, which included the lines:

> *'O sudden steep! O hill*
> *towering above!*
> *Chasm from the road falling*
> *suddenly away!*
> *Sure no men talked of you*
> *with more love'*

THINGS TO WATCH

Watch *Harry Potter* to see... Gloucester Cathedral, used in several of the films as part of Hogwarts. Many additional Hogwarts scenes were filmed at Oxford University's Christ Church College. You can see the fan-traceried vaulted ceiling in the tower housing the staircase and landing used in *Harry Potter*

and the Philosopher's Stone (2001) and *Harry Potter and the Chamber of Secrets* (2002). The Tudor architecture of the grand Dining Hall in Christ Church College was the inspiration for the set design of Hogwarts Great Hall.

Watch 2002 James Bond film *Die Another Day* to see... parts of Bourton-on-the-Water – albeit mostly a local car park, which was covered in artificial snow for the filming so that Bond and his Aston Martin could be dramatically chased across it. The film also made use of an ex-RAF aircraft runway at nearby Upper Rissington in the same ice chase scene.

Watch *Bridget Jones's Diary* (2001) to see... pretty Snowshill, near Broadway. Filming included the village green and a local house featuring as the home of Bridget's parents. For the scene when she visited them at Christmas time, the village was covered in artificial snow.

Watch *Emma*, the 1996 TV dramatisation of Jane Austen's famous novel (starring Kate Beckinsale and Prunella Scales), to see... Sudeley Castle and Stanway House, near Broadway, both of which formed parts of Mr Knightley's home, Donwell Abbey.

Watch 2004's *The Libertine* to see... Stanway House. Johnny Depp plays a debauched 17th century poet, the womanising Earl of Rochester. Stanway House also featured in 2004's

Vanity Fair, which starred Reese Witherspoon.

Watch 2010 TV hit *Downton Abbey* to see… Bampton. Most of the exterior shots of the drama series were filmed in this Oxfordshire village.

Watch *The Bourne Ultimatum* (2007), *Brideshead Revisited* (2008), *The Oxford Murders* (2008), *Inspector Morse* (1987–2000) and *The Madness of King George* (1994) to see… Oxford.

Watch BBC's period drama *Tess Of The d'Urbervilles*, an adaptation of the famous Thomas Hardy novel of the same name, to see… Owlpen Manor and Chavenage House, near Tetbury.

Watch *Amazing Grace* to see… Gloucester's docks.

Watch *Lark Rise to Candleford* (2008), *House of Elliot* (1991–94), *Noel Edmund's House Party* (1991–99), *Poirot: The Mysterious Affair at Styles* (1990) and many more TV programmes to see… Chavenage House.

THINGS TO KNOW

▶ Prince Charles, Princess Anne, Liz Hurley, Jeremy Clarkson, Damien Hirst, Alex James, Lily Allen, Rebekah Brooks and Kate Moss are just a few of the celebrities with Cotswolds abodes. The quickest way to make yourself unpopular with locals, however, is to start asking questions about them. Local people aren't particularly interested in tabloid fodder, especially as the newcomers have helped drive house prices through the roof (excuse the pun). The only exceptions to this general apathy might be the two royals, who've lived in the area a long time.

▶ There's no general agreement on what the word Cotswolds means, though it's probably of Saxon origin and probably originally conveyed something like 'sheep enclosures on the hills'.

▶ Covering nearly 790 square miles and spanning across six counties (Warwickshire, Worcestershire, Gloucestershire, Oxfordshire, Somerset and Wiltshire), the Cotswolds is the largest of the 38 Areas of Outstanding Natural Beauty (AONB) in England and Wales.

▶ About 80 per cent of the Cotswolds is farmland. This farmland is divided by around 4,000 miles of dry-stone walls – that's roughly equivalent in length to the Great Wall of China.

▶ The Cotswolds is crisscrossed with around 3,000 miles of public footpaths, which are often well-waymarked.

▶ The Cotswolds is part of the largest geological feature in the country: a slab of limestone that stretches from Yorkshire to Dorset.

▶ Some Cotswolds plants are so rare that they have specific legal protection under the Wildlife and Countryside Act 1981.

- The Cotswolds region contains five European Special Areas of Conservation, three National Nature Reserves and over 80 Sites of Special Scientific Interest.
- 120,000 people live in the Cotswolds Area of Outstanding Natural Beauty. Seventy-three per cent of them commute to jobs outside it.
- The highest point in the Cotswolds is Cleeve Hill (330m or 1083ft), near Winchcombe.
- Some of the most important research in the early days of geology was undertaken in the Cotswolds, so the area is strongly connected to the development of the subject. The theory of strata was developed near Bath.
- The first officially recognised dinosaur was found in the Cotswolds in 1824, at Stonesfield.

THINGS TO PACK

Map and walking boots
To get up into those beckoning hills

Camera
To capture the views from the top

Wild flower book
Even the locals don't know what half of them are

Autograph book
In case you catch sight of any of the wearisome Cotswolds-lite celebrities

Sunglasses
So you can pretend you might be a celebrity

Credit card
It's not the cheapest holiday destination

Trousers a size too big
You'll need them after a couple of big Cotswolds dinners

▼ A finger signpost for Stow on the Wold and Toddington

Hand cream
For repairing the damage after you end up taking that dry-stone wall-building course (see cotswoldsruralskills.org.uk)

Reading glasses
For *Cider With Rosie*

HOW TO GET AROUND
Though trains call at the region's cities (Gloucester, Oxford) and some of the larger towns (Cheltenham, Banbury, Kemble, Moreton-in-Marsh, Stratford-upon-Avon, Stroud), and local buses will get you to most of the villages eventually, the Cotswolds aren't blessed with a great public transport network. Your own wheels – two or four – are definitely the way to go. Plus, then you'll have better access to quiet little Cotswolds secrets like Bisley and Minchinhampton.

That said, the traffic can be a headache at peak times, particularly in midsummer on the A429 between Stow-on-the-Wold and Cirencester. Likewise, you should try to avoid the A40 between Burford and Cheltenham on Bank Holidays and Sunday evenings, especially when travelling eastwards. Coming and going, the M4 and M5 are good bets – just check the traffic reports first.

Cars aside, there are two very enjoyable train journeys to be had in the Cotswolds, more for leisure's sake than for reasons of practicality. The historic Gloucestershire Warwickshire Railway (gwsr. com) offers a chuffing steam train ride. The much-loved Cotswold Line goes between Oxford and Hereford, through some of the north Cotswolds most beautiful scenery, especially the stretch from Evenlode to Moreton. The Line also features in two notable poems: *Adlestrop*, by Edward Thomas, and Sir John Betjeman's *Pershore Station, or A Liverish Journey First Class*.

WHERE TO STAY
Even before the Cotswolds were a tourist destination, places such as Broadway were popular stop-offs for long-distance coaching journeys. The region's thus very well prepared for visitors. There are all types of accommodation, though the scale is weighted more towards the boutique and luxury B&B end than the budget end – there aren't many hostels or campsites compared to, say, Devon or Wales. Though of course the cities and larger towns, particularly Cheltenham and Oxford, are appealing, and have more amenities, if what you're after is a classic Cotswolds experience, the more obvious honeypot villages are in the north. These include Chipping Campden, the most elegant of the lot, Burford, Bibury, Bourton-on-the-Water and Broadway. All are very photogenic, but all get crowded in the summer and most weekends. To dodge the coach-loads a little, perhaps look to stay in Winchcombe,

Blockley or Snowshill in the north, or further south in Painswick, Nailsworth or Tetbury. All are picturesque places with great character.

Also think about what it is you want from the Cotswolds. If it's to tag as many syrupy villages, manor houses and gardens as possible, the north has more A-listers. The central area (Painswick, Nailsworth, Stroud, etc.) has fewer crowds and more varied walking. It's also closest to the best farmers' markets and restaurants, which are, loosely speaking, located at the Tetbury-Stroud-Cirencester axis.

For a list of hotels and B&Bs in picturesque stone cottages, visitcotswolds.co.uk is a good starting point. You could also contact the tourist board for a free Welcome to the Cotswolds brochure (01285 623545; cotswold.gov.uk).

If you're keener on camping, see Campsites, page 56. Other good Cotswold campsites include Thistledown Farm near Stroud (01453 860420; thistledown.org.uk), Cotswold Camping near Charlbury (01608 810810; cotswoldscamping. co.uk) and Far Peak Camping near Northleach (01285 720858; farpeakcamping.co.uk).

WHEN TO VISIT

Every season has good reason to visit. Crowd-free winters are ideal for crisp, enlivening walks, long pub lunches by the fire – and lower hotel prices. Spring brings bluebells, daffodils and bleating lambs. Summer's great of course, but the honeypot villages in the north get swamped with bus tours and day-trippers. But then again, the more sunlight, the more those buildings glow. Autumn's just peachy: the villages and hills are quieter, plus those beech woodlands are gloriously ablaze, especially at the magnificent Westonbirt and Batford Arboretums.

VISITING WITH KIDS

Kids might get bored being dragged around to village after village, which may all look the same to them after a while. However most village visits can easily be combined with short but rewarding walks. Animals are usually crowd pleasers, and Cotswold Wildlife Park (Burford), Cotswold Farm Park (Kineton), Slimbridge Wetland Centre or Bourton-on-the-Water's Birdland should keep them young 'uns entertained. If the weather's looking uncooperative, then think about visiting manor houses and mansions (see 10 Mansions and Manor Houses, page 245), castles (Sudeley or Berkeley) and, if there's a break in the clouds, get out to those spectacular gardens. The historic Gloucestershire Warwickshire Railway (gwsr. com) is another option. If the weather's good, the Cotswold Water Park (near Cirencester, waterpark.org) is well worth splashing out at.

▲ Gloucestershire Warwickshire Railway

THINK LOCAL

In places such as Chipping Norton, it may look like everyone's a lord or a millionaire. But that's not the case across most of the Cotswolds. In fact an influx of wealthy Johnny-and-Jenny-come-latelies has pushed house prices beyond the reach of some locals. Good new business fail here as they do elsewhere, bullied by global-brand competitors. Wherever you can, please shop locally in the independent cafes and shops rather than grabbing something from one of the ubiquitous chains. Being independently-minded is very much what the Cotswolds are about.

FURTHER INFORMATION

The best starting point, especially for the great outdoors and things like dry-stone walling courses, is escapetothecotswolds.org.uk. Another good resource is the-cotswolds.org, and the area's official tourist information site is glos-cotswolds.com (01452 425673).

Local tourist information centres include Bourton-on-the-Water (01451 820211); Chipping Campden (01386 841206); Cirencester (01285 654180); Moreton-in–Marsh (01608 650881); Stow-on-the-Wold (01451 831082); and Tetbury (01666 503552). Most are open usual office hours, as well as on weekends.

FESTIVALS & EVENTS

As well as various arts, literary and music festivals in the Cotswolds, there are many original, traditional and quirky celebrations...

MAY

▶ **Cotswold Olimpick Games, Chipping Campden**
If you can only make one Cotswolds event, make it this one. The Cotswold Olimpicks started in 1612, and they continue today with torch-lit processions, Morris dancing, tug of war, shin kicking and welly wanging. Unique and brilliant. olimpickgames.co.uk

▶ **Cheese-Rolling at Cooper's Hill, Brockworth, Spring Bank Holiday**
A mock double Gloucester cheese is rolled down a precipitous slope and people run/fall after it, breaking a few bones while someone from nearby Brockworth inevitably nabs the prize. Idiosyncratically Cotswoldian. cheese-rolling.co.uk

▶ **Randwick Wap & Spring Time Cheese Rolling Ceremony, Randwick (near Stroud)**
Randwick also has a cheese rolling ceremony, preceded by a colourful procession of costumed villages led by the Mop Man, who wields a wet mop to clear crowds. Plus there's a dunking in the pond. The festival is thought to date back 700 years.

▶ **Tetbury Woolsack Races, Tetbury**
Men and women race up an impossibly steep hill carrying 60lb (35lb for the ladies) sacks of wool on their backs. The event, celebrating Tetbury's past as a prosperous wool town, dates to the 17th century. There's also a street fair. tetburywoolsack.co.uk

▶ **Levellers' Day, Burford**
This day of music, fancy dress, debate and entertainment celebrates three Levellers who quit Oliver Cromwell's New Model Army, and were executed here.

▶ **Morris Dancing, May Day**
Dancing with bells and sticks is still a strong tradition here, thought to date to at least the 13th century. The dances are a celebration of rural life, and often include elements that mimic country skills, such as harvesting and sewing. May Day and St George's Day are good times to catch the spectacle.

JUNE

▶ **Ramsden Fete, Ramsden**
Not just your average collection of cupcake and second-hand Lego stalls. The Ramsden Fete offers a strong man contest,

jousting, egg throwing, morris dancing (of course) and much more glorious silliness. ramsdenvillage.co.uk

▶ **Summer Solstice, Rollright Stones**
Join the Cotswold Order of Druids at the mysterious Rollright Stones, near Chipping Norton, to see in the longest day of the year. There's also a Samhain ceremony in early November. rollrightstones.co.uk

▶ **Loghborough Festival Opera, near Moreton-in-Marsh**
A boutique opera event, set in a converted barn on a country estate. 2013's edition played Wagner's entire Ring Cycle to celebrate the composer's bicentenary. lfo.org.uk

JULY

▶ **Banbury Hobby Horse Festival, Banbury**
When they all turn out for this parade, the number and variety of horse-related costumes that exist in the world will stagger you. There's Maypole dancing and lots of horsing around. hobbyhorsefestival.co.uk

▶ **Art Couture, Painswick**
At this lively festival of wearable art, you'll likely see costumes running the whole gamut between weird and wonderful. There are also street shows and music. acpfestival.co.uk

AUGUST

▶ **Treefest, Westonbirt Arboretum**
A celebration of traditional woodcrafts and woodland skills. See falconry and axe carving. forestry.gov.uk/westonbirt

▶ **Football In The River, Bourton-on-the-Water**
Six-a-side, 15 minutes each way, kicks off at 4pm – only the pitch is the Windrush River,

which runs through the centre of Bourton-on-the-Water. This tradition of moist matches has been around for over 70 years. Spectators should expect to get wet too.

SEPTEMBER

▶ **Painswick Ancient Clypping Ceremony, Painswick**
Painswick's church yard is famous for its 99 yew trees and many failed attempts to grow a hundredth (see page 176). In the 'Clypping' ceremony, children carry flowers and join hands around the church while singing the Clypping Hymn. The annual observance is thought to date back to 1321.

▶ **Tetbury Food and Drink Festival, Tetbury**
From Gloucester Old Spot sausages to wines from Bow in the Cloud Vineyard, this festival is all about local Cotswold produce. There's crafts, music and cookery demonstrations. tetburyfooddrinkfestival.com

DECEMBER

▶ **Boxing Day Duck Race, Bibury**
Hundreds of festive fans gather in pretty Bibury for the increasingly popular duck races. Two races orchestrated by the local cricket club, one of 150 'decoy' ducks and a second of over 2,000 plastic yellow fellows. It's a good quack. biburycricketclub.co.uk

▶ **Marshfield Paperboys, Marshfield, Boxing Day**
The town crier leads a procession of 'Mummers' dressed in paper costumes through the streets, as the 'paper boys' perform the town's unique mumming play. There are carols and encores along the street, with six performances in total.

CAMPSITES

For more information on these and other campsites, visit theaa.com/self-catering-and-campsites

Tudor Caravan & Camping ▶▶▶▶

tudorcaravanpark.com

Shepherds Patch, Slimbridge, GL2 7BP | 01453 890483 | Open all year

This park benefits from one of the best locations in the county, situated right alongside the Sharpness to Gloucester canal and just a short walk from the famous Wildfowl & Wetlands Trust at Slimbridge. The site has two areas, one for adults only. As it's next to the canal, there are excellent walks plus the National Cycle Network route 41 can be accessed from the site.

Apple Tree Park Caravan and Camping Site ▶▶▶▶

appletreepark.co.uk

A38, Claypits, Stonehouse; GL10 3AL 01452 742362 & 07708 221457 Open Feb–Nov

This family-owned park is on the A38, not far from the M5. A peaceful site with glorious views of the Cotswolds, the park is well located for visiting Slimbridge Wildfowl &

Wetlands Trust and makes an excellent stopover for M5 travellers.

Mayfield Touring Park ▶▶▶▶

mayfieldpark.co.uk

Cheltenham Rd, Cirencester, GL7 7BH | 01285 831301 | Open all year

Mayfield is a gently sloping park on the edge of the Cotswolds, with level pitches and a warm welcome. It's an ideal base for exploring the Cotswolds and its many attractions, and for walking the nearby Monarch's Way and Cotswold Way.

Bo Peep Farm Caravan Park ▶▶▶▶

bo-peep.co.uk

Bo Peep Farm, Aynho Rd, Adderbury, Banbury, OX17 3NP | 01295 810605 Open Mar–Oct

Charmingly named Bo Peep Farm is a park with good views and a spacious feel. Four well laid out camping areas are planted with maturing shrubs and trees. In keeping with the area the two facility blocks are built in attractive

Cotswold stone. The newly refurbished 'Dovecote Barn' offers on-site food at selected times. There are four miles of walks on site.

Lincoln Farm Park Oxfordshire ▶▶▶▶▶

lincolnfarmpark.co.uk
High St, Standlake, OX29 7RH
01865 300239 | Open Feb–Nov
This attractively landscaped family-run park, is in a quiet village near the Thames. There are top class facilities throughout the park, and excellent leisure facilities in the Standlake Leisure Centre. A warm welcome is assured from the friendly staff. As an added bonus, there's outdoor chess.

Cotswold View Touring Park ▶▶▶▶

www.cotswoldview.f9.co.uk
Enstone Rd, Charlbury, OX7 3JH
01608 810314 | Open Easter or Apr–Oct
This is a good Cotswold site, well screened, but with attractive views across the countryside. Breakfasts and takeaway food are available from the shop, and the site has camping pods for hire. Fans of old-fashioned games will enjoy the skittle alley and boules.

Briarfields Motel & Touring Park ▶▶▶▶

briarfields.net/
Gloucester Rd, Cheltenham, GL51 0SX | 01242 235324 | Open all year
Briarfields is a well-designed level park, with a motel, where the facilities are modern and very clean. The park is well-positioned between Cheltenham and Gloucester, with easy access to the Cotswolds. And, being close to the M5, it makes a perfect overnight stopping point.

Greenhill Leisure Park ▶▶▶▶

greenhill-leisure-park.co.uk/
Greenhill Farm, Station Rd, Bletchingdon, OX5 3BQ | 01869 351600 | Open all year (restricted opening Oct–Mar no dogs, shop & games room closed)
Greenhill is an all-year round park set in open countryside near the village of Bletchingdon. Fishing is available in the nearby river or in the park's two well-stocked lakes. Pitches are very spacious and the park is very family orientated. The owner's motto is 'Where fun meets the countryside'. The facilities are also very good.

Wysdom Touring Park ▶▶

Cheltenham Rd, Burford, OX18 4PL
01993 823207 | Open all year
Owned by Burford School, this small 'adults' only' park is very much a hidden gem being just a five minute walk from Burford, one of prettiest towns in the Cotswolds. The pitches have good privacy; all have electric and there are many hardstandings for caravans and motorhome. The unisex toilet facilities are very clean.

VISIT THE MUSEUMS | GET OUTDOORS | EXPLORE BY BIKE | GO BACK IN TIME | TAKE A TRAIN RIDE | MEET THE WILDLIFE

TAKE IN SOME HISTORY | HIT THE BEACH | EAT AND DRINK | GET INDUSTRIAL | VISIT THE GALLERIES | GO CANOEING

TRY HORSE-RIDING | PLACES NEARBY | CATCH A PERFORMANCE | GO ROUND THE GARDENS | TAKE A BOAT TRIP

A–Z of
The Cotswolds

▶ Badminton

Badminton joins Mexico's Tabasco as a place a lot less famous than its name has become. Unlike the sauce, however, the sport of thwacking a feathery flying thing across a high net doesn't strictly come from this place of the same name. The game was imported here from India in 1873 and takes its name from Badminton House, the demesne of the Dukes of Beaufort. But this little village is also pretty famous for its annual, high-profile three-day horse trials. They've taken place on the estate since 1949, and the roads get pretty gridlocked around here when they're on in early May. The village is worth a quick look, even if Badminton House itself is closed to the public. The village's yellow, lime-washed houses seem out of step with their Cotswolds neighbours.

Badminton House is a Palladian structure, built for the first Duke of Beaufort in 1682 and remodelled by William Kent in 1740. It's considered a fine example of period style and the interior – which, unfortunately, you won't be seeing – is wonderfully decorated. The park was partly the work of famous landscape architect 'Capability' Brown. Some of the formal layout is on a quite extraordinary scale: the tree-lined Great Avenue is several miles long.

Great Badminton, the 18th-century church on the grounds of the estate, is notable for its monuments to the Beaufort family. One of these, by Grinling Gibbons, is so big that the church had to be altered to accommodate it. The boxpews are exceptionally large, like old-fashioned snug bars.

The area around Badminton was known locally as 'Beaufortshire' famous as home to the Beaufort Hunt.

▶ PLACES NEARBY

The brilliantly named Sodburys – the villages of Chipping, Old and Little – (see page 189) and an impressive Iron Age hill-fort are only about five minutes away, across the other side of the A46. And it only takes another five minutes to tootle down the A46 to visit Dyrham Park (see page 119), an excellent National Trust site with a manor house, gardens and herds of deer.

▶ Barnsley & Barnsley House

barnsleyhouse.com

GL7 5EE | 01285 740000 | Usually open daily; contact first

Little Barnsley is right up there with the very prettiest Cotswolds villages. And there, coyly keeping its charms hidden until the last moment, stands Barnsley House. After the abrupt

▲ Badminton Horse Trials

entrance drive has been negotiated, the first and lasting
impression is one of harmony. The House is both a restaurant
(offering mainly Italian-inspired mains) and a hotel, but
chances are that even if you only popped in for a nose about,
you'll end up at least buying lunch. And if you only popped in
for lunch, chances are you'll be staying the night. The
honey-coloured Queen Anne house stands serenely amid
4 acres of intimate gardens, which are well worth a visit.
Restaurant guests have free access to these, but call ahead.
Rosemary Verey and her late husband, David, began to design
the gardens in the 1960s. On an axis from the drawing-room
door, a stone path – its texture softened by clumps of
geraniums and rock roses – runs straight to the centre of the
south lawn, which is flanked by the soft, muted colours of
aquilegias, stachys, phlomis and other flowers. Beyond this,
a purple sycamore, an atlas cedar and a silver-grey white
poplar provide a marvellous contrast of foliage colours,
textures and shapes.

A delightful knot garden sits near to the house's western
side, its little box hedges set amid gravel in the manner of
16th and 17th century formal parterres. In the 1960s David
Verey moved a temple from Fairford Park to the southeast
corner of the garden, creating a peaceful vista that leads the
eye over the richly covered lily pond, through two iron gates
flanked by statuesque cypresses, and finally to a charming
wall fountain beyond.

Alongside Mrs Verey's potager, or decorative kitchen garden, runs a wonderful laburnum tunnel. In spring this tunnel is thickly covered with yellow panicles that reach down to meet the tall, mauve alliums that rise from beneath its shade.

The potager, inspired by the one at the Chateau de Villandry in the Loire valley, and by *The Country Housewife's Garden*, written in 1617 by William Lawson, is a remarkable creation. The layout of the potager is typical of Barnsley House garden– a charming mixture of nonchalance and formality. Brick paths in many different patterns criss-cross the area. The beds themselves are planted with red and green varieties of lettuce and other vegetables, while sweet peas grow close to gooseberries, onions, cabbages, lavender and strawberries.

In perfect harmony with the stone wall behind them, two stone statues of country girls holding baskets generously filled with flowers flank the gateway to the potager beyond.

10 classic towns & villages

▶ **PLACES NEARBY**

Barnsley's church has unusual Norman features, and the village also has a fine pub. Painfully picturesque Bibury (see page 66), one of the Cotswolds' most photographed villages, is only a little way west on the B4425. Also on the B4425, nearer Cirencester, you'll find Abbey House Farm's excellent Organic Farm Shop.

Abbey House Farm Shop
theorganicfarmshop.co.uk
GL7 5HF (though they warn that satnavs will misdirect you)
01285 640441
Offers lots of sumptuous stuff to eat in its own right, but there's also an award-winning cafe with vegan options, as well as accommodation (including yurts and a lakeside cabin).

The Village Pub ◉
thevillagepub.co.uk
GL7 5EF | 01285 740421

Owned by Barnsley House and frequented by actress Elizabeth Hurley, The Village Pub's beds and food are more affordable than those of its parent institution. It has an uber-sleek interior and high quality nosh, plus six very inviting bedrooms.

▶ Berkeley Castle

berkeley-castle.com
Berkeley, GL13 9BQ | 01453 810303 | Open Apr–Oct, Sun–Wed
11–5 (last admission 4)

We probably shouldn't grumble really – at least not within earshot of locals – but if the Cotswolds do lack something, it's castles. Well, and beaches. But let's deal with the castles for now. Not including Castle Combe, which is a misleadingly-named village, there are only two castles in the Cotswolds: Sudeley (see page 217) and Berkeley. And really, Sudeley is a Renaissance manor house rather than a genuine military fort. Berkeley, on the other hand, is a real castle, belonging to the more aggressive Middle Ages.

For 850 years the gaunt profile of Berkeley Castle has kept watch over the Severn and the Welsh Borders, seeming to grow powerfully out of the outcrop of rock on which it stands. With its forbidding towers and dense walls of purple stone, it was for centuries the home of one of the region's most powerful families. Few can trace their ancestry back to the Anglo-Saxons, but the Berkeleys of Berkeley Castle descend directly from the Master of the Horse to Edward the Confessor. Their descendants have lived here for more than 800 years.

Events of great importance have taken place inside its thick walls. The West Country barons met in the castle's great hall before placing their demands before King John at Runnymede in 1215. In 1327, the unfortunate Edward II was first imprisoned and then murdered in a room in the keep. During the Civil War Berkeley Castle was besieged for three days by Parliamentary forces, and though the castle was not seriously damaged, the large breach the Parliamentarians made in the wall of the keep remains to this day.

Berkeley Castle was founded after Henry II granted a Charter to Robert Fitzharding in 1153. Visitors still enter the shell keep via a Norman doorway in the inner courtyard. Most of the building that we see today dates from the 14th century. The Drake Room and Tower Room contain a later – but nonetheless remarkable – collection of ebony furniture from the Portuguese East Indies, which, by tradition, once belonged to Sir Francis Drake. In the picture gallery there are seascapes by van de Velde, portraits by Lely, a groom and horses by Stubbs and a hunting painting, *The Old Berkeley Hounds*, by Benjamin Marshall. Hunting is an ever-present subject at Berkeley. The dining room is hung with portraits of three Masters of the Berkeley Hounds, by Raoul Millais, William Orpen, and John Teesdale. Beyond the medieval kitchen is the housekeeper's room, where the Godwin Cup – believed to have belonged to King Harold's father – is displayed.

The great hall still retains a medieval atmosphere, with its 13 foot- (4m-) thick walls hung with Oudenarde tapestries illustrating the story of Queen Esther, an unusual painted screen dating from the 16th century and a magnificent timber roof. Over the fireplace hangs a fine portrait of Admiral Sir Cranfield Berkeley by Gainsborough. A well-preserved Berkeley Arch gives access to the grand staircase. This lovely wooden stair (1637) leads to the morning room, which was once the chapel. The ribs of its ceiling are painted with verses from the Bible, translated into Norman French in 1387 by John Trevisa, a friend of scholar and philosopher John Wycliffe. The verses are an early example of the practice of rendering the Bible in the vernacular. The walls of the staircase are hung with

▼ Berkeley Castle and gardens

magnificent early Brussels tapestries depicting the stories of Isaac and Rebecca and Sodom and Gomorrah, woven by the de Pannemaekers from cartoons by Raphael. Among the wall decorations is a Doom painting above the chancel arch, intended to urge people away from the path of sin.

From the castle, the views over the gardens to the river are superb. The terraces have grass walks with borders of low plants, backed by shrubs and climbers, while the bowling alley is flanked by a high wall and ancient clipped yews. Beyond, cattle graze in the water meadows, creating as beautiful and peaceful a scene as can be found anywhere in the country.

The Butterfly House has close to 42 species of fluttery things, including specimens from as far afield as Japan and Indonesia, and the Atlas, the world's largest moth. All are of course kept in one of those super-humid rooms that makes you feel instantly sleepy.

TAKE IN SOME HISTORY

Dr Jenner's House

jennermuseum.com
Church Lane, High St, GL13 9BN | 01453 810631 | Open early Apr–early Oct, Sun–Wed 12–5 (also Sat Jul–Aug and Oct half term)

At the risk of being morbid, you might never have been born if it wasn't for Edward Jenner. This fine fellow pioneered a vaccine against smallpox in 1796, and this beautiful Queen Anne house was Jenner's home. The house and the garden, with its thatched Temple of Vaccinia, are much as they were in his day. The displays record Jenner's life as an 18th-century country doctor, his work on vaccination and his interest in natural history. You can discover the story of a man who changed the world in the house where history was made. Jenner is buried in the chancel of the church.

EAT AND DRINK

The Malt House

themalthouse.uk.com
Marybrook St, GL13 9BA
01453 511177

In the middle of Berkeley and near the castle, this pub is popular with walkers tackling the spectacular Severn Way, which runs along the nearby estuary shoreline. Comfy accommodation and good food tempt passers-by into making overnight stops.

▶ PLACES NEARBY

The Slimbridge Wetland Centre (see page 187), which has the world's largest collection of swans, geese, ducks and flamingos, isn't far away. If you're in the mood for a walk, head east towards Dursley (see page 117) or Wotton-under-Edge (see page 252) to meet the Cotswolds Edge and to see some spectacular views from the top.

▶ Bibury

Bibury is the perfect place to capture pleasing Cotswolds clichés with your camera. Poet, artist, socialist and Arts and Crafts Movement luminary William Morris described Bibury as the 'most beautiful village in England', which is quite a claim in an area as blessed with handsome villages as this. Bibury is certainly in the upper echelon. Trout-filled River Coln glides alongside the almost-never-not-being-photographed row of picturesque cottages on the main street.

Bibury has Saxon origins, though most of what makes the village, as well as neighbouring settlement Arlington, so attractive dates from around the 17th century, when it prospered as a weaving centre. The interest-filled church sits in a well-tended churchyard at the far end of the main street, at the heart of the original village. It retains some of its original Saxon work – the chancel arch jambs, and fragments of a cross shaft.

TAKE IN SOME HISTORY
Arlington Row

Arlington Row, a terrace of low-gabled weavers' cottages just across the river, towards the church end of the village, is the most photographed street in Bibury, and perhaps in the entirety of the Cotswolds – and

▼ The River Coln and Arlington Row

for good reason. Seeing them may provoke one of those 'have I just stepped back in time?' moments. Originally they were used by workers weaving wool for Arlington Mill at the other end of the village – they used the Rack Isle in front of the cottages, now a bird sanctuary, for drying wool. The cottages are owned by the National Trust, and still occupied. The path in front of Arlington Row continues up the amusingly named Awkward Hill, which is lined with attractive cottages, or skirts Rack Isle, parallel to the river, and continues on to 17th-century Arlington Mill.

SEE A LOCAL CHURCH
St Mary's Church

The church has a Saxon core, which can be seen in the lower parts of the chancel arch and in the Saxon cross shaft set into the chancel wall. The original church was extended and embellished throughout the Middle Ages: there's a 13th-century south aisle with lancet windows, a large Perpendicular window to the right of the porch, and a Norman north doorway. The churchyard has a fine assortment of tombs and gravestones, a number of which commemorate the local clothiers and weavers who financed the development of the church over several centuries. Part of the churchyard is known as the Bisley Piece as a result of a curious story. It seems that the village of Bisley once possessed what was called a 'bone hole', into which bones were thrown when old graves were broken into. Some 600 years ago, a priest is supposed to have fallen in and died. The incident apparently angered the Pope himself, and consequently the pontiff forbade burials in Bisley (see page 216) for two years. Instead, at considerable inconvenience, the residents had to bury their dead at Bibury, 15 miles away.

EXPLORE BY BIKE
Capital Sport
capital-sport.co.uk
HP22 5EZ | 01296 631671
Cycling holidays in the Cotswolds, including a Cotswolds Valleys Luxury Tour that takes in Bibury and Burford.

GO FISHING
Bibury Trout Farm and Fishery
biburytroutfarm.co.uk
GL7 5NL | 01285 740215

10 hidden gems

Open April–Sep 8–6; closes at 5 Mar–Oct, 4 Nov–Mar Next door to Arlington Row you'll find Bibury Trout Farm and Fishery, where you can catch your own fish or buy them from the shop.

EAT AND DRINK
Swan Hotel ®
cotswold-inns-hotels.co.uk
GL7 5NW | 01285 740 695
The Swan Hotel was once a fashionable haunt for the followers of Bibury Races, which flourished during the 17th century. Now it's an elegant place to stay or to take afternoon tea.

▶ **PLACES NEARBY**

Nearby are two villages with good pubs, while Barnsley (see page 60) lies to the west.

Ablington

The pretty neighbouring hamlet of Ablington is comprised of a collection of cottages, barns and manor houses. It was home to Reverend Arthur Gibbs, the 19th-century author of *A Cotswold Village*.

Catherine Wheel

catherinewheel-bibury.co.uk
Ablington, GL7 5ND
01285 740250

Catherine Wheel is a former blacksmith's that opened as an inn in 1856. A warm welcome, good ales and quality food remain its hallmarks. The beautiful Cotswold-stone building, stable courtyard and orchard date back to the 15th century, and plenty of historical features remain. Catherine Wheel holds a beer festival held every August Bank Holiday.

The New Inn

new-inn.co.uk
Coln St Aldwyns, GL7 5AN

The main draw of Coln St Aldwyns, south of Bibury, is The New Inn, an attractive bar with a flower-filled courtyard and a superb restaurant. It's also an appealing place to stay.

▶ Blenheim Palace

See **Woodstock & Blenheim Palace**, page 246

▶ Blockley

This pretty village with a rather unpretty name sits beside the fast-flowing Blockley Brook. It's less well known than many of its more crowded neighbours – partly because the big tour buses struggle on the narrow lanes around here. So with a satisfying degree of privacy you can visit Blockley and discover its subtle appeal. The village, with its pretty mill stream, is dotted with houses of varying ages. It was formerly a silk town, employing 600 people in the six mills here in 1880, just before the failure of the industry in the area. Many of the weavers' cottages remain, with the older ones clustered towards the village centre and the 19th-century silk workers' cottages terraced along the northern edge. One of the old mills can be seen beyond a pool near the church. A beautiful garden, Mill Dene, has been created around another of the old mills.

The church of St Peter and St Paul, with its Norman chancel, is unusually large, a testament to the village's early status. Within are a Jacobean pulpit and some interesting brasses. There are plenty of good walks to be taken around Blockley and the surrounding area.

▲ Blockley

GO ROUND THE GARDENS

Mill Dene Garden

milldenegarden.co.uk
School Lane, GL56 9HU
01386 700457 | Open Apr–Sep,
Wed–Fri 10–5, Sat 9–2

A charming English garden
that triumphs against its
steep gradient and is full of
humour. Remarkably, the
creators admit that they
knew nothing about gardening
when they started out
decorating this 2.5 acre site.
There are plenty of inviting
seats dotted about so you can
take it easy, and they serve
cream teas too.

▶ PLACES NEARBY

To the north of Blockley
you'll find the busier and
prettier Chipping Campden (see
page 96) or yellow Broadway
(see page 77), a village of
great popularity with tourists,
but one that's nevertheless well
worth a look. To the south is
Moreton-in–Marsh (see page
151), which is better than it
sounds. Nearby Batsford (see
page 154) is an estate village
with a Victorian church which
contains some excellent
monuments, while Batsford
Park has an arboretum and a
falconry centre.

▶ Bourton-on-the-Water

▲ The River Windrush, Bourton-on-the-Water

Bourton-on-the-Water – especially in photographs – looks the very epitome of Cotswolds loveliness. But so many people visit that this must be the busiest place in the Cotswolds, and it's become something of a a victim of its own success. *All* the bus tours seem to stop here, and they seem to have brought with them an abundance of tacky gift shops and shockingly-priced ice cream. Bourton is fast becoming a Cotswolds parody.

The frustrating thing about all this – and probably the chief reason for Bourton's overpopularity – is that it offers a lot more attractions than most Cotswolds villages, where there's sometimes little to do other than look about a bit and click your camera a few times. These attractions range from the excellent Birdland (featuring everything from penguins to birds of prey) to a model village (representing Bourton in miniature), a perfume factory, a motor museum, the Dragonfly Maze, and a model railway exhibition – all near the High Street, within walking distance of each other. Bourton has loads to do and is particularly child friendly in a region that isn't always obviously so.

Bourton's church, St Lawrence's, is likewise comprised of a mixture of elements. It has a medieval chancel, a Victorian nave and a distinctive domed Georgian tower – complete with skull on the exterior, which serves as a salutary reminder of our mortality.

As well as this collection of attractions, 'the Venice of the Cotswolds' – as it likes to call itself in a rather bold and un-English manner – does have unique features not found in other Cotswolds honeypots. Namely, these consist of the five graceful footbridges that the River Windrush flows under in the village centre. They're backed by an appealing combination of Jacobean and Georgian facades in classic Cotswolds stone.

The region isn't particularly hilly, but there's good valley-walking to be enjoyed nearby – especially the circuit linking Upper Slaughter, Lower Slaughter and Naunton. Alternatively, the climb up to the Rissingtons is a shorter and quieter option. Nearer at hand, to the east of Bourton there are a series of disused gravel pits which, now filled with water, have become sanctuaries for waterfowl. Following the path across Station Road from the car park makes for a very pleasant walk.

If you can visit Bourton on a winter, spring or autumn weekday, and you may well love it. During standard visiting hours at any other time, you'll have to fight with the hordes for your prized photo – don't say you weren't warned. The absolute best day to visit Bourton, though – and to embrace the crowds, figuratively rather than literally – is the August Bank Holiday, when the typically quirky Cotswoldian Football on the River festival occurs (see page 54). A 30-minute game of football takes place in the normally calm Windrush River, with bridges for goalposts. Spectators shouldn't expect to remain dry.

VISIT THE MUSEUMS

Cotswold Motoring Museum & Toy Collection
See highlight panel opposite

Bourton Model Railway Exhibition
bourtonmodelrailway.co.uk
High St, GL54 2AN | 01451 820686
Open Jun–Aug 11–5, weekends only
Sep–May
Covering over 500 feet, these guys have some of the finest operating indoor model railway layouts in the country – so they say, anyway, and who are we to argue? Over 40 British and continental model trains run automatically on three main displays. There's also memorabilia, working fun fair models, and much more for those who love to keep it rail.

MEET THE BIRDLIFE

Birdland
See highlight panel overleaf

ENTERTAIN THE FAMILY

The Model Village
theoldnewinn.co.uk
Old New Inn, Rissington Road, GL54 2AF | 01451 820467
Open daily 10–6 (4 in winter)
The Model Village is a fascinatingly intricate one-ninth-scale replica of the centre of Bourton-on-the-Water. The best bit (or, depending on the viewer, the bit most likely to provoke *Inception*-style existential horror)? There's a model village within the model village. Mini Bourton took local craftsmen five years to build and was opened in 1937, on the Coronation Day of King George VI and Queen Elizabeth.

Dragonfly Maze
thedragonflymaze.com
Rissington Rd, GL54 2EE
01451 822251
Slowly negotiate your way to the centre (if you're lucky) of the high-hedge maze using clues on the flagstones en route. And if it isn't challenging enough, simply ask about 'the extra puzzle'. Perfectly suited to equally frustrate and amuse both children and adults.

TOUR THE FACTORY

Cotswold Perfumery
cotswold-perfumery.co.uk
GL54 2BU | 01451 820698
Open Mon–Sat 9.30–5, Sun and BH 10.30–5
This is one of Europe's few combined manufacturers and retailers of perfume, offering excellent factory tours and perfumery courses. 'We started with just one perfume – it was dreadful,' remembers John Stephen, the owner who turned his hobby into a business more than 40 years ago.

TAKE OFF

Ballooning In The Cotswolds
ballooninginthecotswolds.co.uk
GL5 3EX | 01453 753221
Get in a basket to appreciate the Cotswolds from above. You can get an early morning start, or wait for the late afternoon/evening time slot. Flights are subject to weather. Allow up to four hours, with about an hour in the air.

▸ Cotswold Motoring Museum & Toy Collection

cotswoldmotoringmuseum.co.uk

The Old Mill, GL54 2BY | 01451 821255 | Open daily, Feb–Nov 10–6

Vintage car collections, classic cars and motorcycles, quaint caravans, original enamel signs and an intriguing collection of motoring curiosities might sound like an enthusiast's special delight, but this museum is very much aimed at child visitors, too. A regularly changing exhibition takes a sideways look at some of the 20th century's motoring icons. Past exhibitions have included *Wallace & Gromit: The Curse of the Were-Rabbit*, and The Who film *Quadrophenia*.

▶ Birdland

birdland.co.uk

Rissington Road, GL54 2BN, 01451 820480 | Open all year, Apr–Oct 10–6, Nov–Mar 10–4 (last admission 1hr before closing)

Birdland has the only group of king penguins in England. There are also flamingos, pelicans, penguins, cranes, storks, cassowaries, waterfowl, over 50 aviaries of parrots, falcons, pheasants, hornbills, touracos, pigeons, ibis and many more feathered friends. The Toucan and Desert Houses are home to the more delicate species. Plenty to keep the kids – and adults – entertained.

EXPLORE BY BIKE

Hartwells Cotswolds Cycle Hire

hartwells.supanet.com

High Street, GL54 2AJ

01451 820405

Hartwells offers a large choice of mountain bikes, hybrid and touring cycles, and even tandems. Rentals include free car parking.

SADDLE UP

Bourton Vale Equestrian Centre

bourtonvaleequestrian.co.uk

GL54 2HN | 01451 821101

Escorted riding in small groups around the Slaughter villages for 1-2 hours. All ages and abilities. Pre-booking essential.

EAT AND DRINK

The Mad Hatter

Riverside, GL54 2BX

01451 821508

An afternoon spent here will transport you back to a bygone era, its olde worlde atmosphere brought to life by exposed wooden beams and an inglenook fireplace. The 18th-century building looks out onto the River Windrush.

▶ **PLACES NEARBY**

The Cotswold Farm Park (see page 133) is only 10 minutes' drive away. The Slaughters – Upper and Lower – are almost as good-looking as Bourton, and slightly less crowded. West of Bourton is a group of interesting villages – **Notgrove**, **Turkdean**, **Hazleton** and **Cold Aston** – that are worth a visit.

10 places to take the kids

▶ Birdland and Dragonfly Maze, Bourton-on-the-Water, page 72 and opposite

▶ Blenheim Palace, page 250

▶ Chedworth Roman Villa, page 87

▶ Cogges Manor Farm, page 243

▶ Cotswold Farm Park, page 133

▶ Cotswold Water Park, page 191

▶ Cotswold Wildlife Park, page 81

▶ Minchinhampton, page 148, Rodborough, page 213, Selsley, page 212, or Cleeve Common, page 236, for a kite-flying, Frisbee or a good old-fashioned run around

▶ Prinknash Bird and Deer Park, page 179

▶ Slimbridge Wetland Centre, page 187

▶ Westonbirt Arboretum, page 220

Naunton

Normally a place like Naunton, tucked into the bottom of a classic shallow but steep Cotswold valley, would be a pleasing attraction by itself. But because it's close to three other attractive villages it gets overlooked. The best way to visit it is on a walking loop from Bourton-on-the-Water, taking in both Slaughters as you stroll.

▶ Bredon Hill

Bredon Hill is quite the oddity around these parts. A traditional hill – one you can walk all around the bottom of in one go and everything – in the Cotswolds. Imagine! The landscape north of Tewkesbury, just within the borders of Worcestershire, is dominated by the 997-foot high bulk of Bredon. This huge outlier was part of the escarpment many centuries ago. The countryside here is quite different from that of the Cotswolds proper. The landscape is more in tune with the surrounding Vale of Evesham, and building in stone is much less common. The hill itself is an excellent place for both rambling and brambling: in the autumn, the lanes and tracks that criss-cross Bredon's slopes are thick with blackberries.

The earthworks at the summit are the remains of Iron Age hill-fort Kemerton Camp, probably abandoned in the 1st century AD after a big battle against the invading Belgae. The slashed remains of 50 bodies were discovered here, grouped around the main entrance where they presumably fell in battle.

There are also Roman earthworks and ancient standing stones here. The Banbury Stone is nicknamed 'Elephant Stone', for reasons that become obvious once you see it, while two stones near the summit are called the King and Queen Stones. Locals once believed that passing between the King and Queen stones would cure illness. The summit's chunky tower is called Parsons Folly, and was built in the mid-18th century as a summer house.

Bredon Hill features in plenty of poetry, writing, and art, most famously in A E Housman's poem 21 from *A Shropshire Lad:*

> *'In summertime on Bredon*
> *The bells they sound so clear*
> *Round both the shires they ring them*
> *In steeples far and near*
> *A happy noise to hear'.*

▶ PLACES NEARBY

Below the hill are several villages of interest. At **Beckford**, silk continues to be printed by hand, while at **Kemerton** a footpath takes you through the exotic gardens of the old priory. **Overbury**, with its variety of half-timbered and stone houses, is one of the loveliest villages in Worcestershire. **Bredon** itself was immortalised in John Moore's affectionate story of mid-20th century rural life, *Brensham Village.* The village is noted for its magnificent 14th-century threshing barn with its aisled interior, now owned by the National Trust.

▶ Broadway

Without wishing to cause an argument, Broadway is one of the five, or possibly three, most handsome villages in the Cotswolds. Yet, with its broad main street – there's a clue in the name – ploughing busily up the lower slopes of the escarpment, it's hardly a typical one. Most of the houses on the high street date from the 16th, 17th and 18th centuries. Some were inns, for Broadway was an important staging post on the London to Worcester route, following the construction of the road up Fish Hill in the early 18th century. The Lygon Arms, now one of the most famous hotels in the country, is a reminder of that period. Later the village was the object of the attentions of William Morris and other creative luminaries, including American novelist Henry James and pioneering designer Gordon Russell.

Most of the village can be discovered on foot. In Russell Square, you'll find a museum devoted to 20th-century furniture designer Gordon Russell. Broadway's original church, St Eadburgha's, is out on the Snowshill Road, and is worth a visit. Broadway Tower, an impressive Gothic folly built on the second highest point in the Cotswolds, overlooks the town. From here you can look out over a 62-mile radius and peer (allegedly) into 16 counties. The view is definitely worth the steep climb up the hill when following the Cotswold Way.

VISIT THE MUSEUM
Gordon Russell Museum
gordonrussellmuseum.org
15 Russell Square, WR12 7AP
01386 854695 | Open Mar–Oct,
11–5 Tue–Sun, Nov–Feb closes at 4;
closed Jan and Mon
Schooled in the Arts and Crafts tradition of the Cotswolds, Gordon Russell was a furniture designer and maker, calligrapher, entrepreneur, educator, and a champion of accessible, well crafted design. He believed that good design has a lasting impact on people's lives. The Museum celebrates his life and work during his 60 years in Broadway with a collection of furniture that embraces styles from the Arts and Crafts to 1930s streamlined Modernism, and from Utility Furniture to 1980s luxury postmodernism.

GET OUTDOORS
Broadway Tower Country Park
broadwaytower.co.uk
Broadway, WR12 7LB
01386 852390
Members of the Arts and Crafts Movement used the Tower, which was completed in 1798, as a holiday retreat – artists William Morris, Dante Gabriel Rossetti and Edward Burne-Jones were frequent visitors. The vantage point was also used to track enemy planes during the World Wars. Nowadays there's a telescope,

a dog-friendly cafe, a shop, a museum and lots of stairs to climb to the top. There are deer in the park, too.

EAT AND DRINK

Tisanes

tisanes-tearooms.co.uk
21 The Green, WR12 7AA
01386 853296
They serve wonderful cream teas, as well as an unusual and extensive variety of sandwiches and lunches, in this pretty 17th-century stone building on the High Street.

▸ PLACES NEARBY

Buckland, within walking distance of Broadway, is a pretty village with a fine 15th-century parsonage that is said to be England's oldest. The church contains Jacobean seating, 15th-century glass and a panel thought to have come from Hailes Abbey (see page 235), near Winchcombe.

Buckland Manor

bucklandmanor.com
WR12 7LY | 01386 852626
Privately owned 13th century Buckland Manor is one of those places that's so fancy you won't ever feel you belong – which can make a visit all the more pleasurable. Everything's dripping in luxury, expense and elegance. In summer, take tea on the garden patio. And you could always add a glass of champagne to your order...

▸ Burford

Yet another memorably handsome, classic Cotswolds town. Albeit not quite as oooh-inducing as the Biburys of this world, it's more characterful than instantly cute. Just off the main Oxford road, Burford is all but invisible to passing motorists. Drive north from the roundabout, however, and almost immediately, from the brow of the ridge, Burford slips away before you in a cascade of attractive inns and charming cottages. The wide main street, lined with shops and pubs, passes the church on the right before crossing the Windrush on a medieval bridge (1322) by the old mill. Burford's prosperity has historically depended on wool, quarrying, and coaching. There were burgesses here in the 13th century, and the town grew rapidly in the first Elizabethan era to become an important wool centre. The nearby quarries at the Barringtons, Upton and Taynton produced some of the Cotswolds stone used in the construction of some of England's finest buildings – Blenheim Palace, St Paul's Cathedral and the colleges of Oxford. In the 18th century, at the dawn of the coaching era, Burford became an important stop on the route east to Oxford and London. In the days immediately following the opening of the turnpikes, when Burford was an established coaching

▲ Burford

town, its inns competed with each other for travellers' custom. 'Burford Bait' was the name given to the famously large meals they provided, which probably relied on venison poached from Wychwood Forest. The coaching era, however, came to an end with the ascendancy of the railway, which had the audacity to bypass Burford.

Burford provides some enjoyable strolling. While the High Street is the main thoroughfare, Sheep Street to the west and Witney Street and Church Lane to the east have much to offer too. Sheep Street has some very fine inns – the Bay Tree Hotel and the Lamb Inn (the old brewery next door houses the Tourist Information Centre) – while Witney Street boasts perhaps the finest building in town, the 17th-century Great House. From Witney Street, Guildenford leads to Church Lane, where a row of lovely almshouses (founded in 1457) are close to St John the Baptist church. Opposite the almshouses sit the old buildings of Burford Grammar School, which was founded in 1577 by wealthy cloth merchant Simon Wysdom. He also constructed the Weavers' Cottages, which are grouped near the medieval bridge.

The 15th-century parish church is impressive. Among the chapels and monuments, perhaps the finest is the effigy of Sir Lawrence Tanfield, James I's Lord Chief Baron of the Exchequer, erected in 1628. Another fine memorial honors Edmund Harman, barber-surgeon to Henry VIII, and includes Britain's first representation of Amazonian Indians from the New World. The autograph of a Leveller, one of 340 Roundhead mutineers kept in the church for three days during the Civil War, is inscribed on the rim of the font: 'Anthony Sedley prisner 1649' (sic). Taking Priory Lane, which meets the High Street near the bridge, leads you past the handsome Elizabethan Priory and around to Falkland Hall (1558).

At the corner of High Street and Sheep Street you'll find the pillared Tolsey, a Tudor house where wool merchants used to meet and which now houses a museum of considerable interest. Further down you'll see the wide arch of the old George Hotel, where Charles II used to stay with his mistress Nell Gwynn, which later became an important coaching inn. Their son was created Earl of Burford.

Due to the proximity of the Bibury races, which used to take place near Aldsworth, Burford was also once famous for its saddlery business. As a result of Charles II and Nell Gwynn's visits to the town when the races were on, Burford saddles received an unspoken royal appointment.

ENTERTAIN THE FAMILY
Cotswold Wildlife Park and Gardens
See highlight panel opposite

SEE A LOCAL CHURCH
The 'wool' Church of St John the Baptist
Lawrence Lane, at the lower end of Burford High Street, beside the River Windrush, OX18 4RY
St John's began life as a Norman church, as the central tower and west wall, with its typical Norman door, can attest. It was rebuilt in the 13th century, but in the 15th century the nave was remodelled to add enormous Perpendicular windows. A fine clerestory and a splendid three-storey porch were also constructed.

One curiosity to be found at St Johns is the memorial tablet to Edmund Harman, barber-surgeon to Henry VIII. It is carved with one of the earliest known representations of South American Indians.

The brightly coloured pulpit was assembled in 1878 from fragments of 15th-century wooden tracery. The tiny wooden chantry chapel opposite the door survived the Reformation thanks to the local squire, who used it as a private pew.

In a small chapel north of the chancel, there is an early 17th-century canopied tomb

▶ Cotswold Wildlife Park and Gardens

cotswoldwildlifepark.co.uk

OX18 4JP | 01993 823006 | Open all year, daily from 10
(last admission 4.30 Mar–Sep, 3.30 Oct–Feb)

Three miles south of Burford, this 160-acre landscaped zoological park (surrounding a Gothic-style manor house) contains more than 260 different animal species. Many of the animals, such as Asiatic lions, leopards, white rhinos and red pandas, are endangered. Visit the reptiles, hide away in the bat house, spot the sloths or walk through the lemur enclosure. There's an adventure playground, a children's farmyard, and train rides during summer. There are bird of prey demonstrations on weekends in August and on Bank Holidays. The park has also become one of the Cotswolds' leading attractions for garden enthusiasts. Its exotic summer displays and varied plantings offer something of interest all year round.

occupied by Sir Lawrence Tanfield, Lord Chief Baron of the Exchequer, and his wife. At their feet kneels their grandson, Lucius Cary, Viscount Falkland, the Cavalier courtier and poet who was killed at the Battle of Newbury in 1643.

G E Street restored the church in 1877, removing most of the original plaster in the process – much to the ire of William Morris, who founded the Society for the Protection of Ancient Buildings (SPAB) as a direct consequence. Thankfully this new society ensured that many of the region's fine churches and other buildings were preserved as they were.

A plaque on the outside of the church commemorates three Roundhead soldiers who were executed here in 1649. They were the ringleaders of a large band of mutinous troops known as Levellers, 340 of whom were imprisoned by Cromwell in the church during the Civil War. One inscribed his name on the lead font, which can still be seen.

EXPLORE BY BIKE
Capital Sport
capital-sport.co.uk
01296 631671
Cycling holidays in the Cotswolds, including a Cotswolds Valleys Luxury Tour that takes in Burford and Bibury.

EAT AND DRINK
The Bay Tree Hotel ⊛
cotswold-inns-hotels.co.uk
Sheep Street, OX18 4LW
01993 822791
A Cotswold country inn smothered in wisteria with flagstone floors and leaded windows overlooking a garden is an appealing prospect, and The Bay Tree fits the bill. Candlelit in the evenings, the dining room is a cream-coloured space offering cooking that takes a modern approach.

The Bull at Burford ⊛⊛
bullatburford.co.uk
105 High Street, OX18 4RG
01993 822220
The Bull started life as a coaching inn in 1610, so it's seen some high-profile visitors over the centuries – Lord Nelson and Charles II, to name just two. The Bull's classy restaurant features bare Cotswold-stone walls, age-blackened beams and original artwork. The modern French-influenced dishes show welcome ambition.

The Angel at Burford ⊛
theangelatburford.co.uk
14 Witney Street, OX18 4SN
01993 822714
The Angel is a gem of a pub, albeit an upmarket one, with a row of Hook Norton ales on the pumps and a roaring fire during cooler months. It's the kind of place where your dog is made welcome. There's a serious approach to food, too, with due respect paid to local suppliers and the seasons.

▶ PLACES NEARBY
South of Burford is the
excellent Cotswold Wildlife
Park (see page 81), the
only place to see descendants
of the Cotswold Lion
sheep. To the east are
pretty Minster Lovell (see
page 149) and Witney (see
page 242).

▶ Castle Combe

Wiltshire's Castle Combe is Stanton's (see page 192) biggest
rival to the coveted Prettiest Village in the Cotswolds title – that
is, if it's not the prettiest in the whole country. The historical
village, which always seems to be sun-kissed, is tucked away in
a stream-threaded, wooded combe.

So beautifully preserved in aspic is it that, as well as the
garnering regular clusters of tourists, it has also captured the
attention of filmmakers and thus earned itself a tidy living in
recent years as a film-set. Steven Spielberg's *War Horse* (2011)
is among its more recent credits. When the sound technicians,
makeup artists and Jeremy Irvine have left town, though,
Castle Combe settles back into unruffled pastoral tranquillity, a
picture of serenity.

Entering Castle Combe, you'll see 15th-century Cotswold-
stone cottages with steep gabled roofs, all surrounding a
turreted church and a stone-canopied market cross. There is
also a medieval manor house, a fast-flowing stream in the
main street leading to an ancient packhorse bridge, and a
perfectly picturesque river. The timeless valleys and tumbling
wooded hillsides that surround the village make for some
lovely strolls.

The nearby castle, which gave the village its name and of
which little more than earthworks remain, began life as a
Roman fort. The Saxons used it before it became a Norman
castle in 1135, and the home of the de Dunstanville family. In
the 13th and 14th centuries, the village established itself as an
important weaving centre. Sir John Fastolf, the lord of the
manor, erected fulling mills along the By Brook and 50
cottages for his workers. Castle Combe prospered greatly with
the growth of the cloth trade in Wiltshire, becoming more like a
town. It hosted a weekly market and an annual fair. For
centuries the villages produced a red and white cloth, known as
'Castle Combe'. Cloth manufacture began to decline in the
early 18th century when the diminutive By Brook was unable to
power the larger machinery being introduced. People moved to
larger towns seeking work, and Castle Combe became
depopulated and returned to an agricultural existence. An
annual fair, centred around the market cross, continued until

1904, and Castle Combe remained an 'estate' village until 1947, when the whole village was sold at auction.

A favourite view of the village can be had from the old weavers' cottages, across the bridge. The small Village Museum, staffed by Castle Combe residents, contains many items of local interest. The greatest tribute to the wealth of the weaving industry is reflected in St Andrew's Church, which probably dates from the 12th century; one of the museum's interesting items is the clock that used to chime from the tower. The church's impressive Perpendicular tower was built in 1436, when the church was enlarged.

Outside the village is the motor racing circuit which hosted national championship races until the 1990s. Motor sports and other popular events are still held here.

There's almost no parking in the village itself, so when you're encouraged to park up at the top of the hill – a request that may leave you eyeing the maker with suspicion – you're better off obeying.

PLAY A ROUND

Manor House Hotel and Golf Club

www.manorhousegolf.co.uk
SN14 7JW | 01249 782982
Open Mon, Tue, Thu, Fri & BHs.
Other days pm only
Set in a wonderful location within the wooded estate of the 14th-century Manor House, this course includes five par 5s and some spectacular par 3s. Manicured fairways and hand-cut greens, together with the way the River By Brook meanders through the middle, make for a picturesque and dramatic course.

EAT AND DRINK

The Bybrook at The Manor House Hotel ◉◉◉

manorhouse.co.uk
The Manor House Hotel, SN14 7HR
01249 782206
The interiors look delightfully dated, while the cooking aims to cut a contemporary dash with tip-top ingredients and a tendency towards complexity. Much of the produce is grown in the kitchen garden, and much of the rest is sourced from organic growers in the village.

▶ Charlbury

The Evenlode valley area of the Cotswolds hides its villages well. Charlbury is a small, busy town looking across the valley towards Wychwood Forest. It has a large number of shops and inns, and a railway station designed by Isambard Kingdom Brunel. Although primarily a sheep town, it was also a centre of glove manufacture. Behind the main street is a small green, the Playing Close, which has a Jacobean-style drinking fountain at one end and which is surrounded by handsome villas and cottages tucked behind solid iron railings. Charlbury's church, on the other side of the main street, is largely Perpendicular in style, with Norman pillars and arches on the north side. Unexpectedly, it has a rather Victorian interior. The town museum in Market Street is dedicated to the traditional crafts and industries of the area.

SEE A LOCAL CHURCH
Church of St Mary the Virgin
Church Lane, OX7 3PS

The interior of this church is something of a surprise. It was much altered in the 19th century, and in the early 1990s the main altar was moved to the nave's west end, creating more space and enhancing the church's architectural features – particularly the fine Norman arcade on the north aisle. The five-light windows at the east end of both chancel and aisle are good examples of 14th-century Decorated tracery. A sundial from 1776 is preserved on a south-facing buttress.

EAT AND DRINK
The Bull Inn
bullinn-charlbury.com
Sheep Street, OX7 3RR
01608 810689

This handsome stone-fronted 16th-century free house presides over Charlbury's main street. Log fires and the beamed interior add to the charming period character. Outside, the vine-covered terrace is a lovely backdrop for a drink or meal in summer. The Bull Inn serves a range of Cotswold ales by Goffs.

▶ PLACES NEARBY
Cornbury Park
OX7 3EH

Beyond the River Evenlode is Cornbury Park, which was a gift from Elizabeth I to Robert Dudley. A pleasant walk can be had through the forested grounds, though the largely 17th-century house itself is not open to the public.

Ditchley Park
ditchley.co.uk
OX7 4EP | 01608 677346

Ditchley Park, west of Charlbury, is open to the public by appointment only. James Gibbs built this 18th-century mansion for the 2nd Earl of Lichfield, while 'Capability' Brown did the landscaping. The grounds consist of a 300-acre park, a lake, temples and woodlands. The house was the meeting place of Winston Churchill and the US Secretary of Defense during World War II.

Finstock
At Finstock, a couple of miles south of Charlbury, the great poet T S Eliot was baptised into the Church of England in 1927. Novelist Barbara Pym, who died in 1980, lived here for the last eight years of her life.

▶ Chavenage House

chavenage.com

Nr Tetbury, GL8 8XP, 01666 502329 | Open May–Sep, Thu, Sun & BHs 2–5 (last tour 4). Also Easter Sun & Mon; other days by appointment only

Numerous TV programmes and films have been shot at this beautiful, Elizabethan house. It served as Candleford Manor in the BBC's *Lark Rise to Candleford*, and appeared in the 2008 adaptation of *Tess of the D'Ubervilles*, as well as several tales related to ghosts, ghouls or spectral goings on; this creaky old manor house has a long history of hauntings that dates back to original owner, Nathaniel Stephens. A relative of Oliver Cromwell, Nathaniel was Parliament's member for Gloucestershire. Cromwell visited Chavenage to persuade him to vote for the arrest and trial of Charles I – and convinced him to state in Parliament that the best cure for a sick plant is 'cutting off its head'.

Nathaniel's daughter was horrified and predicted a curse on the family, and sure enough, a few months later Nathaniel was struck down by a fatal illness. When he died, a black coach and horses arrived, driven by a headless coachman, and the ghost of Nathaniel was literally spirited away – or so the story goes.

The room where Cromwell slept has reputedly witnessed several ghostly happenings. One visitor was apparently so terrified that she packed her bags and fled, walking the seven miles to Kemble Station in the middle of the night. Other weird occurrences include appearances from a 'grey lady', an apparently restless heavy wooden bed that lifts off its legs, and sightings of a ghostly monk in the chapel.

▼ Chedworth Roman Villa

Built in 1576, the Elizabethan house contains stained glass from the 16th century and even earlier, as well as fine furniture and tapestries. Chavenage is a typical Elizabethan E-shaped house, with a central porch and two projecting bays. The main door also has a sanctuary ring and a spy hole, which probably came from the priory. With its tall windows containing late-medieval glass, its fine 16th-century screen and the minstrels' gallery above it, the main hall retains the atmosphere of Elizabeth's reign.

Queen Anne is thought to have lodged at Chavenage. The splendid bed that stands in her room is supposed to have been converted for the use of her personal physician.

At the bottom of the stairs there is a memorial chest which dates from the beginning of the 17th century, while the ballroom has fine court cupboards and Cromwellian chairs upholstered in leather. The present chapel was built in the early years of the last century, but it contains a lovely Elizabethan monument and an important Saxon font.

▶ **PLACES NEARBY**

The nearest place to this surprisingly remote manor is handsome Tetbury (see page 219), a former wool town. To the north is Nailsworth (see page 157), a mill town tucked into a steep wooded valley.

▶ Chedworth Roman Villa

nationaltrust.org.uk

Yanworth, GL54 3LJ | 01242 890256 | Open end Mar–Oct, Thu–Sun 10–5, mid–end Mar and early–mid-Nov Thu–Sun 10–4

With the obvious exception of Bath's baths, you'll struggle to find a better insight into Roman Britain than the one offered by this National Trust property. Chedworth Roman Villa was rediscovered in 1864 by a gamekeeper. Set in a wooded combe, with 50 rooms, it was one of the largest mansions in the country and was home to some of the richest people in the country during its heyday in the 4th century. What remains are the lower parts of the walls – which give us enough information to identify the purposes of each of the rooms – and compelling 4th century mosaics featuring, among other things, representations of the four seasons. The mosaics can be viewed via state-of-the-art walkways. Two bath houses and a temple with spring provide us with insight into non-mod cons such as latrines and underfloor heating. In terms of mod cons, there's also a cafe. You can park on site, but consider parking in Chedworth and enjoying a half-hour or mile long walk from the village. There is, in general, good walking to be had nearby.

▶ **PLACES NEARBY**

Chedworth

Most people will come to the area the visit the Villa, but relaxed little Chedworth, a mile away, is worth a look as well. Because it's spread around a valley head, the village is said to be the longest in England. The church has a 12th century tower, and the 17th century Seven Tuns pub has a waterwheel and good beer.

Four miles north of Cirencester on the A429, you'll find the Chedworth Farm Shop.

The Hare and Hounds

hareandhoundsinn.com

Foss Cross, GL54 4NN

01285 720288

A mile closer to Chedworth on the same road, the Hare and Hounds is a fine pub in a 14th-century building. Open fires, a mix of old-world and contemporary cuisine and locally brewed Arkell's bitter welcome ramblers undertaking the local walks. In summer you can eat alfresco in the suntrap garden.

▶ Cheltenham

Some cruelly refer to Cheltenham as the poor man's Bath. It's not an architectural match for its similarly-spa-boasting rival at the bottom end of the Cotswolds, but Cheltenham is a fine place nonetheless – and, crucially, unlike its southern cousin, Cheltenham is not usually swamped with tourists. Built against the base of the Cotswolds escarpment, overlooked by Cleeve and Leckhampton Hills, it's a useful base for visiting the escarpment hills, as well as the Severn Vale, the Forest of Dean and the Wye Valley. It also doesn't have quite the reputation it should for its festivals: there's a Folk Festival in February, the National Hunt Festival horse racing festival in March; Jazz in April; the Science Festival in June; the Summer Cricket Festival the Music Festival in July; and the Literature Festival in October. That's a lot of festivals.

The discovery of a spring in 1716 rocketed what was then a market town of comparative insignificance to prominence as a fashionable spa town. The wealthy rushed to Cheltenham to bathe and to try to cure their myriad ills, which ranged from worms to constipation. The Regency era (1811–1820) building boom has left behind a town of considerable elegance, with handsome, wide streets lined with tasteful villas and terraces.

The centre is fairly compact and easy to explore on foot. The original town ran along the current High Street, which is now home to major chain stores and shopping arcades. The Regency town spread southwards along the Promenade, one of the finest thoroughfares in the country, and which is today lined with elegant shops. The magnificent terrace at the northern end, built to house those coming to take the waters, now houses the Municipal Offices and the Tourist Information Centre. In front of this terrace stand the Neptune Fountain and a statue of Edward Wilson, the Cheltenham botanist and explorer who accompanied Captain Scott on his ill-fated expedition to the South Pole. The Promenade continues gently uphill, passing the Imperial Garden and the Town Hall on the left, and reaching the imposing, porticoed facade of the Queens Hotel, which was built on the site of the Imperial Spa.

The road narrows between the shops here. It is worth walking along Queens Circus and a short way down Fauconberg Road – on the right is Cheltenham Ladies' College, part of which conceals the original Royal Well. On the left is one of Cheltenham's loveliest lanes, Montpellier Street, which is lined with interesting shops. A small alleyway on the left leads back towards the main road, passing old Montpellier Arcade on the left. At the top of the road is the Rotunda. Although it's now a bank, this was originally the Montpellier Spa. Its design was apparently based on the Pantheon in Rome. The well-preserved interior is worth a look.

There's plenty more Regency architecture to enjoy in the area close to Montpellier, notably to the west in Lansdowne. Heading southeast will take you to Suffolk Square, just beyond which, along Suffolk Parade and Suffolk Road, are some independent antique and curio shops. North of the High Street is Pittville. Its showpiece, the Pittville Pump Rooms, were designed between 1825 and 1830 by John Forbes, a local man. The Pump Rooms constitute a magnificent architectural ensemble, and they were to have been the focal point of Joseph Pitt's Pittville Estate. The project ran out of money before reaching completion, but Forbes still left his mark on his hometown. His legacy survives in the Pump Rooms, Pittville Park (with its lake surrounded by villas in an array of fantastic styles), Pittville Lawn, Clarence Square and Wellington Square. In the Pump Rooms, which are often used for concerts and recitals, you can taste the waters or visit the museum on the upper floor.

Cheltenham is noted for the ironwork that decorates many of the early buildings of the town. Distinctive balconies of finely wrought iron adorn many of the elegant buildings, adding a continental atmosphere to the streets and squares. Particularly fine examples are to be found along Oxford Parade, Royal Parade and Suffolk Square.

Cheltenham also has a growing reputation as a great place for eating.

VISIT THE MUSEUMS

The Wilson
cheltenhammuseum.org.uk
Clarence Street, GL50 3JT
01242 237431 | Open daily
9.30–5.15
This recently revamped gallery and museum has four floors, with archive collections and space for local heroes, including explorer Edward Wilson, Captain Robert Scott's right-hand man on his 1912 Antarctic expedition. There are also large galleries for temporary exhibitions: international and national touring shows, highlights from other collections and family-focused stuff. The Arts & Crafts collection is housed in a new gallery, and there's a Tourist Information Centre of the ground floor.

Holst Birthplace Museum
holstmuseum.org.uk
4 Clarence Road, GL52 2AY
01242 524846 | Open Tue–Sat and BH Mon 10–4 (Mon by arrangement); closed mid-Dec–early Feb
Cheltenham's other famous son is the composer Gustav Holst, the composer of *The Planets Suite*. Holst was born in

Cheltenham in 1874. The house in Clarence Road where he grew up is now a museum dedicated, in part, to the life of the composer, and in part to an evocation of life in the Regency and Victorian city. There's a Gustav Holst Way medium-distance trail in the north Cotswolds too, which calls in at places relevant to his life.

Pittville Pump Room and Museum

cheltenhamtownhall.org.uk
Pittville Park, GL52 3JE
01242 523852
Cheltenham's elegant signature building is the Pump Room (free admission), designed between 1825 and 1830 by local man John Forbes as a grand spa. Though the project ran out of cash before it could be fully realised, at least this centrepiece was finished. Inside, you can sample the (honking) spa waters from a marble fountain. The rooms are often used for concerts and recitals, and there's a museum on the upper floor.

GO TO THE RACES

Cheltenham Racecourse
cheltenham.co.uk
GL50 4SH | 01242 513014
16 race days per year
The track is best known for the Cheltenham Festival, which is held there in March. This is the top three-day meeting of the National Hunt season. The Hunt features the Gold Cup and Champion Hurdle, and attracts more than 50,000 spectators.

The Hall of Fame tells the story of the history of the racecourse.

GO SHOPPING

The Courtyard
Montpellier Street, GL50 1SR
Generally open Mon–Sat 9–5.30
Escape the chain stores by visiting this two-level complex of chic boutiques and specialist shops, clustered around a piazza and an elevated walkway.

GO TO THE THEATRE

Playhouse Theatre
playhousecheltenham.org
47–53 Bath Road, GL53 7HG
01242 522852

Everyman Theatre
everymantheatre.org.uk
Regent Street, GL50 1HQ
01242 572573

▼ Holst Statue, Imperial Gardens

▲ View over Cheltenham

TAKE OFF
Ballooning In The Cotswolds
ballooninginthecotswolds.co.uk
Cheltenham, GL5 3EX
01453 753221
See page 72

EXPLORE BY BIKE
Compass Holidays
compass-holidays.com
Cheltenham Spa Railway Station,
Queens Road | 01242 250642
This local Cotswold company
runs walking and cycling
short breaks and holidays
around the region.

SADDLE UP
**Ullenwood Court
Riding Centre**
ullenwoodriding.co.uk
Ullenwood, Cheltenham, GL53 9QS
07801 732090
Ullenwood offers escorted rides
through lovely countryside or
tuition by BHS qualified staff, as

well as pub rides.
They also cater for people
with disabilities.

**UK Chasers Cross
Country Course**
www.notgrove.com
Notgrove Estate, Notgrove,
Cheltenham, GL54 3BT
07776 077271
A cross-country course
professionally designed by Tim
Bennett, offering, over a
distance of three and a quarter
miles of spectacular
countryside, a varied mix of 28
off-road jumps.

GO WALKING
**Cotswolds Walking
Holidays**
cotswoldwalks.com
As their name suggests, this
husband and wife team run
walking holidays in the
Cotswolds area.

PLAY A ROUND

Cotswold Hills Golf Club

cotswoldhills-golfclub.com
Ullenwood, Cheltenham, GL53 9QT
01242 515264

A beautiful, free draining, gently undulating parkland course situated high on the Cotswolds, with stunning panoramic views of the surrounding countryside.

Lilley Brook Golf Club

lilleybrook.co.uk
Cirencester Road, Charlton Kings, GL53 8EG | 01242 526785

This challenging parkland/downland course on the lower slopes of Leckhampton Hill also has outstanding views of Cheltenham, the Malverns and the Black Mountains.

EAT AND DRINK

The Daffodil ⊚

thedaffodil.com
18–20 Suffolk Parade, Montpellier, GL50 2AE | 01242 700055

Where converted banks were once the dominant restaurant trend, old Art Deco cinemas now follow. The Daffodil occupies what was once Cheltenham's first picture palace, which opened in the silent film era of the early 20s with a screening of now-forgotten horse-racing thriller, *Thunderclap*. Nothing of the drama is lost in the building's refashioning as a modern eatery. Its open kitchen sits where the screen once did, and the sizzling Josper charcoal oven is matched by sizzling live jazz.

Le Champignon Sauvage ⊚⊚⊚⊚

lechampignonsauvage.co.uk
24–28 Suffolk Road, GL50 2AQ
01242 573449

The cookbooks that have issued forth from this supremely civilised place over the years provide fascinating snapshots of British restaurant dining of the past quarter-century. Food is served in a sunny yellow and cornflower blue room hung with striking modern paintings. The scene is refined, comfortable and relaxing.

Cheltenham Park Hotel ⊚

pumahotels.co.uk
Cirencester Road, Charlton Kings, GL53 8EA | 01242 222021

Whether you've had a winner or lost your shirt on the gee gees at nearby Cheltenham Racecourse, this smart hotel's Lakeside Restaurant is the place to end the day with a meal of celebration or consolation. The bright and airy space is flooded with light from walls of floor-to-ceiling windows that overlook the gardens and lake – a setting that sits well with the uncomplicated, please-all repertoire of classic and gently modern cooking.

Ellenborough Park ⊚⊚⊚

ellenboroughpark.com
Southam Road, GL52 3NH
01242 545454

With its impressive facade and its elevated position in rolling parkland overlooking Cheltenham racecourse, historic Ellenborough Park's palatial grandeur cannot be overstated. Ellenborough has a swanky spa, business facilities, smart bedrooms and two restaurants. The Brasserie is a useful second string to its bow, but the establishment's event is the fine-dining Beaufort Dining Room, with its Tudor fireplaces, stained glass Oriel windows and acres of burnished oak panels. It's an impeccable setting for the finely-crafted, inspired cooking. There are first-rate cheeses, too, with a fabulous selection from across the British Isles to choose from.

The Gloucester Old Spot

thegloucesteroldspot.co.uk
Tewkesbury Road, Piff's Elm,
GL51 9SY | 01242 680321
With its quarry tile floors, roaring log fires, farmhouse furnishings and real ales, local ciders and perries, this pub ticks all the boxes. There's a May Day bank holiday cider festival, too. Game and rare-breed pork make appearances on a menu that includes Old Spot pork loin steak with hand-cut chips and cannelloni with braised rabbit and black pudding.

Lumière ⊛⊛

lumiere.cc
Clarence Parade, GL50 3PA
01242 222200
Refurbishment has given Lumière an elegant and serene ambience, with its crisply starched linen, pinstriped carpet, banquettes and gilt mirrors.

Monty's Brasserie ⊛⊛

montysbraz.co.uk
George Hotel, 41 St Georges Road,
GL50 3DZ | 01242 227678
The George delivers all the Regency style one hopes for in Cheltenham, with plenty of period details inside and out. Monty's matches its good looks with a lively menu backed with daily specials, all of which are based on good-quality ingredients. There's also a cocktail bar in the basement.

▶ PLACES NEARBY

A number of villages in the vicinity of Cheltenham are worth visiting, including **Prestbury**, which is both home to a racecourse and said to be the most haunted village in Britain. It has a good pub.**Syde** and **Brimpsfield**, 5 miles to the south of Cheltenham, are noted for their interesting churches. Two other churches of note can be found at Bishop's Cleeve and Stoke Orchard.

Church of St James the Great

Stoke Orchard, GL52 7SH
If churches are your thing, north of Cheltenham in Stoke Orchard, near the M5, is the Church of St James the Great (GL52 7SH), which dates from 1170. It's the inside that makes the church so special. Its walls are covered in a wonderful jumble of paintings, the fragments and layers of which were painted over the course of several centuries, including the early 13th. This arrangement of paintings is unique in Britain.

St Michael and All Angels Church

Bishop's Cleeve, GL52 8LJ

Bishop's Cleeve's St Michael and All Angels Church has excellent Norman architecture and decorative work. Built on a Saxon foundation that may date back to the 700s, the current church takes its shape and character from the 1170s, when the Normans rebuilt it. There is a small museum about the church's history over the south porch, which includes charming murals. These were painted by a thoughtful Georgian schoolmaster as visual lessons.

Miserden and Misarden Park Gardens

misardenpark.co.uk
GL6 7JA | 01285 821303
Garden open Apr–end Sep
Tue–Thu 10–4.30

Perched above the wooded valley of the River Frome, stately Miserden is another off-the-beaten-track little village worth visiting if you've time. The main attraction, other than walks in the valley, is Misarden Park Garden home to flowers, shrubs, fine topiary, roses, and much more. The 17th century Manor House (not open) stands high overlooking the Golden Valley. And no, no one knows why the two are spelled differently.

Camp Riding Centre

ridingschoolgloucestershire.co.uk
Miserden, GL6 7HJ | 01285 821219
Open daily all week & some evenings
Camp Riding Centre offers

tuition for adults and children, as well as half-day and full-day treks, in beautiful hill country.

The Royal Oak Inn

royal-oak-prestbury.co.uk
The Burgage, Prestbury, GL52 3DL
01242 522344

Close to the racecourse, this 16th-century pub serves local cask ales, real ciders and delicious food in a snug dining room or the patio overlooking the pretty beer garden. There is a beer festival at Whitsun bank holiday and an August bank holiday cider festival.

10 arts festivals

▶ Cheltenham Folk Festival, cheltenhamfolkfestival.co.uk

▶ April/May, Cheltenham Jazz Festival, cheltenhamfestivals.com

▶ May, Stroud Arts & Music Festival, sitefestival.org.uk

▶ May, Nailsworth Festival, nailsworthfestival.org.uk

▶ May/June, Wychwood Music Festival, wychwoodfestival.com

▶ June, Longborough Festival Opera, lfo.org.uk

▶ July, Guiting Festival, guitingfestival.org

▶ August, Stroud Fringe, stroudfringe.co.uk

▶ August, Didmarton Blue Grass, didmarton-bluegrass.co.uk

▶ October, Tetbury Music Festival, tetburymusicfestival.org.uk

▶ Chipping Campden

The loveliest village in the Cotswolds? It depends on your definition. It's certainly the most elegant, though it arguably gets a bit too busy to be the loveliest overall (that's Stanton, surely). But it has character, history and handsomeness, and you should definitely visit, ideally for May's unfathomably brilliant Cotswold Olimpicks (see page 54). The curving main street is lined with houses. Each is grafted to the next, but each also has its own distinctive embellishments. As the name suggests (chipping means market, via the word 'cheap'), Chipping Campden was once a market town. In fact it was one of the most important of the medieval wool towns in the Cotswolds. Campden then dozed for centuries until C R Ashbee moved his Guild of Handicraft here from London in 1902. The Court Barn Museum displays work from that era.

Campden's church, at the north end of the town, is the finest wool church in the Cotswolds, with a magnificent tower and a spacious, almost austere interior. It contains the largest brass in the county, memorializing wool merchant and church patron William Grevel. The Gainsborough Chapel houses the fine 17th-century marble tomb of Sir Baptist Hicks and his wife. The Hicks built the nearby stone almshouses in 1612, as well as Campden House, which was razed during the Civil War.

Grevel House is on the High Street, opposite Church Street. It once belonged to the aforementioned William Grevel who, in addition to being largely responsible for the church's current form, is supposed by some to have been the original model for the merchant in Chaucer's *Canterbury Tales*.

Just off Leysbourne, which is the northern extension of the High Street, is the Ernest Wilson Memorial Garden, a charming little botanical enclave snug in the shadow of the church. The garden is named for and commemorates an eccentric plant collector who was born here in 1876. In the middle of the village, supported by stone pillars, is the 1627 Market Hall.

Dover's Hill, the scene of the annual Olimpick Games, overlooks the village. The Cotswold Way, a glorious, 102-mile National Trail, starts here, and goes all the way down the limestone escarpment to Bath.

VISIT THE MUSEUM

Court Barn Museum

courtbarn.org.uk

Church Street, GL55 6JE

01386 841951 | Open Apr–Sep Tue–Sun 10–5, Oct–Mar Tue–Sun 10–4; closed Mon except BH

Artists, designers and craftspeople have worked in and around Chipping Campden since the time of the Arts and Crafts movement. This museum celebrates these practitioners, including

Chipping Campden

200 m

the talented C R Ashbee, and their skill. There are informative displays and video, a shop, and even workshops. It's great stuff.

SEE A LOCAL CHURCH
St James wool church
Church Street, GL55 6JG
This is the quintessential Cotswolds wool church. The tower is the first feature you see: solid and square, it was built in about 1500 and houses eight bells that date from 1618 to 1737. Inside, the first impression is of grace and light. This is in part due to the window over the nave arch, a Cotswolds speciality.

The church's treasures include a unique pair of altar hangings from about 1400. There are also excellent monuments, many to the rich wool merchants who poured their wealth into the creation of the building.

GO WALKING
For some cracking views along the escarpment and across the Vale of Evesham, simply follow Cotswold Way markers (which start at the Market Hall) for about 30 minutes. These will guide you along the high street, out of town and uphill to Dover's Hill.

EAT AND DRINK

Badgers Hall

badgershall.com

High Street, Chipping Campden

GL55 6HB | 01386 840839

The building is 15th-century, with honey-coloured stone, exposed oak beams, mullioned windows and open fireplaces. Homemade cakes, scones and pastries are freshly baked on the premises using local produce. They also have charming rooms available.

The Bantam Tea Rooms

bantamtea-rooms.co.uk

High Street, GL55 6HB

01386 840386

This traditional, welcoming, family-run tea room is situated amongst the wonderfully preserved buildings of golden Cotswold stone, many of which date back to the 14th and 17th centuries. Try one of their freshly-baked cakes, or even a Bantam Afternoon Tea. You can choose from a veriety of traditional, fruit or herbal brews. If you fancy a picnic or a snack for the road, all of their tasty treats are also available to take away.

Eight Bells

eightbellsinn.co.uk

Church Street, GL55 6JG

01386 840371

Originally built in the 14th century to house the stonemasons who

▼ Chipping Campden

constructed nearby St James' church, this lovely inn was rebuilt in the 17th century and used to store the peal (or the set) of eight church-tower bells while they awaited installation. The cobbled entranceway leads into two atmospheric beamed bars with open fireplaces and, in the floor of one fireplace, a surviving priest's hole. Outside, an enclosed courtyard and terraced garden overlook the almshouses and church. Enjoy the Hook Norton and Purity real ales and freshly prepared, locally sourced, seasonal dishes. Specials, a prix-fixe menu and a children's menu are also available.

The Kings ◉◉
kingscampden.co.uk
The Square, High Street, GL55 6AW
01386 840256

Sympathetically restored and packed with character, The Kings' oldest parts include the 16th-century stone mullioned windows on the first floor. The Kings may be a classic Georgian townhouse built out of honey-hued Cotswold stone, but the place wears the style of a smartly casual modern operation, with comfy banquettes, mismatched furniture and polished wooden floors in the brasserie, and, in the beamed restaurant, unclothed antique tables and a log fire. The large grassed garden and dining terrace is good to find in a town centre pub.

The bar offers at least two real ales, including local Hook Norton, as well as daily papers and traditional pub games (but no noisy gaming machines). Bar snacks include a good range of sandwiches and baguettes, while main meals are served in the informal bar brasserie or the relatively formal two AA-Rosette restaurant overlooking Chipping Campden's square. The packed, imaginative formal restaurant menu features modern food built on splendid seasonal ingredients.

Noel Arms Hotel
noelarmshotel.com
High Street, GL55 6AT
01386 840317

This golden Cotswold-stone 16th-century coaching inn is one of the oldest hotels in the Cotswolds. Charles II reputedly stayed here. Packhorse trains used to carry bales of wool, the source of Chipping Campden's prosperity, through the carriage arch and on to Bristol and Southampton. The Noel Arms' traditional appeal has been successfully preserved and seamlessly interwoven with contemporary comforts. You can absorb the history while sipping a pint of Hook Norton in front of the log fire in Dover's Bar, reading the papers over a coffee and pastry in the coffee shop or enjoying brasserie-style food in the restaurant. Indunil Upatissa provides an alternative to the modern English dishes by creating his trademark curries daily. Enthusiasts arrive for his Curry Club on the last Thursday evening of every month.

Seagrave Arms ☻

seagravearms.co.uk
Friday Street, Weston Subedge.
GL55 6QH | 01386 840192

This Grade II listed former farmhouse dates from around 1740, and looks out over some of the lushest scenery in England. The Seagrave has been sympathetically restored and retains many of its original features. It offers open log fires in winter and a sheltered courtyard in summer. The kitchen sources from local farms and suppliers, bakes its own bread, and makes its own chutneys and ice creams – local cheeses come with apple chutney. Wash it all down with a sprightly Gloucestershire wine from Three Choirs Vineyard. The Georgian inn also has luxurious accommodation and the bar serves great beers from Purity and Cotswold breweries.

Three Ways House ☻

threewayshousehotel.com
Chapel Lane, Mickleton, GL55 6SB
01386 438429

Three Ways House is the Cotswolds seat of the Pudding Club, so skipping dessert just won't do. The Victorian building has heaps of period charm, although the restaurant itself has a more contemporary, eclectic look, and makes good use of mirrors to increase the sense of space. The cooking is punchy, big-hearted British stuff. A flag-waving dedication to local raw materials is balanced with a multi-cultural approach to flavour combinations.

The Volunteer Inn

thevolunteerinn.net
Lower High Street, GL55 6DY
01386 840688

This convivial, log-fire warmed, honey-coloured stone-floored bar is a welcoming retreat for guests hunting through the town's antique shops or pausing on a stroll along the Cotswold Way. Once a recruiting centre for volunteer militia, today's clients sign on for some very interesting dishes from the Inn's Maharaja Restaurant. These incluce jalali hash, a roasted duck, red onion and peppers combination, and venison tikka, which can be washed down with a pint of Doom Bar bitter. The grassy beer garden is a quiet town-centre retreat.

▸ **PLACES NEARBY**

To the north of Chipping Campden are the spectacular gardens of Hidcote Manor (see page 135). To the west is another north Cotswolds honeypot, Broadway (see page 77). The town itself, and Broadway Tower in particular, are definitely worth a visit. A little further to the east is Shipston-on-Stour (see page 181), formerly an important wool town.

▶ Chipping Norton

Chipping Norton is unspectacular but perfectly pleasant. However depending on your politics and your views on what makes good journalistic practice, you may find its inhabitants less pleasant. So look away now if you want to experience this market town without bias. [SPOILER ALERT] Current Norton residents include Rebekah Brooks, former editor of *The Sun*, David Cameron (though he's got another house in London, apparently), and Elisabeth Murdoch, daughter of Rupert, who lives at nearby Burford Priory. The 'Chipping Norton set', as the media-coined phrase goes, achieved notoriety during the 2011 News International phone hacking scandal. Television's Jeremy Clarkson is also a Chipping Norton resident, and former Blur bass guitarist Alex James lives nearby too.

Other than all that, it's busy market town. The Bliss Tweed Mill, built in 1872 by Lancashire architect George Woodhouse, sits in a fold to the west of the town. For the Cotswolds, the large Victorian structure serves as an unusual reminder of the Industrial Revolution – although it's now been converted into flats. The Market Square, dominated by the 19th-century Town Hall, with its Tuscan-style portico, is the heart of Chipping Norton. Opposite the Town Hall, you'll find a museum with displays on the town's history.

Elsewhere you'll find a varied collection of shops, hotels and houses, some dating back to the 17th century, though most are 18th-century – a testimony to the wool trade. From the square, the town slopes down Church Street, past a row of almshouses dating back to 1640, towards St Mary's, a Perpendicular church containing some fine brasses and impressive tombs. Its most unusual feature is a hexagonal porch with a vaulted ceiling. Behind the church are motte-and-bailey earthworks that show the town was of some importance in the Norman period. In Middle Row, look out for the 16th-century Guildhall.

VISIT THE MUSEUM
Chipping Norton Museum
chippingnortonmuseum.org.uk
High Street, OX7 5AD
01608 641712 | Open Easter–end Oct Mon–Sat 2–4
The pleasingly unglamorous volunteer-run museum and history society has a large collection of artefacts, which range in provenance from Roman Britain to World War II. It also possesses impressively extensive archives.

GO FISHING
DiscoveryCarp
discoverycarp.com
Chad Lakes Fishery, Bledington, near Chipping Norton, OX7 6XL
01451 831470
Coarse fishing in the heart of the Cotswolds countryside.

PLAY A ROUND
Wychwood Golf Club
thewychwood.com
Lyneham, OX7 6QQ | 01993 831841
Wychwood was designed to use the natural features of its location. It's set in 170 acres on the fringe of the Cotswolds, and blends superbly with its surroundings. Lakes and streams enhance the challenge of the course, with water coming into play on eight of the 18 holes. All greens are sand-based, built to USGA specification.

EAT AND DRINK
The Chequers ◉
thechequerschurchill.com
Church Road, Churchill, OX7 6NJ
01608 659393
This unassuming stone building has modern gastro-pub style in spades, but that's not to say you can't just have a pint in the cosy bar. The ambience is relaxed. The small oyster bar is also home to a delicious array of charcuterie and cheeses. The kitchen has an eye for top-notch local produce; this place is all about simple dishes done well.

The Crown Inn
crowninnenstone.co.uk
Mill Lane, Church Enstone,
OX7 4NN | 01608 677262
Run by an award-winning chef, this 17th-century stone inn is cosy and welcoming, with log fires in the inglenook and old historic photos. The Crown specialises in fresh fish. All the ingredients comes from local suppliers. There's also a picturesque cottage garden.

Daylesford Organic
daylesfordorganic.com
Daylesford, Nr Kingham,
GL56 0YG | 01608 731700
Enjoy organic handmade bread, pastries, seasonal-fruit yoghurts and even handmade brown sauce at this beautifully designed cafe, or a traditional afternoon tea. There's also a cookery and farm school, and a farm shop. There's even a yoga studio with a lovely rural view. You could spend a full day here.

The Kingham Plough ◉◉
thekinghamplough.co.uk
The Green, Kingham, OX7 6YD
01608 658327
The Plough is quintessentially English, with stylish rustic-chic décor, venerable beams and exposed stone walls. In the bar there are real ales and scrumpy, and large comfy armchairs and sofas to enjoy them in. There's also proper bar food, such as Scotch quail eggs, or homemade pheasant sausage and mash. Exec chef Emily Watkins, who used to work at Heston Blumenthal's The Fat Duck, happily deploys traditional and trendy cooking techniques to deliver intelligent interpretations of modern British cuisine.

The King's Head Inn ◉
kingsheadinn.net
The Green, Bledington, OX7 6XQ
01608 658365

The King's Head is a textbook example of a switched-on village pub. Outside, honey-hued Cotswold houses huddle around the village green, where ducks and bantams play in a trickling brook. Inside, you'll find wobbly flagstone floors, log fires and head-skimming beams. The place is still the village boozer, serving a fine pint of Hook Norton, while the cooking is a definite notch or two above your average pub.

Wild Thyme Restaurant with Rooms ⊚⊚
wildthymerestaurant.co.uk
10 New Street, OX7 5LJ
01608 645060
The mood is relaxed and the food is bathed with Mediterranean warmth at this charming, chic restaurant. Black beams are all that attest to the age of the building. Otherwise the scene is one of rustic modernity – chunky country-style tables, bare wooden floors and exposed stone or whitewashed walls hung with modern art. The kitchen sends out robust flavours based on plenty of seasonal ingredients.

Wyatt's Tea Room
wyattsgardencentre.co.uk
Hill Barn Farm, Great Rollright, OX7 5SH | 01608 684835
Part of a farm shop, this spacious and very clean tea room is justifiably popular. Light lunches – homemade soups, freshly-baked bread, quiches, ploughman's, home-baked cakes and 'luxurious lattes' – and mouth-watering teas can be enjoyed throughout the year.

10 places to eat
- **The Bell**, Sapperton, bellsapperton.co.uk
- **Le Champignon Sauvage**, Cheltenham, lechampignonsauvage.co.uk
- **Cotswolds88 Hotel**, Painswick, cotswolds88hotel.com
- **The King's Head Inn**, Bledington, kingsheadinn.net
- **The Kingham Plough**, Chipping Norton, thekinghamplough.co.uk
- **Lumière**, Cheltenham, lumiere.cc
- **Lords of the Manor**, Upper Slaughter, lordsofthemanor.com
- **The Priory Inn**, Tetbury
- **Three Ways House**, Mickleton, puddingclub.com
- **Wild Garlic Restaurant**, Nailsworth, wild-garlic.co.uk

▶ PLACES NEARBY
The Rollright Stones
The Cotswolds only has one stone circle of note, but it's a pretty good one, not to mention a sneaky beast. It's one of three distinct ancient monuments on the side of the A3400 road between Shipston-on-Stour and Chipping Norton, near Long Compton. The monuments are believed to have been built at different times for different

▲ The Rollright Stones

purposes. The names of the megaliths, the King's Men, the Whispering Knights and the King Stone, derive from a legend explaining their origins. Long ago a band of soldiers met a witch. She told them that their leader might take seven long strides, and then 'if Long Compton thou canst see, King of England thou shall be'. The aspiring monarch risked all, saw nothing and was, along with his followers, turned to stone. The Whispering Knights, clustered together off in their own tight circle, were traitors who planned to overthrow the king once he became ruler of all England.

There's a more banal origin story for the Stones too. The three monuments are said to date from 3000–2000 BC, during the Bronze Age. Scholars believe that there were originally 105 King's Men, but there are now only 77, each 100 feet in diameter. The remaining 77 are mysteriously difficult to count. If you can count them three times in a row and get the same total, it's said you will receive a wish. The Whispering Knights are believed to be all that remains of a Neolithic long barrow. The Stones are open to the public, but note that parking is limited.

Little and Great Rollright
The nearby village of Little Rollright has a fine 17th-century manor house and a handsome little church built in the Perpendicular style, which contains some magnificent 17th-century stone monuments. Great Rollright has fine views looking southwards over the rolling countryside. Its historic buildings include the Norman church, with its gargoyles and carved doorway. Wyatt's Tea Room is close by, and you can purchase organic food and plants there.

Churchill
Just 3 miles southwest of Chipping Norton and close to Stow-on-the-Wold is the village of Churchill, the birthplace of

Warren Hastings, the first Governor-General of Bengal. It was also the birthplace of William 'Strata' Smith, 'the Father of English Geology', who produced the first geological map of England. Their stories are well told in the Churchill and Sarsden Heritage Centre in the Old Church, which also contains village records and maps dating back to the 17th century.

Hook Norton

Hook Norton, east of Great Rollright, is known these days, above all, for its beer, which is brewed in a Victorian red-brick brewery next door to the village museum. A huge railway viaduct running across the valley shows the village's past importance as an ironstone centre.

Hook Norton Brewery

hooky.co.uk

Brewery Lane, Hook Norton, OX15 5NY | 01608 730384

Tours Mon–Fri 11–2, Sat 10.30–1.30

Knock back a beer after taking a tour around the over-150-year-old Hook Norton Brewery. In business since 1849, Hook Norton is one of only 32 family-owned breweries left in the country. It's also the finest extant example of a Victorian tower brewery. The owners still transport the beer to pubs around the village using a traditional shire-horse-drawn dray.

Long Compton

Long Compton, strung out along the A3400 and not far from the Rollright Stones, is an attractive village with a handsome Perpendicular church. You approach the church through a lychgate, which is thought to be a cottage with its lower floor removed.

Jurassic Way

Not far from the Rollright Stones is the Jurassic Way, a long-distance footpath connecting Banbury and Stamford. It runs for 88 miles and follows the line of a Jurassic limestone ridge, passing through a wide variety of different landscapes. It links with the Macmillan Way, which passes through Stow-on-the-Wold.

▶ Cirencester

It's hard to imagine that, after London, Cirencester was once the most important city in England. Very hard indeed – as handsome as it is in places, Cirencester's just, well, comparatively *small* and Cotswoldsy. Part of the Cotswolds' charm is that its best places don't feel important in a political or business sense. But once, this place really was.

The town was founded as a military headquarters in AD 49 during Roman occupation. It was then called Corinium

Dobunnorum. A number of important roads radiated from the city – the Fosse Way, Ermine Street and Akeman Street. The Saxons renamed Corinium 'Cirencester'. Ciren, from coryn, means the 'top part'. This refers to the River Churn, the highest source of the Thames. Ceastre means 'fort'. One wonders why the Saxons bothered with the rebranding effort when they also practically destroyed the town, preferring instead to build smaller settlements outside the walls. Only in the Middle Ages did Cirencester regain something of its former glory, when it became the most important of the Cotswold wool towns. Satisfyingly, markets still take place each Monday and Friday.

The town is most easily explored on foot. There are a number of well-signposted car parks within easy reach of the city centre, while the market square is the most convenient place to begin discovering the town. The 15th-century parish church of St John the Baptist, one of the largest parish churches in England, is the main attraction. Its magnificent Perpendicular tower was built by a group of local earls with the reward Henry IV gave them for foiling a rebellion. The church's east and west windows are filled with medieval stained glass, and clerestory windows illuminate its fine roof. The exterior's best-known feature is its three-storeyed south porch, which overlooks the market square. The abbots built the porch in the late 15th century as an office for the abbey, and after the Dissolution destroyed the abbey itself the porch became the town hall. One of the finest examples of its type in the country, the building was returned to the church only in the 18th century. Inside you'll find several memorial brasses bearing the matrimonial histories of well-known wool merchants, some interesting church plate and a decorative, painted, wine goblet-style pulpit.

The Victorian Corn Hall, on the Market Place opposite the church, has been beautifully restored and hosts several markets throughout the week. The Brewery Arts Centre, on Cricklade Street (which runs south from the square), is a hub of visual and performing arts. The old brewery also houses craft studios.

On Park Street, close to Cirencester Park, is Corinium Museum. The museum brings many aspects of local history and various finds to life, including the mosaics that were made in the area in the Roman era. Many are displayed in tableaux form. The museum is also the home of the Tourist Information Centre.

Close by is Thomas Street, on which you'll find a 15th-century Weavers Hall almshouse, also known as St Thomas's Hospital. Nearby Coxwell Street is lined with merchants'

▲ Corinium Museum

houses. Farther north, on Spitalgate Lane, you'll find another group of almshouses and the arcade of the nave of the Hospital of St John. East from here is the mysterious-looking Spital Gate, all that remains of the old abbey. From here, a walk through the Abbey Grounds – where the remnants of the Roman walls can be seen at the eastern boundary – will take you back to the town centre.

No visit to Cirencester would be complete without a glimpse, at the very least, of Cirencester Park, probably the finest example of geometric landscaping in the country. It is approached by walking up Cecily Hill, one of the prettiest streets in Cirencester, which leads to the wrought iron entrance gates. The first Lord Bathurst conceived the park in the early 18th century. The house (not open to the public), hidden behind one of the largest yew hedges in the world, was built to his own design. The park was landscaped with the help of, among others, the poet Alexander Pope, who celebrated the construction of the park in verse. In fact there is a corner known as Pope's Seat near the polo ground. The grounds are privately owned, but open to walkers and riders. Cirencester Park is an excellent place for walking, especially along the Broad Ride, which stretches from the entrance almost to Sapperton.

Apart from the wall in the Abbey Garden, the only other surviving local souvenir from the Roman occupation is the superb 2nd-century Roman Amphitheatre, which is one of the largest and best preserved in the country. It now lies on Cotswold Avenue, just south of the ring road.

The King's Head, complete with royal keystone over the door, sits on the Market Square. Despite outward appearances, the hotel dates back to 1340. In 1642 the Royalist Lord Chandos took refuge in the hotel, thus saving his life, while in 1688 Lord Lovelace, of William of Orange's army, was captured here.

The plate of Cirencester's parish church is among the most interesting in the country. The Boleyn Cup, made in 1535 for Anne Boleyn, second wife of Henry VIII, is particularly interesting. The church is also notable because it has the oldest 12-bell peal in the country, which rings out the 'pancake bell' every Shrove Tuesday.

VISIT THE MUSEUM
Corinium Museum
coriniummuseum.org
Park Street, GL7 2BX
01285 655611 | Open Mon–Sat 10–5, Sun 2–5; closes 1hr early Nov–Mar Mon–Sat

Corinium was one of Britain's largest Roman towns, and as such the museum is known for its Roman mosaic sculpture and other Roman material. The museum also features archaeological and historical material from prehistoric times to the 19th century from Cirencester and the Cotswolds generally, housing Medieval, Tudor, Civil War and 18th-19th century displays. Anglo-Saxon treasures from Lechlade bring this little-known period to life.

SEE SOME LOCAL CHURCHES
Church of St John the Baptist
Gosditch Street, GL7 2PE
Dubbed the Cathedral of the Cotswolds, Cirencester's brilliant 'wool' church is the largest and, many would say, the finest of them all. The richly ornamented three-storey south porch and imposing tower certainly preside over the Market Place with all the grandeur of a cathedral. The interior is just as astonishing.

Roman Cirencester (Corinium) had become the second most important town in Britain, and by late Saxon times there was already a very large church here. By the early 12th century Cirencester had an Augustinian abbey, and it was about then that the first church was built on this site.

Parts of it survive in the present church, most of which dates from successive renovations and additions throughout medieval times. The Lady chapel dates originally from 1235–50, the tower from around 1400, various chantry chapels from the mid-15th century, and the porch from about 1490. The nave was rebuilt between 1515 and 1530, acquiring the soaring, slender pillars and huge Perpendicular clerestory windows that are such key factors in creating the church's light-filled, elegant interior. Little more than a hundred years after these improvements were made, this glorious building was a temporary prison. In 1642 the Royalists locked up more than 1,000 citizens of Cirencester here overnight after a Civil War battle.

Many interior features are worth seeking out. Don't miss the exquisite fan vaulting or the wineglass pulpit – a stone masterpiece from about 1440, with delicate openwork tracery and decorative paintwork in burgundy and gold.

North Cerney All Saints
Dark Lane, a lane running west from the A435, GL7 7BX

This unusual and lovely church gets its character from an eclectic mix of work from the 12th, 15th and 20th centuries. Transepts and a new roof were added to the original Norman church in the 1470s, creating a cruciform shape that makes for an oddly charming juxtaposition with the saddleback tower at the west end.

The interior, full of colour and beautiful craftsmanship, owes much to a 20th-century benefactor. William Iveson Croome, a knowledgeable local historian, worked with architect F C Eden to restore and refurnish the church. They thoughtfully executed work on the rood loft and the gilded reredos, also purchasing contemporary glass and period furnishings.

GET CRAFTY
New Brewery Arts
newbreweryarts.org.uk
01285 657181
Arts and crafts workshops and courses.

TAKE OFF
Ballooning In The Cotswolds
ballooninginthecotswolds.co.uk
Cirencester | 01453 753221
See page 72

SADDLE UP
Talland School of Equitation
talland.net
Dairy Farm, Ampney Knowle, Nr. Cirencester, GL7 5ED
01285 740155
Talland offers flexible courses, including residential, and tuition for all ages and abilities. Large indoor and outdoor schools. People with disabilities catered for.

PLAY A ROUND
Cirencester Golf Club
cirencestergolfclub.co.uk
Cheltenham Road, Bagendon, GL7 7BH | 01285 652465
An undulating open Cotswold course with excellent views.

EAT AND DRINK
The Crown Inn
thecrowninn-cotswolds.co.uk
Frampton Mansell, GL6 8JG
01285 760601
This old inn, a 17th-century cider house in the Golden Valley, is full of low beams and has cosy open fireplaces and real ales. Fresh, local food is served in the restaurant and at the three

inviting bars. In warm weather, there is plenty of seating in the garden.

The Crown of Crucis

thecrownofcrucis.co.uk
Ampney Crucis, GL7 5RS
01285 851806

This 16th-century former coaching inn retains its historical charm while feeling comfortably up-to-date. 'Crucis' refers to the Latin cross in the nearby churchyard. The pub overlooks the village cricket green and stands beside Ampney Brook in the heart of the Cotswolds. The quiet stream meandering past the lawns creates a perfect picture of quintessential rural England. With its traditional beams, log fires and warm, friendly atmosphere, the busy bar offers a large selection of draught and real ales, including their own Crown Bitter, and a choice of wines by the glass. Bar food is served all day, and the restaurant offers a fine dining menu.

The Fleece at Cirencester

thefleececirencester.co.uk
41 Market Place, GL7 2NZ
01285 658507

Charles II reputedly hid in this 16th-century pub disguised as a manservant. Settle by one of the log fires with a pint of Wainwright, and select your fare from a menu that mixes traditional and modern influences, using produce from ethical suppliers. The Fleece also serves afternoon tea, offers rooms, and is conveniently located in the heart of Cirencester.

▶ PLACES NEARBY

South Cerney and the Cotswold Water Park (see page 190) lie to the south of Cirencester. The Cotswold Water Park is the best place in the region for sporting activities (if you don't mind getting a bit soggy), from windsurfing to sailing, bike riding and more. Travelling west towards Stroud (see page 211) makes for a lovely drive. You'll pass **Sapperton**, with its Arts and Crafts Movement connections, and then travel on through the Golden Valley and Chalford (see page 212), where there are fine walks to be had in the steep wooded valleys and abandoned canals to explore. The area can also yield great insights into Stroud's industrial past as the centre of the cloth trade. Then pop up onto Minchinhampton Common (see page 148) to enjoy vast views from the Jurassic grasslands, or down to Nailsworth (see page 157). Chedworth's Roman Villa (see page 87) and its mesmerising mosaic are to the north, and unfairly pretty Bibury (see page 66) is to the northeast.

The Duntisbournes

A string of villages along the small River Dunt just to the north of Cirencester, the Duntisbournes have a special character. Their saddleback church towers have something almost French about them. Duntisbourne Abbots was the home of Dr Matthew Baillie, the Scottish-born physician who attended George III during his many years of illness. Duntisbourne Leer is prettily forded by the Dunt, as is Middle Duntisbourne, which is barely more than a farm at the bottom of a steep valley. The church at Duntisbourne Rouse is particularly dramatically situated.

Rodmarton Manor

rodmarton-manor.co.uk
GL7 6PF | 01285 841442
Open May–Sep Wed, Sat and
BHs 2–5

Rodmarton Manor is one of the finest legacies of the Arts and Crafts Movement, and one of the last country houses to be built and furnished in the old traditional style when everything was done by hand with local stone, local timber and local craftsmen. There are gardens to wander about too.

St Michael's Church

Duntisbourne Rouse, GL7 7AP

This enchanting little church, on the slope of a Cotswold hillside, is just as ancient as it looks and feels. The nave reveals its origins: here are two Saxon doorways, in addition to other distinctive Saxon herringbone masonry and quoins with long-and-short stonework. There are traces of early wall paintings. The tiny crypt chapel below the Norman chancel has a small, unglazed, round-headed east window to let in the morning sun. A medieval cross in the churchyard completes the idyllic scene. The saddleback tower that helps lend the building its timeless air was actually a later addition to the church, and dates from 1587.

▶ The Coln Valley

The River Coln, a tributary of the Thames, carves through the Cotswolds. It rises on the escarpment not far from Cheltenham (see page 88) then gently descends the slopes, passing through a number of pretty villages en route.

One of these, **Withington**, has an unusually large church with a fine Norman doorway and a handsome wall monument to Sir John Howe and Lady Howe of Cassey Compton. The 17th-century mansion of **Cassey Compton** is now a magnificent farmhouse. It lies in splendid isolation in the middle of the valley, and forces the Yanworth road to curve around it. As you approach it you may see a sculpture in a nearby field, a product of artist Jonathan Poole's Compton Cassey Gallery, which now occupies the house.

Near here the river passes close to Chedworth Roman Villa (see page 87) and **Fossebridge**, a steep point on the Roman

Fosse Way where an ancient inn continues to attract passing customers. On the other side of the Way, the Coln furrows across the meadows of **Coln St Dennis** – a small, quiet village built around a modest green, with a small Norman church. Look for the mysterious inscription to Joan Burton on the interior wall of the tower, as well as the Norman corbel stones that now line the nave.

Further on you'll find the pretty hamlet of **Calcot**, and then almost immediately **Coln Rogers**, a village with a church remarkable for its Saxon plan and the Saxon window north of the chancel. At the old mill in **Winson**, where the road zigzags, there are charming gardens, and towards the centre of the village you'll find some converted barns. The compact green is overlooked by a classical-looking manor house. After Winson come Ablington (see page 68) and gorgeous Bibury (see page 66).

Finally, before going on to Fairford (see page 121) and Lechlade (see page 144), the Coln arrives at **Coln St Aldwyns**, where a magnificent horse chestnut tree shades the green.

▼ The River Coln, Cassey Compton

The New Inn is a fine local pub. A pretty churchyard surrounds the church, which has memorial windows commemorating John Keble, the 19th-century reformer, and his father. It is possible to walk along the Coln from here to Bibury.

▸ Corsham Court

corsham-court.co.uk

SN13 0BZ | 01249 701610 | Open 20 Mar–Sep daily (ex Mon & Fri, but incl BHs) 2–5.30, Oct–19 Mar open weekends only 2–4.30 (last admission 30mins before closing); closed Dec

If you fancy visiting a classic Cotswolds manor house but don't fancy the attendant crowds, come here – it's an interesting place in a quiet corner of the region.

Corsham Court is an Elizabethan manor house. It was built in 1582 on the site of a medieval royal manor that had, for centuries, been part of the dower of the Queens of England. Paul Methuen, a wealthy clothier and ancestor of the present owner, bought Corsham in 1745. 'Capability' Brown's designs were employed in the house as well as the grounds, and John Nash made further changes to Corsham.

In the 19th century Frederick Methuen, Lord-in-Waiting to Queen Victoria, married Anna Sanford. The young heiress who brought with her a collection of Old Masters, many of which were outstanding and important. Since then the Methuens, though primarily a military family, have shared a love of art and a commitment to preserving their inheritance. The fourth Lord Methuen studied painting under Walter Sickert (of the Camden Town Group) and, as a soldier in liberated France, served as Field Marshal Montgomery's advisor on the preservation of monuments and art. In later years Methuen let a large part of the house to the Bath Academy of Art, although the present Lord Methuen continues to make Corsham Court his home.

The character of the house as we see it today dates principally from the middle of the 19th century. The staterooms are splendid, as much for their architecture and furnishings as for the paintings they contain. The picture gallery, designed by Brown, is a triple cube, 72 feet in length, with an intricately plastered ceiling and walls of crimson silk that match the Chippendale furniture. Van Dyck's superb *Betrayal of Christ* hangs here, together with Rubens's *Wolf Hunt* and works of the Italian School. In the elegant dining room are two Reynolds portraits of the children of Paul Methuen. Corsham also possesses an exquisite *Annunciation* from the studio of Filippo Lippi, a haunting portrait of the ageing Queen Elizabeth I and a sculpture of a sleeping cherub by Michelangelo. It further contains furniture by Chippendale, Adam, Cobb and Johnson. The garden has flowering shrubs, herbaceous borders, a Georgian bath house and peacocks.

Corsham itself, right on the edge of the Cotswolds, is worth a wander around. You won't find many tourists here, but you will find a handsome, historical market town, which was once prosperous due to the thriving wool trade and a quarry. The high street's 17th century buildings are the best-looking things in town: a row of gabled Flemish cottages and the Hungerford Almshouses and Schoolroom. The Georgian town hall is also impressive. There are some good independent shops about, including good-value cafes and bookshops.

EAT AND DRINK

Guyers House Hotel ◉◉
guyershouse.com
Pickwick, SN13 0PS | 01249 713399
Set in six acres of lovely English gardens, which include a tennis court and croquet lawn, Guyers House is a classic country-house hotel. When it comes to dining, the kitchen keeps fruitful connections with the local food network, as well as furnishing the larder with fresh, seasonal ingredients from its own vegetable and herb garden. Although the setting is traditional, the menu comes up with some surprising compositions that work well.

The Methuen Arms ◉◉
themethuenarms.com
2 High Street, SN13 0HB
01249 717060
The Methuen Arms is a contemporary boutique inn situated at the hub of Corsham village life. Bare elm floorboards, log fires, ancient beams and exposed stone walls give the Methuen a rustic-chic look. There are hand-pulled real ales at the bar, and the extensive menu offers confident, up-to-date dishes. The kitchen promises top-grade local ingredients.

▶ PLACES NEARBY

Box
Travelling west on the A4 towards Bath takes you downhill to pretty little Box and the gorgeous valley of By Brook. There's a spectacular viewpoint by a bus stop were people often stop to take photos. You'll know when you see it. Limestone has been quarried here since the 9th century, but Box is more famous for its tunnel. Isambard Kingdom Brunel constructed the Great Western Railway link between Bristol and London from 1835 to 1841, and it included what was then the world's longest tunnel (2 miles). The tunnel, which passes through Box Hill, has a dramatic neo-classical facade and pillars. That's bold enough, but apparently Brunel also planned for the sun to shine directly down the tunnel on his birthday, 9 April. Unfortunately

atmospheric refraction meant that he was two days out. Nevertheless, the tunnel entrance is still an impressive sight today. Box also provided a home for and inspiration to *Thomas the Tank Engine*-author Wilbert Awdry. It's also home to musician Peter Gabriel and his recording studio, as well record-breaking adventurer David Hempleman-Adams. There's some fine walking to be done in the By Brook valley, which has woods and combes worth exploring.

Little Box Cafe

littleboxcafe.com
On the A4, next to the Post Office, Box, SN13 8NA

Why aren't there more cafes like this one? Winningly bohemian, down to earth and friendly, it's a small space – as the name suggests – but the food's fantastic and excellent value. Their vegetable dhal curries have a loyal following, and their hearty vegetable soups are similarly homemade and very tasty. They also do all-day breakfasts, and the cakes are as good as they look.

The Northey Arms

ohhpubs.co.uk
A4, Box, SN13 8AE | 01225 742333

The Northey has stylish, relaxing décor, and ingredients are sourced through local suppliers and the bar features regular guest ales and beers.

The Quarryman's Arms

quarrymans-arms.co.uk
Box Hill, Box, SN13 8HN
01225 743569

The food can be hit-and-miss at the ivy-clad Quarryman's, but for somewhere to sit with a local real ale or crisp cider on a summer's day, with views out across the valley, this place takes some beating. The appealing decor is mostly wood and stone. As a nod to the local history that gives the pub its name, the bar is decorated with mining paraphernalia. They'll even arrange a guided tour of nearby mines.

▸ Deerhurst

Deerhurst is an attractive farming village. Its cottages, which come in a variety of architectural styles, include some fine examples of cruck timber-framing. Deerhurst is splendidly located on the wide, grassy east bank of the Severn. Its claims to fame are a largely Saxon parish church and an almost-complete Saxon chapel.

Dating from the 8th century, St Mary's Priory was once part of an important 10th-century monastery. The priory is the only remaining Saxon monastic church in the country, and has several Saxon doors and windows. The extremely rare 9th-century font is said to be the finest in England. The double-headed window high up on the west wall, which is possibly made up of Roman stones, is particularly striking. The animal-headed label stops (the carved ends of dripstones) in the middle doorway below this window date from the early 9th century. On the surviving arch of the Saxon apse, now on the east exterior, you'll find the Deerhurst Angel, a carving from the 9th century.

SEE SOME LOCAL CHURCHES

Odda's Chapel

english-heritage.org.uk
0870 3331181 | Open daily
Apr–Oct 10–6, Nov–Mar & 31 Dec
10–4

Odda's Chapel used to be concealed behind walls added over the course of later centuries. The chancel had been divided by floors, while the nave had become a kitchen. Only in 1865 was this complete Saxon chapel revealed. The Odda Stone, an inscribed tablet discovered inside, dates the chapel's construction to 1056.

St Mary's Priory Church

Deerhurst, GL19 4BX
St Mary's is one of the most complete buildings to survive from before the Norman conquest. The building has many Saxon features, including a carved baluster, tiny triangular windows, and, high up on the west wall, a beautiful pair of windows with pointed tops. There are several excellent pieces of Saxon sculpture here, thought to date from the 9th century, including an angel in the ruined apse. The font is especially interesting, covered in intricate interleaving carved patterns. At some point the font was appropriated for use as a washtub on a farm. It was reclaimed in the course of restoration work.

An early painted figure was recently discovered on a panel high up in the east wall of the nave. It may date from the 10th century, which would make it the oldest wall painting in any church in Britain.

▶ PLACES NEARBY

To the north of Deerhurst is historic Tewkesbury (see page 223), which has plenty of stories and is hardly unattractive. There's also a stunning collection of ancient wall paintings at the Church of St James the Great (GL52 7SH) at **Stoke Orchard** to the east.

▼ St Mary's Church

▶ Dursley

J K Rowling used the name of this town for the unpleasant Dursley family in her popular books about a bespectacled schoolboy who can do a few magic tricks. Although the busy market town beneath the Cotswold Edge has been severely modernised, its old centre remains intact. Dursley was once an important cloth manufacturing town. The delightfully arcaded market hall, built in 1729, and the Georgian Market House (which is now the town hall) sit bang in the centre, along with a statue of Queen Anne.

The church is not blessed with a harmonious interior, but it does have a fine vaulted porch in the Perpendicular style. The Gothic tower's spire collapsed in 1698, and it was rebuilt at the beginning of the 18th century with a grant from Queen Anne. The north door of the church was blocked to prevent the church from being used as a thoroughfare for the collection of water from the Broad Well. Although in the immediate area Woodmancote offers a better selection of 18th-century houses, Dursley is a pleasant, old-fashioned sort of place, and exploration of its centre is rewarding.

GO WALKING

Twinberrow Wood, on the slopes of Stinchcombe Hill, is home to the Dursley Sculpture and Play Trail. Various community groups created the trail to encourage children to walk in the woods, and the result is worth checking out. To find the trail, take the A4135 from Dursley towards Tetbury. At the top of the hill take a sharp right. Continue along this road until you see the sign for the Sculpture and Play Trail. There's parking on both sides of the road. Map available from valevision.org.uk.

EAT AND DRINK

The Old Spot Inn
oldspotinn.co.uk
Hill Road, GL11 4JQ
01453 542870
This classic 18th-century free house is a former Campaign For Real Ale Pub of the Year, so it's worth visiting to sample the regularly changing, tip-top real ales on pump and to savour the cheerful buzzing atmosphere of this cracking community local. It sits smack on the Cotswold Way, and was once three terraced farm cottages known as 'pig row.' It's apt, then, that it should take its name from the Gloucestershire Old Spot pig. Devoid of modern-day intrusions, the traditional low-beamed bars are havens of peace. Only the comforting sound of crackling log fires and the hubbub of chatting locals fills the rambling little rooms. Food is wholesome and homemade. There's also a pretty garden for summer alfresco sipping.

▶ **PLACES NEARBY**

Sleepier more old-fashioned Wotton-under-Edge (see page 252) is just down the road from Dursley, while historic and moody Berkeley Castle (see page 63) is to the west. Nailsworth (see page 157) and handsome Tetbury (see page 219) are about 15 minutes' drive to the east. Closer to hand, the dramatic hill-fort at Uley Bury and Owlpen Manor (see page 230) are to the northeast.

Cam

The village of Cam, just to the north of Dursley, still has a single factory which produces high quality cloth for dress uniforms and for snooker-table covers. Cam church, apparently built by Lord Berkeley to save his soul after the murder of Edward II took place at Berkeley Castle, contains a Jacobean pulpit. Nearby Cam Peak and Cam Long Down are Cotswold outliers – formerly part of the Cotswold escarpment, the surrounding softer rock has been eroded around them, leaving them stranded.

Stinchcombe Hill

Just to the northwest of Dursley is Stinchcombe Hill, considered by many to be the marker for the most westerly point of the geographic Cotswolds. From its summit, Drakestone Point, you can take in far-reaching views along the escarpment to the Forest of Dean and the River Severn.

Stinchcombe Hill Golf Club

stinchcombehillgolfclub.com
Stinchcombe Hill, GL11 6AQ
01453 542015

Stinchcombe sits high on the hill, offering splendid views of the Cotswolds, the River Severn and the Welsh hills. It's a downland course with good turf, some trees and an interesting variety of greens. Protected greens make this a challenging course in windy conditions.

Nibley Knoll

Southwest of Dursley is Nibley Knoll, with its distinctive needle-shaped monolith rising out of the hillside. This is the Tyndale Monument. It was built in 1866 to honour William Tyndale, born in nearby North Nibley. In 1484, Tyndale was the first man to translate the Bible from Latin into English. It is possible to climb the 111-foot-tall monument to get an excellent view.

▲ Dyrham House

▶ **Dyrham Park**

nationaltrust.org.uk

SN14 8ER | 0117 937 2501 | House, Garden, shop & tearoom open 29 Jun–1 Sep, daily, 2 Sep–27 Oct, Fri–Tue 10–5 (House 11–5); House also open 9 Mar–28 Jun, Fri–Tue 11–5; Garden also open 16 Feb–28 Jun, Fri–Tue 10–5 2 Nov–15 Dec, Sat–Sun 10–4; Basement & Kitchen open 16 Feb–8 Mar, Fri–Tue 11–4, 2 Nov–15 Dec, Sat–Sun 11–4; Park open daily (ex 25 Dec) 10–5. Whole property closed until 1pm 4 & 18 Sep, 6, 13 & 20 Nov & 4 Dec (last admission 1hr before close)

Dyrham, a picturesque and flowery village eight miles to the north of Bath, bears a name associated with a battle of enormous consequence for Britain. It took place on nearby Hinton Hill in AD 577. The invading Saxons defeated the Britons, permitting the capture of the Romano-British cities of Bath, Cirencester and Gloucester.

There was once a Tudor house here. The National Trust-owned Dyrham Park we see today, however, was built for William Blathwayt, Secretary at War during the reign of William III. The present house is entirely a creation of the William and Mary period at the end of the 17th century. From fairly modest beginnings, Blathwayt rose through the Civil Service to hold a number of top government jobs. He found favour with William III, both for his administrative abilities and because he spoke Dutch. Blathwayt also made an advantageous marriage to the heiress of the Dyrham estate. After the death of both his in-laws and his wife, he began to replace their family home.

The baroque mansion, set in a valley and surrounded by 272 acres of gardens and rolling parkland, was constructed in two stages. Huguenot architect Samuel Hauduroy presided over the first wave in 1692. William Talman, designer of Chatsworth, and one of the foremost architects of his day, undertook the second phase of the work around the turn of the century. Between them they created a splendid house that displays unusual restraint for the time. The Blathwayt family lived here until 1956, when the government acquired the house. In 1961, the National Trust acquired it in turn. In 1993, the house was used as a backdrop for the film *Remains of the Day*.

Dyrham Park has changed little over the years. All the furniture, paintings and china you can see in the house today were collected by Blathwayt himself. The magnificent collections of blue-and-white Delftware and Dutch paintings of the period reflect Blathwayt's regular journeys to Holland in the company of William III.

There are Dutch-style gardens, too. These include a statue of Neptune and one of the earliest-known greenhouses. Thanks to the great landscape architect Humphry Repton, swathes of the park are now designed in accordance with the more naturalistic English style. A herd of fallow deer grazes in the parkland, as they have done since Saxon times.

EAT AND DRINK

Tollgate Teashop
tollgateteashop.co.uk
Oldfield Gatehouse, On the A46,
SN14 8LF | 01225 891585
On the side of the busy A46, in a distinctive stone building with arched windows and wooden floors, you'll find Tollgate Tea Shop. You can indulge in a delicious cream tea while listening to peaceful classical music and smelling their fragrant wood-burning stove.

Tollgate offers a selection of ten good teas. Their use of traditional blue and white willow-pattern china perfects this teatime experience. You can buy gift vouchers and treat someone to a cream tea, as well.

▶ Evesham

Feeling fruity? If not, you soon will be. Built in a protective loop of the River Avon in the middle of a fertile vale that has become Britain's foremost fruit-growing area, Evesham is an agricultural centre and a market town.

The medieval town grew up beside the 8th-century Benedictine abbey, one of the grandest ever built. Abbeys like Evesham once dominated this region, and were instrumental in developing orchards and gardens for the production of fruit and vegetables. Unfortunately little of this once-mighty abbey survives today. Detached Evesham bell tower is probably England's finest example of the kind. The tower, 14th- and 16th-century gateways and two medieval churches, constitute the principal remains of the once mighty abbey. The churches were originally the abbey chapels, and the bell tower was a combined gatehouse and campanile. The bell tower's peal of 12 bells certainly lives up to the grandeur of their setting, and is nationally acclaimed as a benchmark against which other English-hung rings are compared.

One of the abbey buildings houses the Almonry Museum and Heritage Centre, which contains a mock-up Victorian kitchen and exhibits that commemorate the Battle of Evesham (1265). Here the troops of Prince Edward, later King Edward I, killed Simon de Montfort, the leader of the opposition to Henry III. After the rebellion of 1263-1264, de Montfort had become de facto ruler of England. He had also called the first directly-elected parliament, securing his place in history as an important founder of modern democracy.

▶ PLACES NEARBY

With two Cotswolds A-listers, Chipping Campden (see page 96) and Broadway (see page 77), to the southeast (and practically on Evesham's doorstep), you'd be foolish to go in any other direction. If you've already been, travel southwest. Tewkesbury's (see page 223) not far away, and Cheltenham (see page 88) and Winchcombe (see page 233) are not far from there.

▶ Fairford

Every July the Royal International Air Tattoo is held at RAF Fairford. But the town, located on the River Coln and the A417, is more than an airfield. It has a busy lowland feel not entirely characteristic of the Cotswolds.

Fairford's magnificent 'wool' church of St Mary deserves a place in any roll call of fine Cotswold churches. Rebuilt in the 1490s by John Tame and his son Edmund, the most influential of Fairford's medieval wool merchants and hardly altered since, the building's impressive fame is, however, often eclipsed by the renown of its virtually complete set of spectacular late medieval glass. Made between 1500 and 1517, they comprise the only surviving complete set in the country, and narrate the highlights of the Biblical story. They are most likely the work of Flanders craftsman Barnard Flower, whom Henry VIII commissioned to make the windows of the King's College Chapel in Cambridge and the Lady Chapel at Westminster Abbey. Flower probably didn't complete the massive undertaking alone, and almost certainly had help from English and Dutch craftsmen. The 28 windows tell many stories from the Old and New Testaments, culminating in the great west window that depicts Christ in Glory. Episodes from the early history of the Christian Church and its saints are also depicted. The great west window, which shows the Last Judgement, is particularly riveting and luminous. The amusing carved misericords – which include a drunkard and a woman beating her husband – underneath the choir stalls are not to be missed either.

The glass miraculously survived the Reformation, only for the west windows to be badly damaged in a storm in 1703. The windows were removed from the church and put into safe storage during World War II. The glass has been restored, repaired, partially renewed and cleaned through the centuries, but its survival as a set makes it unique.

Outside the church, don't miss the fascinating series of carved figures just below the roof parapet. The churchyard contains fine Cotswold tombs and monuments, some dating back to the 17th century. A favourite with visitors is more recent: a 1980 memorial with a stone sculpture of Tiddles, Fairford's much-loved church cat.

The church overlooks the green water meadows and the old mill by a picturesque bridge. From the church a pleasant circuit is possible and will bring you back to the main street. Most of the houses that line the street date from the 17th or 18th century. Along with the many inns, these houses serve as a reminder of Fairford's former role as a coaching town. John Keble, the 19th-century church reformer, was born at Keble House, on the north side of the road main street at the east end of the town.

To the north you'll find the picturesque twin villages of Eastleach Turville and Eastleach Martin, which are separated by the River Leach, one of the Thames' many tributaries. The influence of the Tame family and the proximity of the river led

Henry VIII's librarian, John Leland, to observe – dreadful pun alert – that 'Fairford never flourished afore the cumming of the Tames onto it.' Wool merchant John Tame, who built Fairford's church, became Fairford's lord of the manor. His son, Sir Edmund Tame, is responsible for St Peter's at Rendcomb, 5 miles north of Cirencester (see page 105). His initials can be found there on some of the corbels and on an old glass pane in a nave window. The church tower at Barnsley probably also owes its existence to his patronage.

▶ **PLACES NEARBY**

Uber-historic Cirencester (see page 105), once the second most important city in the country, is to the west. South Cerney and the activity-tastic Cotswold Water Park (page 190) are slightly further south. The delightfully named Filkins (see page 123) and the excellent Cotswold Wildlife Park (see page 81) are to the northeast; Lechlade (see page 144) is to the east; gorgeous Bibury (see page 66) is north and shouldn't be missed either. You're in trouble here: too many choices.

▶ **Filkins**

This quiet Cotswold village has a distinctly bypassed feel. Its cottages are distinguished for their solid craftsmanship rather than their beauty. Their story can be read in *Jubilee Boy,* an entertaining book by local resident George Swinford, which you can find on sale at the woollen mill (among other places). Swinford worked as a foreman on the estate belonging to statesman Sir Stafford Cripps, and also gave his name to Swinford Museum in the village. The last people to work some of the quarries in the Filkins' area before George Swinford reopened them in 1929 were French POWs from the Napoleonic Wars.

The village is best known for its working woollen-weaving factory. It's one of the last, if not *the* last, in the Cotswolds – which is poignant when you think about how the whole constitution of the area owes its character to sheep. Cotswold Woollen Weavers keeps the flag flying, producing quality clothes on clattering old looms. The factory's located in an attractive old barn. Visitors can watch all the processes of production, and while the enterprise is a serious and forward-thinking business concern with an online shop and an attractive website, it also takes time to pay tribute to the historical relevance of wool production with a permanent exhibition devoted to sheep and wool.

VISIT THE MUSEUM AND GALLERY

Cotswold Woollen Weavers

naturalbest.co.uk

GL7 3JJ | 01367 860491 | Open all year daily, Mon–Sat 10–6, Sun 2–6

This traditional 18th-century woollen mill is home to the Cotswold Woollen Weavers. Located in the idyllic village of Filkins, the mill houses a textile museum, design studio, shop and gallery. See traditionally-woven cloth, interior textiles and traditionally-made upholstered furniture, all hand-worked on site. Enjoy constantly changing collections inspired by the limestone landscape of the Cotswolds.

There is also a cafe, an art gallery and an excellent shop. Adjoining buildings contain more workshops devoted to other traditional crafts.

▶ **PLACES NEARBY**

A short distance east of Filkins, you'll find some interesting little villages. The Norman south doorway of the church at **Kencot** dates back to the 12th century, and is decorated with a carving of Sagittarius shooting an arrow into the mouth of a monster. The church at **Alvescot**, which is set in a quiet location to the north of the village, has a splendid 16th-century brass.

▶ Gloucester

For a town with so much history, Gloucester isn't as much of a looker as you might expect. It's not without its charms: Gloucester has an uber-magnificent cathedral, historic docks, remnants of Roman wall, and some great museums. These would probably draw more tourists if not for the fact that some of Gloucester's other bits, namely its large shopping arcades and other unappealing buildings, are rather offputting. There is in fact quite a lot to see here, but with the exception of the obvious, magnificent cathedral, it has to be sought out.

For many centuries, Gloucester was one of the most important cities in the kingdom. It was founded as Roman Glevum, a garrison town on the western edge of occupied England. It later became a 'colonia', a retirement community for legionnaires, who were rewarded after completing their service with a villa and a sinecure. In the 7th century, the Saxons established the monastery of St Peter in Gloucester. The town's current street plan takes after its Saxon incarnation, having changed significantly since the Roman period. Once Gloucester became the capital of a Saxon shire, Edward the Confessor held his winter court there. William I continued the tradition, and announced the creation of the Domesday Book, the great project of his reign, in the town. Soon after this announcement, work started on the Cathedral Church of St

Peter, the abbey church that was to become the city's chief landmark. In 1216, Henry III was crowned in Gloucester. He remains the only king of England proper not to have been crowned at Westminster. In 1327 the murdered Edward II was buried here, which turned Gloucester into a place of pilgrimage up until the Dissolution of the Monasteries.

Points of interest are scattered throughout the city, which makes an early visit to the tourist office in Southgate Street a good idea. St Michael's Tower stands on the former site of the city's 13th-century stone cross, removed in 1751 'for the better conveniency of carriages'. It is also the meeting point of the city's four principal streets – the neatly-named Westgate, Eastgate, Southgate and Northgate.

Gloucester Cathedral is just to the north of St Michael's Tower, and its own monumental tower is visible from afar. William I appointed Serlo, a Benedictine monk from Mont St Michel, as abbot. Serlo resuscitated the ailing Saxon abbey, and began its reconstruction during the reign of William II. It was consecrated in 1100 and completed in 1120, although additions were made over the following centuries. During the Dissolution

of the Monasteries the Abbey Church of St Peter was rededicated to the Holy and Invisible Trinity, becoming the cathedral church of the new diocese of Gloucester. It's an outstanding example of medieval ecclesiastical design that successfully blends Norman and Perpendicular influences.

The tower was built around 1450, and replaced an earlier, smaller tower and spire. It contains Great Peter, the last medieval Bourdon bell. The nave is lined with magnificent Norman arcading. The nave's vault dates back to 1242. Its equally antique roof was constructed from 110 oak trees from the Forest of Dean. The south transept is a very early example of the Perpendicular style, while the Norman crypt reflects the original Norman church above. The massive east window (from 1349), the beautifully carved 14th-century choir stalls, the late Perpendicular-style Lady chapel, the tomb of Edward II and the Norman chapter house are all worth a look. Indeed, you may have already given Gloucester Cathedral a look without even knowing it: the cloisters feature in two of the Harry Potter films. Houses from the 16th, 17th and 18th centuries surround the cathedral green. The cathedral also looks out on the 15th-century half-timbered Parliament Room where Richard II held Parliament (weren't expecting that, were you?) in 1378.

Gloucester's docks, another of the city's major historical attractions, have long been redundant. The area has been restored, however, and is worth perusing. Warehouses have been resurrected as offices, restaurants and museums, among them the National Waterways Museum. In another warehouse you'll find the Gloucester Antiques Centre, which has 100 shops to browse. At the north end of the docks, the Old Custom House is home to the Soldiers of Gloucestershire Museum.

A walk through the bustle of the city's main streets reveals Gloucester's rich history. The medieval New Inn sits on Northgate Street, a short way from St Michael's Tower. Designed to accommodate the growing number of visitors to the tomb of Edward II in the 15th century, the Inn is built around a beautiful galleried courtyard. On Southgate Street, the Church of St Mary de Crypt is a fine example of the Perpendicular style. Despite refined appearances however, St Mary has an interestingly chequered past: the crypt once seved as a tavern, and the church became an explosives factory during the Siege of Gloucester in 1643. Blackfriars, the finest surviving Dominican Friary in the country, has recently been restored. This religious institution also has a somewhat irreligious backstory – it was built on the site of a Norman military fortification.

◀ Gloucester Cathedral

Aficionados of museums will find several worth seeing, besides those located in the old docks. Visitors can see the remains of the city's Roman Wall under the City Museum. Ecclectic Gloucester City Museum and Art Gallery on Brunswick Road contains Roman mosaics and the Birdlip Mirror, together with a Natural History section with a freshwater aquarium and an excellent art collection. The Folk Museum is housed in half-timbered houses on Westgate Street. Not far from here is Ladybellegate House, the finest town house in Gloucester.

Robinswood Hill Country Park, just a few miles to the south of Gloucester on a Cotswold outlier, offers an impressive view from its 651 feet (198m) height. Presumably the animals of the park's rare breeds farm enjoy the scenery. The old quarry on the hill's west side is a Site of Special Scientific Interest: its exposure of lower and middle lias rock is the finest inland example in the country.

TAKE IN SOME HISTORY
Gloucester Cathedral
gloucestercathedral.org.uk
College Green, GL 1 2LX | 01452 528095 | Open daily 7.30–6; restricted access during Sunday services (7.40am, 8.00am, 10.15am and 3pm); guided tours Mon–Sat 10.45–3.15, Sun 12–2.30
Maintenance on Gloucester, one of the country's great cathedrals, keeps seven stonemasons in full-time employment. Visitors can spot the building's Norman components or, with the aid of a guided tour, see where scenes from Harry Potter were filmed.

VISIT THE MUSEUMS AND GALLERIES
Soldiers of Gloucestershire Museum
glosters.org.uk
Custom House, Gloucester Docks, GL1 2HE | 01452 522682 | Open all year daily 10–4.30 including BHs; closed Mon in winter

Soldiers of Gloucestershire tells the remarkable stories of those who have served in the regiments of Gloucestershire since 1694. Their courage, humour, sacrifice and moving individual acts of bravery are brought together in exciting and colourful exhibitions. The WWI trench exhibit allows visitors to feel and hear the deafening sound of guns, and engage with interactive displays. The Museum features memorabilia from the 18th, 19th and 20th centuries, including uniforms and medals.

Gloucester City Museum & Art Gallery
gloucester.gov.uk
Brunswick Road, GL1 1HP
01452 396131 | Open Tue–Sat 10–5; closed mid-Dec–1 Jan
The impressive range of artefacts includes the Rufus Sita tombstone; the amazing Iron Age Birdlip mirror; one of

the earliest backgammon sets in the world; dinosaur fossils; paintings by famous artists such as Gainsborough and Turner; full-sized dinosaurs; preserved wildlife from the city and the Gloucestershire countryside; beautiful antique furniture, glass, ceramics and silver; and hands-on displays, computer quizzes and activity workstations throughout the galleries. An exciting range of temporary exhibitions spotlights anything from contemporary art and textiles to dinosaurs and local history. The museum also hosts children's holiday activities and regular special events.

Nature in Art
nature-in-art.org.uk
Wallsworth Hall, A38 Twigworth, GL2 9PA | 01452 731422
Open all year, Tue–Sun & BHs 10–5
Nature in Art is the world's only museum dedicated exclusively to art inspired by nature. Within the fine Georgian mansion, displays embrace two and three-dimensional work in all mediums and styles, ranging from Picasso to Shepherd. Spanning 1500 years, the collection contains work by 600 artists from over 50 countries. As well as a temporary exhibition, you'll find watercolour landscapes, contemporary glass, works by Flemish masters, oriental art, bronze sculpture and even some modern abstract interpretations.

The National Waterways Museum
canalrivertrust.org.uk
Llanthony Warehouse, The Docks, GL1 2EH | 01452 318200 | Open all year daily 10–4.30
Based in Gloucester Docks, this museum takes up three floors of a seven-storey Victorian warehouse and documents the national collection of inland waterways and the history of Britain's water-based transport. The emphasis is on hands-on experience, including working models and engines, interactive displays, actual craft and computer interactions. Boat trips run daily in summer (but call ahead).

Gloucester Folk Museum
gloucester.gov.uk
99–103 Westgate Street, GL1 2PG
01452 396868 | Open all year, Tue–Sat, 10–5
So what exactly does a folk museum cover? Local history, domestic life, crafts, trades and industries from 1500 to the present, the Siege of Gloucester, Victorian kitchen and laundry equipment – you might have an easier time outlining what it *doesn't* cover. The museum is partly housed in three floors of splendid Tudor and Jacobean timber-framed buildings, which date from the 16th and 17th centuries. New buildings contain the ironmonger's shop, as well as a wheelwright's and a carpenter's workshops. Brand new buildings contain

education exhibits and the Folk Tearooms. The Toys and Childhood gallery lets you get hands-on with the toys, including a puppet theatre. Delve further into the history of childhood with the Victorian classroom. Throughout the year, the museum holds a wide range of exhibitions, hands-on activities, events, demonstrations and role-play sessions. The special events often take place in the museum's attractive cottage garden and courtyard, and often include live animals and outside games.

Gloucester Docks

gloucesterdocks.me.uk
The Docks | 01452 311190

Following the opening of the Sharpness Canal in 1827, fourteen warehouses were built here to store grain and other goods. Most of the warehouses have been renovated, transformed into offices and shops. One now houses the Gloucester Waterways Museum. Despite the area's (rather necessary) modernisation, it's still a satisfying place to stroll and soak up some history.

MEET THE ANIMALS

St Augustine's Farm

staugustinesfarm.co.uk
Arlingham, GL2 7JR | 01452 740277
Open most days Mar–Nov 11–5

This 50-acre organic farm is a great place to take the kids. They can hand-feed farm animals, play traditional games in the barn, run free in the toddler play area or, if they're a little older, run free in the wide, safe green spaces. There's also a picnic area.

ENTERTAIN THE FAMILY

House of the Tailor of Gloucester

tailor-of-gloucester.org.uk
9 College Court, GL1 2NJ
01452 422856

Beatrix Potter's *The Tailor of Gloucester* is set in this tiny shop, which Potter sketched while visiting the city. The shop sells books, toys and ornaments, as well as merchandise from other children's classics like *Winnie-the-Pooh*. The building also contains a small museum.

GO SHOPPING

Gloucester Quays Antique Centre

gloucesterquays.co.uk
99a High Orchard Street, Gloucester Quays, GL1 5SH
01452 338912 | Open Mon–Fri 10–5, Sat and BH 10–5, Sun 11–5

Don't miss your chance to riffle through period and 20th-century furniture, ceramics, glassware, gold, silver and antique jewellery, toys clocks, watches and so much more at Britain's largest provincial antiques market. This converted Victorian warehouse in the city's revamped historic dockland contains three fascinating floors of shops and cabinets, representing 100 dealers.

WATCH A MATCH
Gloucester RFC
gloucesterrugby.co.uk
Kingsholm Road, GL1 3AX
Home to a leading rugby
union club, Gloucester's
Kingsholm is a notoriously
raucous ground.

CATCH A PERFORMANCE
Three Choirs Festival
3choirs.org
JGL1 2LX | Jul–Aug
Europe's oldest choral
festival is held at the
cathedrals of Hereford,
Gloucester and Worcester
on a rotating basis.

Guildhall Arts Centre
www.gloucester.gov.uk
23 Eastgate Street, GL1 1NS
01452 503050
The centre hosts live music,
comedy, theatre, film,
exhibitions and talks.

The Kings Theatre
theatresonline.com
Kingsbarton Street, GL1 1QX
01452 396572

Picturedrome Theatre
theatregloucestershire.net
Barton Street, GL1 4EU
01452 560445

TAKE OFF
Ballooning In The Cotswolds
ballooninginthecotswolds.co.uk
Gloucester | 01453 753221
See page 72

▲ Historic Docks, Gloucester

GO SKIING
**Gloucester Ski
& Snowboard Centre**
gloucesterski.com
Robinswood Hill Dry Ski Slope,
GL4 6EA | 01452 501438
Where Eddie 'The Eagle'
Edwards learnt the skills
that enabled him to jump him
to stardom.

PLAY A ROUND
Gloucester Golf Club
gloucestergolf.com
Matson Lane, Robinswood Hill,
GL4 6EA | 01452 411331
This undulating, wooded
course is built around a hill
with superb views over
Gloucester and the Cotswolds.
The formidable 12th hole
consists of a drive straight
up a hill, nicknamed
'Coronary Hill'.

EAT AND DRINK

The Wharf House Restaurant with Rooms ⊛

thewharfhouse.co.uk
Over, GL2 8DB | 01452 332900

Profits from this restaurant (and its rooms) go towards the upkeep of 34 miles of canals in Herefordshire and Gloucestershire. Located on the River Severn, the restaurant is actually owned by the counties' canal trust. It really comes into its own when the weather allows diners to sit on the terrace overlooking the water. But with its wooden tables, parquet floor and fashionably neutral colour palette, it's still a pleasant space if you're dining indoors. The menu suits the relaxed and informal setting, offering a large choice of well-prepared, unfussy dishes.

The Queens Head

queensheadlongford.co.uk
Tewkesbury Road, Longford, GL2 9EJ | 01452 301882

This pretty, 250-year-old, half-timbered pub/restaurant is just out of town, and cannot be missed in summer when it is festooned with hanging baskets. Inside, a lovely old flagstone-floored locals' bar proffers a great range of real ales and ciders. The owners, at the helm since 1995, believe in giving their diners high-quality, freshly prepared modern British food that is great value for money. A couple of caveats: the dress code is smart casual, and the restaurant doesn't admit children under 12.

The Coffee Shop

gloucestercathedral.org.uk
Gloucester Cathedral, GL1 2LX
01452 527701

Situated near the famous cloisters, this friendly place serves teas, coffee, delicious soup, scones and irresistible cakes.

Hayward Coffee Shop

thecityofgloucester.co.uk
Nature in Art, Wallsworth Hall, Twigworth GL2 9PA | 01452 733945

A light and airy conservatory houses the Nature in Art museum's coffee shop, where you'll find a tempting range of cream teas and cakes, all baked on the premises. Admission to the coffee shop is free.

▶ **PLACES NEARBY**

Gloucester is so conveniently close to Cheltenham (see page 88) that the wise thing to do is make the latter your base, as it has better accommodation and dining options. From there, you can visit Gloucester for perhaps a day or an afternoon. Looking southeast, you'll find Painswick (see page 176), the self-proclaimed 'Queen of the Cotswolds'. Its fascinating churchyard and the spectacular hill-fort on the Beacon are a short drive away, and well worth your time.

▶ The Guitings

The valley running east of Winchcombe, following the meandering course of the River Windrush towards Bourton, is sprinkled with some charming and idiosyncratic villages. There are two Guitings, for example – the intriguingly named **Temple Guiting** and the un-Cotswoldsishly named **Guiting Power**.

Temple Guiting takes its name from the Knights Templar, who owned the manor from the mid-12th century until 1308, when the order was violently disbanded. It's a pretty village among trees at the edge of a stream. The church retains fragmentary remains of its original Norman construction, while the stained glass is 16th-century and the tower, pulpit and windows are 18th century. East of Temple Guiting, you'll find the Cotswold Farm Park. Gorgeous and friendly Guiting Power, a couple of miles to the south of Temple Guiting, is clustered around a small green, and is a perfect example of an English village.

The church to the south of the village, also once owned by the Knights Templar, has an exceptionally fine Norman south doorway. Sadly the interior is rather uninspiring. The foundations of a Saxon chapel have been discovered just to the north of the existing church. Guiting Power hosts a small but significant annual music and arts festival in July.

MEET THE ANIMALS
Adam Henson's Cotswold Farm Park
cotswoldfarmpark.co.uk
GL54 5UG | 01451 850307
Open daily mid-Feb–late Dec
10.30–5 (closes 1 hr early in winter)
Meet over 50 breeding flocks and herds of rare farm animals, including the only living descendants of the famous Cotswold Lion – the breed of sheep that made the eponymous area famous and prosperous way back when. There are rabbits and guinea pigs to cuddle, lambs and goat kids to bottle feed, tractor and trailer-rides, battery powered tractors, a Touch Barn, a Maze Quest, Jumping Pillows and safe, rustic-themed play areas both indoors and out. Lambing occurs until early May, followed by shearing and then milking demonstrations later in the season. There's also a 40-pitch camping and caravanning site.

EAT AND DRINK
The Hollow Bottom
hollowbottom.com
Guiting Power, GL54 5UX
01451 850392
Often frequented by Cheltenham race-goers, this 18th-century free house is decorated with all manner of horseracing memorabilia. Its nooks and crannies are warmed by a blazing log fire, and lend themselves to planning an intimate drink

10 places to drink

- **Egypt Mill**, Nailsworth, egyptmill.com
- **The Hollow Bottom**, Guiting Power, hollowbottom.com
- **Howard Arms**, Ilmington, howardarms.com
- **The King's Arms Hotel**, Woodstock, kings-hotel-woodstock.co.uk
- **The Old Spot**, Dursley, oldspotinn.co.uk
- **Rose & Crown Inn**, Nympsfield, theroseandcrowninn.com
- **The Swan**, Southrop, theswanatsouthrop.co.uk
- **The Village Pub**, Barnsley, thevillagepub.co.uk
- **The Wheatsheaf Inn**, Northleach, cotswoldswheatsheaf.com
- **The Woolpack Inn**, Slad, 01452 813429

or meal. There's also a separate dining room, as well as outside tables for use in fine weather. In addition to real ales and ciders, the bar has a grand selection of malt whiskies, wines and champagne. If you're after a snack, the Bottom offers baked potatoes and freshly made baguettes with a choice of fillings. Other dishes include homemade pie and roast of the day, as well as wholetail scampi.

PLACES NEARBY

The Guitings are, approximately, bang in the middle between historic Stow-on-the-Wold (see page 195), scene of the last battle in the English Civil War, spectacular Sudeley Castle (see page 217), which has even more stories to tell, and welcoming Winchcombe (see page 233). To the south, Northleach (see page 155) awaits. The hamlet of **Ford**, just north of Temple Guiting, has a good pub.

Plough Inn

theploughinnford.co.uk
Ford, near Temple Guiting,
GL54 5RU | 01386 584215
This pub likes to wear its horseracing associations on its sleeve, and everywhere else as well. Flagstone floors, burning fires and old furnishings create a very cosy atmosphere. The food is founded on the use of fresh local produce and prepared to a high standard.

▶ Hidcote Manor

▲ Hidcote Manor Gardens

nationaltrust.org
Hidcote Bartrim, near Chipping Campden, Gloucestershire, GL55 6LR
01386 438333 | Open daily May–Sep, and most other weekends and selected
days; check website for details

Hidcote Manor Garden combines restraint with *joie de vivre*. The garden exemplifies the Arts and Crafts movement's landscaping incarnation: it has is a well-defined ground plan, marked by dramatic paths; hedges in strong, straight lines and strict – though sometimes fanciful – topiary shapes. The garden has surprises at every turn.

It was created over 100 years ago by Lawrence Johnston who, with his mother Gertrude Winthrop, bought the property in 1907. At that time, the house was surrounded by nothing but fields and a few mature trees. Johnston read extensively, studying the work of leading garden designers, especially Gertrude Jekyll. He became a recognised horticulturist himself, and sponsored and took part in many plant-hunting expeditions to the Alps, Kenya and South Africa, building up a network of fellow plantsmen around the world with whom he exchanged specimens. As a result of these expeditions, over 40 new species were cultivated in the UK. Many of these bear Johnston's name. The Royal Horticultural Society awarded him three Awards of Garden Merit for his plant-hunting achievements. A yellow climbing rose Johnston bought from a breeder as an unnamed seedling was first dubbed a 'Hidcote

Yellow', but later renamed 'Lawrence Johnston'. It now garlands the north wall of the Old Garden.

Clipped hedges of holly, beech, hornbeam and yew divide the garden into separate compartments – Johnston called it a 'garden of rooms' – each with a distinctive characteristic and colour theme. The use of tapestry hedging in the Circle close to the Old Garden was innovative, though mixed planting was commonplace in ancient hedgerows. Here the blend of different species, such as yew, beech and holly, creates an intriguingly mottled appearance. Unlike an evergreen hedge, this row varies its colour and characteristics by the season. To further reinforce the ground plan, the garden's two axes run uncompromisingly north–south and east–west, with a gazebo at their intersection. The hedges separating the garden rooms are tall, and thus there is no cheating – one has to enter each room to experience its particular explosion of colour, its sensuous planting and its compatible marriage of formal topiary shapes, blowsy, old-fashioned roses, rare shrubs and perennials.

In some cases, the sense of occasion and anticipation is heightened by the style of the entrance. One of the most formal areas, the Bathing Pool garden, has a massive topiary hedge. Shaped in the centre, with a steeply pitched, overhanging roof, it forms a truly triumphal arch. Its reflection in the circular pool increases the impact.

The Red Border is reached via a wide flight of stone steps, flanked by a pair of tall, narrow brick pavilions with incurved roofs topped by ball-shaped finials. Pots of red geraniums and agaves on the stone walls hint at the exciting colour profusion to come. The border is a flamboyant coming-together of red, purple, orange and bronze. The groundwork is laid with the purple-bronze foliage of *Heuchera* 'Palace Purple', which perfectly complements the 1946 blood-red *Floribunda Rosa* 'Frensham', the blazing reds of *Lobelia cardinalis* 'Will Scarlet' and 'Queen Victoria', *Canna indica* 'Roi Humbert' and, as always, the cherry-red verbena. A bright star in this border is the striking daylily *Hemerocallis fulva* 'Flore Pleno' with its orange-going-on-red petals the colours of leaping flames.

Inspired by designer and writer Vita Sackville-West's garden at Sissinghurst Castle in Kent, the White Garden has a billowing profusion of silver-leaved and white-flowering plants, their contrasting forms and textures linked by their uniformity of colour. The beds are bordered with low clipped hedges topped

◀ Hidcote Manor Gardens

by topiary peacocks. Tall, erect spires of white acanthus tower above common wormwood, Artemisia absinthium 'Lambrook Silver', a glorious snow-white Cistus, mop-headed phlox and shrub roses. Later in the season huge clumps of white dahlias hold centre stage.

One of the glories of summer in Hidcote Manor Garden is the flourish of old roses in the Rose Walk. Johnston gradually built up a collection of 18th- and 19th-century damask, gallica and moss roses, many of which were bred in France, and planted them in two long borders. These romantic and sweetly-scented roses bloom in one short-lived but exquisite midsummer burst.

'Mrs Winthrop's Garden', named after Johnston's mother, has a Mediterranean ambience and a largely blue, yellow and lime green colour theme. The edges the garden room's brick paths and circular brick terrace are blurred by billowy hummocks of yellowy-green Lady's mantle (*Alchemilla mollis*) and blue geranium. Clusters of aconitum give the scheme height and structure, and terracotta pots of lemon verbena and aloe vera produce dramatic shape contrast.

Closer to the garden boundaries, Johnston's planting became more cottagey – some would say jungle-like – with such delightful combinations as poppies, alliums and ferns. Azaleas, rhododendrons and rare and unusual trees are evidence of his worldwide plant quests.

Long views in the garden are scrupulously managed to enhance the wow factor of the garden's situation in the beautiful Vale of Evesham. At the end of the Long Walk, the tall iron gates are left open to frame the distant view. Another grass walk slopes up to the Stilt Garden, a wide avenue bordered by tall hornbeams on stilt-like trunks – surely evidence of a French influence.

In 1948 Johnston retired to Serre de la Madone, his property in the south of France, and the National Trust took over Hidcote Manor. It was the first gift they accepted solely because of the garden.

Fellow garden designer and passionate plantswoman Vita Sackville-West wrote of Lawrence Johnston's garden at Hidcote Manor, 'this place is a jungle of beauty. I cannot hope to describe it in words, for indeed it is an impossible thing to reproduce the shape, colour, depth and design of such a garden through the poor medium of prose.'

▸ Kiftsgate Court Gardens

GO ROUND THE GARDENS

Kiftsgate Court Gardens

kiftsgate.co.uk

GL55 6LN | 01386 438777

Open Apr & Sep, Sun, Mon & Wed
2–6, May–Jul, Sat–Wed 12–6, Aug
Sat–Wed 2–6

It's rare to find two spectacular gardens as close together as Kiftsgate and Hidcote Manor Gardens, but Heather Muir, who began work on the Kiftsgate gardens in 1920, was a close friend of Major Lawrence Johnston, the creator of Hidcote. Kiftsgate benefited from Johnston's plant-hunting expeditions to Japan and China. Kiftsgate sits atop the Cotswold Hills, and from the terrace there are spectacular views to the Malvern Hills. A splendid rose, 'Frühlingsgold', which blooms magnificently in June, guards the garden's edge. In springtime the White Sunk Garden is a mass of flowering bulbs. Among the white roses is *Rosa sericea*, 'Heather Muir', a single, early-flowering shrub that grows up to 12 feet in height. But the glory of the rose border is the striking *Rosa filipes* 'Kiftsgate', a white rose which, when last measured, was 80 feet by 90 feet with a height of 50 feet.

▶ PLACES NEARBY

Chipping Campden (see page 96) is southwest of Hidcote, and little Ilmington (see page 140) is to the northeast. Mickleton, the northernmost village in Gloucestershire, is where you'll find the Three Ways House restaurant and hotel and its famous Pudding Club (see page 100), and is closer.

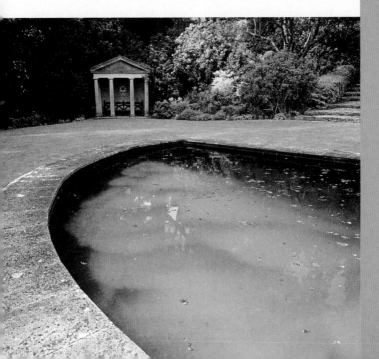

▶ Hills & Commons

Cleeve Hill, the northern part of the Cotswold escarpment offers superb views across the Severn Vale to Wales. Cleeve Cloud, the hill's 1,083 feet (333m) summit, is the highest point of the Cotswolds hills and the highest point in lowland England full-stop. This lonely, windswept plateau straddles the way between Cheltenham and Winchcombe. In an landscape that's relatively unmarked by modern forms of industrial development, the hill is distinctive for the radio towers, which are starkly visible across the area. Part of the hill is now occupied by a municipal golf course, but most of it remains ancient common, bright with gorse bushes on a carpet of coarse grass, studded with orchids and attracting birds and butterflies. A walk up Cleeve Common (see page 236) from Winchcombe is a fine thing. A walk that takes in the atmospheric Belas Knap long barrow (see page 239) as well becomes possibly the finest in the Cotswolds.

Leckhampton Hill offers spectacular views back across Cheltenham and the north end of the Cotswolds escarpment. Like many of the hills along the length of the Cotswold escarpment, Leckhampton attracted the attention of Iron Age locals, who built a hill-fort upon it. It was similarly attractive to the Celtic La Tène people, who arrived from the continent from about 300 BC and built a long barrow here. More recently, Leckhampton's quarries provided much of the stone for Regency Cheltenham. Tramways ran from the limestone quarries directly to Gloucester Docks. Just below the lip on the west side of the hill you'll find local landmark the Devil's Chimney, a pinnacle of stone left behind by 18th-century quarriers and said to arise from Hell.

Crickley Hill, just south of Leckhampton, is in part a country park. It's a good place for family walking, with a number of trails of varying lengths. It too has earthwork remains of a fort used both in the Neolithic and Iron Ages. **Cooper's Hill**, southeast of Gloucester, is an almost sheer slope amid beautiful woodland.

On the slopes near Brockworth, you'll find **Great Witcombe**. In the vicinity, near woodland, are the remains of a Roman villa.

▶ Ilmington

Get out your hankies and bells, and grab a good stick. Yellow-hued Cotswold limestone houses with pretty, well-tended gardens set amid a tangle of intersecting lanes on the Ilmington Downs, the highest point in Warwickshire, give this agreeable village the mellow, rustic feel of a true Cotswolds

▲ Leckhampton Hill

settlement. Less immediately obvious, unless you stumble into the middle of a performance, is the village's strong Morris dancing tradition. The dances are often performed on the grounds of the delightful manor house, especially on the annual Gardens Day in June. During the summer months the Ilmington Morris Men dance on Wednesday evenings in the surrounding villages. The group was formed in 1974. It performs up to twenty traditional 'Ilmington' dances that have been collected over the last hundred years, as well as other forms of the dance. There is evidence of Morris dancing having taken place in Ilmington since the 17th century, when dancers from Ilmington performed their sequences around a flag high up on Dover's Hill at Chipping Campden.

EAT AND DRINK
The Howard Arms
howardarms.com
Lower Green, CV36 4LT
01608 682226
A stunning 400-year-old Cotswold-stone inn on the picturesque village green of Ilmington, The Howard Arms is the starting point and finish line for a number of fabulous local walks, and is popular with ramblers. A detailed guide of walks can

be bought at the bar for a small donation, with all monies going to the church funds. The flagstoned bar and open-plan dining room create a civilised, informal look without sacrificing period charm. A log fire burns for most of the year. Drinkers can choose from award-winning local ales, such as Purity and Hook Norton, or a carefully selected list of over 30 wines by the glass. The inn's efforts to source seasonal ingredients and use local suppliers are equally solid.

▶ **PLACES NEARBY**

Ilmington has the fantastic Hidcote Manor Garden to the west, Stratford-upon-Avon (see page 198) a little way further to the north and Shipston-on-Stour (see page 181) to the east.

▶ Ilmington Manor

ngs.org.uk

CV36 4LA | 01608 682230 | Open for NGS or by appointment

Few who visit the lovely 3-acre gardens of Ilmington Manor today would guess that they are, for the most part, only 90 years old. When Mr and Mrs Spenser Flower came to this delightful village in 1919, the honey-coloured stone manor house, built by Sir Thomas Andrews around 1600, needed massive restoration, and a derelict orchard occupied the position of the present garden. With a flair for design and a clear idea of what they wanted, the Flowers restored and enlarged the manor house, planted many specimen trees and set about creating the interesting and beautiful flower- and topiary-filled gardens that we see today. Their grandson, Martin Taylor, owns the manor today. With his late wife Miranda, Taylor completed the restoration of the manor and its cottages, as well as gardens that have grown into a haven of peace and beauty in all seasons.

The Long Walk has six well-stocked herbaceous borders, which form the centrepiece of the main garden. To the right of the drive, which is lined with hornbeams, sits a little yew-hedge-bordered Pond Garden. The edges of the square pond are decorated with carved stone panels from India, and the surrounding paving is overgrown with many different varieties of scented thyme. The beds are filled with pink diascia, dianthus and other sun-lovers, while trailing sedums continue the patterns on the walls of the pool. This attractive area is bounded to the north and east by walls draped with clematis, a fine banksia rose and other aromatic climbers. It is a surprise to find *Buddleia crispa* here, as the Himalayan Butterfly Bush has a reputation for tenderness.

South of the house beyond the forecourt are three large walnut trees and a dovecote perched high above a neatly clipped hedge. Drifts of naturalised daffodils and brightly coloured crocuses enliven the area in spring.

To the west of the house are steps leading into the large formal Rose Garden, which is planted with old and modern shrub roses.

The so-called Cupid Garden – really more of an informal cottage garden – is one of the most colourful parts of Ilmington Manor. It features an enchanting mixture of roses, lavender and scented mock oranges. Peonies and hardy geraniums stand alongside clematis-clad walls. Nearby is Miranda's Buddha, a white garden walk with white camellias, white roses and hellebores.

▶ Kelmscott

The fame of this small village is strongly linked to the 19th-century poet, artist and Arts and Crafts theorist William Morris. Morris is represented in carved relief on the facade of a terrace of cottages on the main street, seated in the shade of a tree, with his knapsack and hat at his side. Kelmscott Manor, on the edge of the village, was his home from 1871 until his death in 1896. He is buried in the local churchyard in a grave designed by Philip Webb, modelled on a Viking tomb.

This village came to mean much to him, and he named his private printing press in London after it. He wrote of it the following sentimental lines:

'The wind's on the wold
And the night is a-cold,
And Thames runs chill
'Twixt mead and hill.
But kind and dear
Is the old house here
And my heart is warm
Midst winter's harm.'

Ernest Gimson, an important member of the Arts and Crafts Movement, designed the Morris Memorial Hall, Kelmscott's village institute. The playwright, George Bernard Shaw opened it in 1934 in the presence of British Prime Minister Ramsay MacDonald. The site was a gift from Lord Faringdon, while the stone was gifted by Sir Stafford Cripps, and came from the nearby quarry at Filkins (see page 123). Gimson died before the hall's completion.

TAKE IN SOME HISTORY
Kelmscott Manor
kelmscottmanor.org.uk
Kelmscott, GL7 3HJ | 01367 252486
Open Apr–Oct Wed & Sat, 11–5

Kelmscott Manor (limited public opening) was built in the late 16th century. Morris only rented it, but it now contains a fine collection of items associated with the man and with his craft – most notably those comparatively simple domestic artefacts that he strove to see reinvigorated through the Arts and Crafts Movement. The manor also contains pictures by Rossetti and Burne-Jones.

EAT AND DRINK
The Plough Inn
theploughinnkelmscott.com
GL7 3HG | 01367 253543

This attractive Cotswolds-stone inn (from 1631) stands on the Thames Path, a mere 600 yards from the river and midway between Radcot and Lechlade. Its position makes it a haven for walkers and boaters – the Inn provides moorings for customers. It's just a short walk from Kelmscott Manor. Exposed stone walls and flagstone floors set the scene for the Inn's real ales and its extensive, hearty menu. There's a beer, cider and music festival in August.

▸ **PLACES NEARBY**

From here it's only a hop, skip and jump west to Lechlade (see below). Over the Thames to the south you'll find 18th-century Buscot Park (see page 146), with Rembrandts and other works of art.

▸ Lechlade

Lechlade sits at the confluence of the Coln, the Leach and the Thames rivers. At Lechlade, stone quarried at Taynton used to be loaded onto wagons, which would then set out for London. Among other things, such stone was used in the construction of St Paul's Cathedral. From 1789 the Thames was linked to the Severn via the Thames and Severn Canal. The canal started to the southeast, at Inglesham. There an old round house, built for the men who were responsible for the maintenance of certain lengths of the canal, still stands.

Inevitably, wherever there are rivers, there are bridges. Just south of the town, the A361 crosses the Thames via the old 18th-century Halfpenny (or ha'penny) tollbridge. To the east, the A417 crosses the Thames by means of the 13th-century St John's Bridge. A statue of Father Thames presides here. The Thames' highest lock also provides a fine view of the town.

Lechlade is built around its Market Square and its wool church. A collection of fine 17th- to 19th-century buildings look

▲ Canal at Lechlade

out over the square and the streets that radiate from it – Burford Street, High Street and St Johns Street. The church, with its distinctive spire, dates from the late 15th century. Most of the stone used to build it comes from the same Taynton quarries that later provided the stone for St Paul's. The church contains an east window from 1510 and a fine chancel roof. There's also a brass commemorating the wool merchant John Townsend. One balmy summer evening in 1815, the church inspired the Romantic poet Percy Shelley to write:

> 'Thou too, aerial Pile! whose pinnacles
> Point from one shrine like pyramids of fire'

The bustle of commercial river life has long ago faded in Lechlade, although pleasure craft still bring colour and movement to the river, and it is possible to hire small boats from the boatyard near the Ha'penny Bridge. The walk along the Thames, southwest from the Ha'penny Bridge, is very enjoyable. At Inglesham you'll find the pretty church of St John the Baptist, 30ft (100m) from the river, which was saved from decay by William Morris.

TAKE IN SOME HISTORY
Buscot Park
buscot-park.com
Faringdon, Oxfordshire, SN7 8BU
01367 240932 | Open Apr–end Sep
Wed–Fri, every other weekend 2–6
Buscot Park, a handsome
18th-century house, is just to
the southeast of Lechlade. Its
many works of art reflect the
taste of the 1st Lord Faringdon.
There's a well-known series of
paintings by Burne-Jones in
the saloon, and a trio of
Rembrandts. The house is set
in an attractive park, close to
the village of Buscot. Buscot
also has an interesting
church, and an 18th-century
parsonage, now owned by the
National Trust.

GO FISHING
Lechlade and Bushyleaze Trout Fisheries
lechladetrout.co.uk
Lechlade GL7 3QQ | 01367 253266
Anglers can choose between a
nine-acre lake and 250 yards of
wild brown trout fishing on the
River Leach.

LEARN A NEW SKILL
Southrop Manor
thymeatsouthrop.co.uk
Southrop, GL7 3NX | 01367 850174
The Manor offers cooking,
growing, gardening, foraging,
bread making, charcuterie and
other artisanal skill courses.

EAT AND DRINK
The Trout Inn
thetroutinn.com
St John's Bridge, GL7 3HA
01367 252313

Workmen constructing a new
bridge over the Thames in 1220
built themselves an almshouse
to live in for the duration of the
work. That almshouse became
an inn in 1472. The extensive
menu features meat, fish and
vegetarian options, as well as
pizzas, filled jacket potatoes
and burgers. This family–
friendly pub offers smaller
portions for children, who also
have their own separate menu.
Guests can take advantage of
the Inn's two miles of trout and
course fishing waters, or play
Aunt Sally, an old Oxfordshire
throwing game, on the lawn.
The large garden often hosts
live jazz, and there's a beer
festival in June.

The Swan at Southrop
theswanatsouthrop.co.uk
Southrop, GL7 3NU | 01367 850205
It is worth going out of your way
to find this handsome
gastropub. It's bright and
comfortable, and the first class
food is provided by a top chef
and sourced locally where
possible. There's a skittle
alley, and well-behaved dogs
are welcome.

▶ PLACES NEARBY
Kelmscott Manor (see page
144), William Morris' former
home, is east of Lechlade, while
Fairford (see page 121) is west
and the delightfully named
Filkins (see page 123) are both
to the north.

▶ Minchinhampton

Overlooking the Nailsworth valley on the fringe of the eponymous common, Minchinhampton easily goes unheeded. That just makes it the Cotswolds' best-hidden gem. By the 18th century it was one of the most important cloth towns of south Gloucestershire. Yet it was also a town of small traders, and as such it was unable to withstand the various crashes that periodically afflicted the industry. The town's importance ebbed, and Minchinhampton finally lapsed into rural calm. The church's truncated tower attests to the departure or subsidence of the wealthy patrons who might have replaced its decayed spire.

Still, it's hardly the Detroit of the Cotswolds. Minchinhampton remains an attractive wool town built around an old market square. Its 17th-century Market House, balanced on stone pillars, and the post office that resides in a former coaching inn are worth a look. There are also some excellent cafes.

The church, just off the square, dates back to the 12th century. It contains a particularly fine set of brasses, while the 14th-century south transept contains a stately array of tombs and effigies.

Minchinhampton Common, 580 acres of National Trust-owned grassland, is a wide, windswept expanse of pasture, fringed with the villages of the Frome and Nailsworth valleys. If you circumnavigate the common you'll be rewarded with good views. Princess Anne lives just up the road, at Gatcombe Park.

PLAY A ROUND

Minchinhampton Golf Club (Old Course)
old.minchinhamptongolfclub.co.uk
GL6 9AQ | 01453 832642
This open grassland course, situated 600 feet above sea level, provides panoramic views. It's best described as an inland links course with no water or sand bunkers. The numerous humps and hollows around the greens test the golfer's ability to play a variety of shots – often in difficult, windy conditions.

Minchinhampton Golf Club (New Course)
minchinhamptongolfclub.co.uk
GL6 9BE | 01453 833866
Set high on the Cotswolds, both courses offer scenic countryside and outstanding tests of golfers' skill. The Cherington is a testing inland links course, and was an Open Championship Qualifying venue from 2002 to 2007. The Avening is a parkland course, offering a different – but no less challenging – experience.

EAT AND DRINK

Munchinhampton

munchinhampton.co.uk

3 West End, GL6 9JA | 01453 883382

The punnily-named Munchinhampton is owned and run by a friendly, young but not inexperienced local couple. This lovely, intimate cafe and restaurant has a fast growing clientele. A particularly clever chef freshly home makes almost everything. The pies are melt-in-the-mouth sensational, the chutneys dangerously delicious and the chocolate brownies eye-poppingly amazing.

The Weighbridge Inn

weighbridgeinn.co.uk

GL6 9AL | 01453 832520

Parts of this whitewashed free house date to the 17th century, when the original packhorse trail between Bristol and London passed by here. In the 1820s the B4014 was a turnpike, and the innkeeper would run both the pub and the weighbridge for the local woollen mills – serving jugs of ale in between taking tolls. The inn has been carefully renovated and retains its original features. Up in the restaurant, which used to be the hayloft, the old roof timbers reach almost to the floor. The inn prides itself on its ales and ciders and the quality of its food. Everything is cooked from scratch, including the Inn's famous '2in1 pies'. One half contains your choice of one of seven fillings (such as pork, bacon and celery), while the other half contains your choice of homemade cauliflower cheese, broccoli mornay or root vegetables. The pies are cooked to order and are available for take away, or even to bake at home.

Burleigh Court Hotel 🏵

burleighcourthotel.co.uk

Burleigh, Minchinhampton, GL5 2PF

01453 883804

Guests at this Cotswold stone manor house have famous architect Clough Williams-Ellis to thank for the superb view of the Golden Valley, since he designed the hotel's terraced gardens in the 1930s. Built at the outset of the 19th century, Burleigh Court is every inch the classic English country-house retreat, with an oak-panelled lounge bar and all the rest. The kitchen revisits classical ideas with a modern eye, using top-drawer ingredients and home-grown seasonal herbs and veg.

▶ PLACES NEARBY

Minchinhampton Common

After the Common was granted to the people of Minchinhampton in the 16th century, any weaver was permitted to enclose land here and build a home. The bulwarks on the common are the remains of an Iron Age fort, and may have served as a base for Caratacus' resistance to the

Romans. That wasn't the only time the common saw men rallying. George Whitefield, a Gloucester-born Methodist preacher addressed a 20,000-strong congregation on Whitefield's Tump barrow in 1743. During World War I Australian airmen used the common as an airfield.

▶ Minster Lovell

This village is indeed exceptionally Lovell-y. A fine old bridge spans the Windrush, and the main street is lined with buildings composed of Cotswold stone and thatch. Enjoy an entertaining introduction to the village at the Minster Lovell Heritage Centre, just over half a mile (800m) away from the main street on the Burford Road.

You can park at the far end of the main street and then walk down to the church, dedicated to St Kenelm. The church's beauty isn't terribly evident from the outside, but once you go in, the perfection of its design becomes obvious. It is welcoming and comforting, well-tended like a cared-for drawing room, yet uplifting and peaceful. Cruciform in shape, it was built in 1431 on the foundations of an earlier 12th-century church. The font is original, and the alabaster tomb probably belongs to William, the seventh Baron Lovell, who built the church. The church once had warm stained-glass windows, but unfortunately these have been lost to the centuries.

▼ The ruined hall at Minster Lovell

The romantic ruin of Minster Lovell Hall, which like the church was built by William Lovell, stands on the bank of the Windrush. Originally a fortified manor house on a grand scale, it was sold to Sir Thomas Coke. His descendants dismantled it in 1747, and the remains were used as farm buildings until the 1930s. Several legends are attached to Minster Lovell Hall. The strangest of these concerns Francis Lovell, a Yorkist who fled after the Battle of Bosworth and returned in 1487 to champion the cause of Lambert Simnel, pretender to the throne. Defeated at the Battle of Stoke, Lovell returned to the Hall and locked himself in a secret room, attended by a dog and a servant. Somehow, when the servant died, Lovell became trapped in the room and died there. In 1708, during work on the house, a skeleton was apparently discovered seated at a desk in a sealed room, with the skeleton of a dog at its feet. And if you believe that... A sturdy, round, medieval dovecote, which is also open to the public, can be found a across the field, short stroll's distance from the hall.

The pretty village of Crawley, with its river bridge and old blanket mill, is nearby, and can be reached via a pleasant walk along the river. Just to the south of Minster Lovell lie the Charterville Allotments, the subject of a 19th-century social experiment. Chartists purchased the 300 acres and offered them as smallholdings to poor families, along with £30 and a pig.

TAKE IN SOME HISTORY
Minster Lovell Hall
and Dovecote
english-heritage.org.uk
OX29 0RR | 0870 3331181
Open at any reasonable time,
Dovecote exterior only
The extensive, picturesque ruins of Minster Lovell Hall are beautifully situated beside the River Windrush. Home of the ill-fated Lovell family, the ruins of the 15th-century house consist of a a fine hall, a tower and a complete dovecote. Although initially designed as a symbol of great wealth, after several changes of hands the Hall was abandoned – then dismantled and demolished – in the 18th century.

VISIT THE HERITAGE CENTRE
Minster Lovell Heritage Centre
minsterlovell.com
130 Burford Road, OX29 0RB
01993 775262 | Open Mon–Fri 9–5,
Sat 9–1
The Heritage Centre is a small private collection situated on the outskirts of the village in one room of a busy picture-framing workshop. Owner Graham Kew has devoted a lot of time and energy keeping the history of Minster Lovell alive. Ask him to sing you the ballad of the 'Mistletoe Bough', or ask to see the Minster Lovell Jewel.

EAT AND DRINK

Old Swan & Minster Mill ◉

oldswanandminstermill.com
Old Minster, Minster Lovell,
OX29 0RN | 01993 774441

In a wonderful English setting, the Old Swan is a smart country pub with plenty of rustic charm and a serious approach to food. It's very cosy on the inside, with lots of spaces to tuck yourself away in. There's real ale on tap. There's also a local flavour to the menu, a refreshing lack of pretension, and even ingredients grown in the Old Swan's own kitchen garden. At lunchtime there's a range of tip-top ploughman's, or there's always the option of settling down for three courses. The garden is a gem. The more modishly done-out Minster Mill is next-door.

▶ **PLACES NEARBY**

The biggest nearby settlement is Witney (see page 242), which is famous for its blankets (you're there already, right?).

▶ Moreton-in-Marsh

Doesn't sound very appealing, does it? Yet rather than a shack perched precariously in the middle of a bog, Moreton is a roadside town strung along the Fosse Way in the Evenlode Valley. The market town's historic importance derives from the fact that it has the immediate area's sole railway station. It arrived in 1843, and lines now extend to London.

Moreton is a place for wandering, particularly on a Tuesday when the market swings into action. Presiding over the market, Redesdale Market Hall may *look* Tudor, but it was actually built in 1887. The 16th-century Curfew Tower on the corner of Oxford Street, with its bell from 1633, was used as recently as 1860. Beneath the tower you'll find the town lock-up and a board listing the 1905 market tolls. The Wellington Aviation Museum is on Broadway Road, just outside the town.

Some of the villages near Moreton are worth visiting. Bourton-on-the-Hill climbs the road to Broadway, and has a nice pub and a handsome church. The Bourton House Gardens are open to visitors, while the house's 16th-century tithe barn provides refreshments.

Sezincote House is Bourton's near neighbour. Samuel Pepys Cockerell built the extraordinary, early 19th-century, Indian-style house for his brother Charles. Together with its Mughal-influenced gardens, the house is worth at least strolling by. Charles Cockerell is buried in the attractive church in Longborough, the neighbouring village.

GO ROUND THE GARDENS
Sezincote House
sezincote.co.uk
Near Moreton-in-Marsh,
GL56 9AW | 01386 700444
House open May–Sep, Thu, Fri & BH
Mon 2.30–6; Garden open all year
(ex Dec) Thu, Fri & BH Mon 2–6 or
dusk if earlier; children allowed in
the garden, but not allowed in the
house without special permission.
Groups by appointment only
This wonderfully incongruous
Indian-style house was the
inspiration for the outrageously
ornate Brighton Pavilion. The
Mughal style of India's
Rajasthan region inspired the
house's architecture.
Sezincote's charming Persian
Garden of Paradise features
waterfalls, trees of unusual
size and a temple to the Hindu
sun god.

Bourton House Gardens
bourtonhouse.com
Bourton-on-the-Hill
01386 70754 | Open Apr–end Oct,
Wed–Fri 10–5
An ebullient riot of colour
spreads across 10 interlinked
sections of garden. The garden
abutts a 16th century tithe barn
and a grand house (not open to
the public). The house and
gardens featured in a major
Japanese TV series, so both get
an unusual amount of attention
from fans.

GET ACTIVE
Rob Ireland Activity Days
robireland.co.uk
Aston Magna, GL56 9LQ
01368 701683

Former sporting champion
Rob Ireland will organise
activity days for groups, with
options including quad biking,
archery, paintball and clay
pigeon shooting.

GO FISHING
Lemington Lakes
lemingtonlakes.co.uk
Todenham Road, Moreton-in-
Marsh, GL56 9NP | 01608 650872
Set in 75 acres, Lemington
offers course fishing and
big carp.

SADDLE UP
Durham's Farm Riding School & Livery Yard
cotswoldriding.com
Chastleton, Moreton-in-Marsh,
GL56 0SZ | 07811 339162
Durham's offers picnic rides
and more, and has horses
and ponies suitable for all
levels of riders.

EAT AND DRINK
The White Hart Royal Hotel ◉
whitehartroyal.co.uk
High Street, GL56 0BA
01608 650731
The 17th-century former
coaching inn in the centre of
Moreton looks a picture in
summer, with its Cotswolds-
stone walls festooned with
hanging baskets. Since every
building from this era *must*
have sheltered either Cromwell
or Charles I at some point, let it
be noted that the King holed up
here for a night in 1644 after
the Battle of Marston Moor. He
probably didn't enjoy a starter
of crab salad and avocado

mousse, followed by Balinese-style fish (red snapper, king prawn and catfish) wrapped in a banana leaf, served with lemongrass and coconut broth and saffron rice, but his loss is your gain. Wallow in comfort with the likes of steamed lemon and honey pudding. It's what Charles I would have wanted (admittedly for himself, not for you).

Manor House Hotel ◉◉
cotswold-inns-hotels.co.uk
High Street, GL56 0LJ
01608 650501
Period character rubs along nicely with contemporary tastes in this mellow yellow Cotswold-stone classic. The Manor House comes from blue-blooded stock: Henry VIII bequeathed the house to the Dean and Chapter of Westminster in 1539, and the royal trencherman would no doubt give the kitchen's output his seal of approval. The Mulberry Restaurant focuses on highly refined country-house cooking in the modern British mould.

Redesdale Arms ◉
redesdalearms.com
High Street, GL56 0AW
01608 650308
This fine old Cotswold-stone inn has been a part of the bustling, picture-postcard-pretty Moreton scene for centuries. Today it successfully blends venerable wood panelling, oak floorboards and exposed stone walls with a

10 gardens

relaxed contemporary style, achieved with the use of tobacco-hued sofas, modern art and muted colour schemes. Dinner is served in the modern brasserie-styled rear conservatory. Its please-all menus combine quality, local and seasonal produce, simplicity and flavour.

The Red Lion Inn
theredlionlittlecompton.co.uk
GL56 0RT | 01608 674397
This is one of 15 pubs owned by Donnington Brewery – a family concern that has been brewing since 1865. A pretty Cotswold-stone building quietly located on the edge of the village, set in a large mature garden, the building

has exposed stone walls and beams, inglenook fireplaces and real fires. Public bar games include darts, dominoes, and pool. There's also a jukebox. The restaurant offers a seasonal menu and sensibly priced, daily-changing specials.

▸ PLACES NEARBY

Batsford, northwest of Moreton, is an estate village. Its Victorian church contains some excellent monuments, while Batsford Park has an arboretum and a falconry centre. Chastleton House, a National Trust property to the southeast of Moreton, is one of the finest Jacobean houses in the country.

The **Four Shire Stone**, just to the east of Moreton, is a striking 18th-century monolith surmounted by a sundial and a ball. It marks the original meeting point of Gloucestershire, Oxfordshire, Warwickshire and Worcestershire counties. Due to boundary changes, however, it now stands in Warwickshire.

Batsford Arboretum

batsarb.co.uk
Batsford Park, Moreton-in-Marsh, GL56 9QB | 01386 701441
Open daily 10–5

Charity-run Batsford is home to one of the finest botanical collections in the country. Its position on a south-facing slope means you see the tree and plant collections from an unusual angle, as well as the great views of the Evenlode Valley beyond. Despite extending over 56 acres, Batsford is an intimate and even a romantic place, with interest all year round. There's a garden shop (with different opening hours) and a cafe, too.

Cotswold Falconry Centre

cotswold-falconry.co.uk
Batsford Park, GL56 9AB
01386 701043 | Open daily mid Feb–mid Nov

Conveniently located by the Batsford Arboretum, the Cotswold Falconry Centre gives daily demonstrations in the art of falconry. There are over 150 eagles, hawks, owls and falcons in residence. The emphasis here is on breeding and conservation, and 2013 marks the centre's 25th anniversary.

Chastleton House

nationaltrust.org.uk
Nr Moreton-in-Marsh, GL56 0SU
01608 674981 | Open most of Mar and Oct–early Nov Wed–Sun 1–4, end Mar–end Sep 1–5, end Nov–mid Dec Sat–Sun 1–4

A prosperous wool merchant built Jacobean Chastleton House between 1607 and 1612 to show off his wealth and power. The same increasingly impoverished family owned Chastleton until 1991, and the house remained pretty much unchanged for nearly 400 years. This gloriously unspoilt setting has an intriguing air of timelessness. There's not even a tea shop. Gasp.

▲ Church of St Peter and St Paul, Northleach

▷ Northleach

An important wool town in the Middle Ages, Northleach still just about manages to take you back to that period. People don't still throw buckets of sewage out onto the street or anything – the antique feeling comes more from the fact that one of the finest wool churches in the Cotswolds overlooks the market square. This mighty fine example of the English Perpendicular style, the most striking building in town, dates from the 15th century. Its magnificent south porch is one of the finest in the country. The interior is quite stark, but beautifully proportioned. The church contains the grandest collection of monumental brasses in the Cotswolds, commemorating the medieval wool merchants who brought prosperity to Northleach and passed some of it along to the church.

The A40 road, which replaces the old coaching route that ran through the town, fortunately bypasses Northleach. The Abbey of St Peter in Gloucester established Northleach Borough in 1226. The annual rents were one shilling (5p) for a burgage plot, 6d (2.5p) for a market stall and 1d for a cottage. These medieval property boundaries can still be traced. The High Street features an interesting mixture of houses of all periods, which reflects the burgage plots that belonged to the merchants of yore. Burgage plots were created to enable the maximum number of shops to line the main street. These plots were usually subdivided as time advanced and the population swelled – hence the jumble of buildings from different eras. Unusually for the area, some of these are half-timbered.

Keith Harding's World of Mechanical Music occupies one of these buildings just east of the market place, in what was a school. This is a fascinating shop, but it's also a collection of clocks and mechanical instruments from all over Europe, ranging from barrel organs to pianolas. Harding's gives frequent, entertaining demonstrations of many of these instruments, and some of the restored items are for sale.

There are two sets of almshouses – one at Mill End, another at East End. At the western end of the town the High Street meets the Roman Fosse Way. On the other side of the road, you'll see an 18th-century building that was originally a prison. Sir William Blackburn built it according to the ideas of the philanthropist Sir George Onesiphorus Paul, a member of an eminent family of Woodchester clothiers.

ENTERTAIN THE FAMILY
Keith Harding's World of Mechanical Music
mechanicalmusic.co.uk
The Oak House, High Street, GL54 3ET | 01451 860181
Open all year daily 10–5 (last tour 4)
Harding's keeps a fascinating collection of antique clocks, musical boxes, automata and mechanical musical instruments. These are restored and maintained in the world-famous workshops, displayed in a period setting, presented as a live entertainment, and played during regular tours. Visitors can play coin-operated instruments in an exhibition dedicated to the purpose.

SEE A LOCAL CHURCH
Church of St Peter and St Paul
Mill End, just west of the town centre, GL54 3HG
The church at Northleach is a monument to the 15th-century glory days of this sleepy little town, when Northleach wool was the country's finest and the town's merchants among the country's wealthiest. One of these merchants, John Fortey, raised the nave roof and added a lofty clerestory that fills the church with light. It includes an immense Perpendicular window above the chancel arch – a fine example of a feature that is special to Cotswold 'wool' churches. Fortey's contribution is commemorated in one of the church's fine collection of brasses. Other merchants of the time also provided funds to enrich their church. The Lady chapel and the elegant stone pulpit also date from this period, as does the pinnacled two-storey south porch: be sure to look up at the vaulting inside.

EAT AND DRINK
The Wheatsheaf Inn
cotswoldswheatsheaf.com
West End, GL54 3EZ | 01451 860244
A beautiful Cotswold-stone 17th-century inn on the square of the pretty former wool town

of Northleach, The Wheatsheaf is everything anyone could wish for. With flagstone floors, beams, log fires and a vibrant, smartened-up feel throughout, it's perfect for sampling some seriously good food or chilling out in the bar with the papers after enjoying a bracing walk. Monthly menus evolve with the season.

▶ **PLACES NEARBY**

The hamlet of **Hampnett** is a short drive (or walk) northwest of Northleach. Hampnett has an interesting Norman church, with carved birds on the chancel arch and Victorian stencilling.

▶ Nailsworth

The small, characterful mill town of Nailsworth is set amid steep wooded slopes. It has a growing reputation for three things. First among these is football – not something readily associated with the Cotswolds, where the only league team is Cheltenham Town. The Forest Green Rovers, a Football Conference team, are owned by radical eco-energy tycoon and classic Stroud Valleys-type-person Dale Vince OBE. He's banned meat from the football ground – a world first for the sport – and plans to make the club fully sustainable, organic pitch and all. He also owns Rodborough Fort. If the Rovers ever get promoted, Nailsworth will be the smallest town ever to have League football.

Secondly, talking of food, 'Nelly' has a growing reputation for culinary excellence – a reputation backed by some sensational restaurants and cafes. Thirdly, Nailsworth has an impressive amount of alluring independent shops – it's becoming something of a shopping destination. It's an interesting place, still on the tourist path less trodden – if only just. The town should be proud of still having a town crier – even if most people might not be able to work out what he's going on about. It was also home to poet W H Davies (1871–1940), aka Supertramp, who penned the famous words: 'What is this life if, full of care, we have no time to stand and stare?'

Just outside the town you'll find the fascinating Dunkirk Mill, which has features both a massive overshot waterwheel and a well-presented history of the local textile industry.

VISIT THE GALLERY
Ruskin Mill
College Gallery
rmt.org
Old Bristol Road, Nailsworth

GL6 0LA | 01453 837500
Open daily 10–5; closes 4 at weekends
When visiting this inspiring Arts and Crafts centre, make time to

enjoy tea and organic cake in tranquil green, watery surroundings. Take a stroll round the gardens and ponds, and let yourself be captivated by a local storyteller, whose tales aim to please both children and adults, Come back in the evening for folk music (see website's Events section).

GET INDUSTRIAL
Dunkirk Mill Centre
stroud-textile.org.uk
Just off the A46 near Nailsworth, GL5 5HH | 01453 766273
Open Sat, Sun, Wed and BH 2–4
If you've an interest in the industrial, this is great opportunity to see a see a massive working water wheel powering rare and historic textile machinery. The wheel – 12 feet wide and 13 feet in diameter – was installed in the mill in 1855. It's quite a sight in action, as are the large working model pair of fulling stocks and other industrial-cloth making rarities. There's no on-site public parking (except for disabled visitors), so drive to the car park behind Egypt Mill, just off the A46 on the edge of Nailsworth, and follow the cycle trail to the Mill Centre. It's a lovely walk, too.

TAKE OFF
Bristol and Gloucester Gliding Club
bggc.co.uk
Nympsfield, GL10 3TX
01453 860342
The Gliding Club offers trial lessons, instruction and taster courses for motor-less glider planes.

SADDLE UP
Barton End Stables
bartonendstables.co.uk
Barton End, Nailsworth, GL6 0QF
01453 834915
Lessons are available for riders five and older and riders with disabilities are catered for at this indoor/outdoor school.

WATCH A MATCH
Forest Green Rovers
forestgreenroversfc.com
The New Lawn, Another Way, Nailsworth, GL6 0FG
01453 834860 | Season Aug–May
Watch a game of football at one of the most unique clubs in the land – and definitely the greenest.

EAT AND DRINK
The Britannia
food-club.com
Cossack Square, Nailsworth, GL6 0DG | 01453 832501
Occupying a delightful position on the south side of Nailsworth's Cossack Square, The Britannia is a stone-built, 17th-century building. The interior is bright and uncluttered, while outside you'll find a pretty garden with plenty of tables, chairs and parasols for sunny days. The menu offers an interesting blend of modern British and continental food, made with ingredients bought from both local suppliers and London's Smithfield Market. Go lightly with just a starter, perhaps moules marinière, or

plunge into hearty mains such as chargrilled rump steak or confit pork belly. Other options include stone-baked pizzas and impressive meat-free options. There are also great wines.

The Canteen

Day's Mill, Nailsworth, GL6 0DU
07531 505629

This distinctive cafe sells good-value coffee, cakes and light lunches. They cook with fresh, local ingredients from around Nailsworth and Stroud, creating great tasting food that shows off those ingredients well. Everything in the shop is for sale, including the chairs you sit on and the cups you drink from.

Egypt Mill

egyptmill.com
Nailsworth, GL6 0AE
01453 833449

This good-looking 16th-century building is a stylishly converted three-floored, stone-built mill, which still has working waterwheels. The original split-level bar, where the decor is mainly tripped beams and elegant ironwork from old machinery, has Stroud Budding and Wye Valley Bitter on pump. There's an irresistible terrace outside by the river for summer. They have comfortable rooms and a restaurant-proper, too.

Hobbs House

hobbshousebakery.co.uk
4 George Street, Nailsworth,
GL6 0AG | 01453 839396

This innovative, multi-award-wining cafe, featured in Rick Stein's *Food Heroes*, sells an amazing range of breads and patisserie. The open plan kitchen allows you to watch chefs making breakfasts, lunches and, on Fridays and Saturdays, dinners from locally sourced ingredients.

Number 28

28 Fountain Street, Nailsworth,
GL6 0BL | 01453 298545

An unassuming exterior gives way to a small but welcoming cafe, where you can chow down on colourful, healthy food. The tapas are excellent-value, and they also have a massive range of teas. The leather armchairs and eclectic bookshelf entice you to stay long after your meal has finished. At weekends they have a BYOB policy.

The Olive Tree

theolivetree-nailsworth.com
28 George St, Nailsworth, GL6 0AG
01453 834802

Some places just have that intangible but infectious vibe. You came in reluctantly to see through that dinner date you agreed to weeks ago, but now feel too tired for... And suddenly – woof – the fatigue's gone, and your mojo's back. With an informal setting (and a patio for sunny days), this may just be the most welcoming restaurant you've ever been to. The staff always seems not just willing, but happy to accommodate your whims. The menu is wonderful and fresh.

Tipputs Inn

food-club.com

Bath Road, Nailsworth, GL6 0QE

01453 832466

Mellow Cotswolds stone and stripped floorboards blend nicely with modern, clean-lined furniture in this 17th-century inn. The giant candelabra adds a touch of grandeur. Owners Nick Beardsley and Christophe Coquoin create the menus for all their Gloucestershire food pubs (such as The Britannia, also in Nailsworth), and import some ingredients and wines from France. There are dishes for every eventuality, starting with tapas-style appetisers and starters and extending through to well-loved pub classics (fish and chips; homemade burgers), classy options and South Indian cuisine.

Wild Garlic Restaurant and Rooms ◉◉

wild-garlic.co.uk

3 Cossack Square, Nailsworth, GL6 0DB | 01453 832615

Chef-propieter Matthew Beardshall and his enthusiastic staff take a hands-on approach making everything in-house, from organic bread and pasta to sorbets and ice cream. The brasserie-style menu of this small-yet-perfectly-formed modern restaurant changes monthly to reflect the seasons and to make the best use of the regional larder.

▶ **PLACES NEARBY**

The drive up the 'W' to visit cute little Minchinhampton Common (see page 148) is quite an experience. The drive back down offers the best possible view of Nailsworth.

Just outside the town, you can appreciate the massive overshot waterwheel at **Dunkirk Mill**, at the same time as taking in a well-presented exhibit on the history of the local textile industry that made this region what it is today. Take a beautiful drive to see curious little **Avening**. Handsome Tetbury (see page 219) is a bit further east.

Rose & Crown Inn

The Cross, Nympsfield, GL10 3TU

01453 860240

Occupying a central position in the village, this imposing 400-year-old coaching inn of local golden stone could well be the highest pub in the Cotswolds. Its close proximity to the Cotswold Way makes it a popular stop for hikers and bikers. Inside, the inn's character is preserved with natural stone, wood panelling, a lovely open fire and local Stroud Organic and Wickwar Cotswold Way real ales. In the galleried restaurant, the owners offer fresh, homemade food cooked to order. In the large garden, children will enjoy the playground area, which has a swing, slides and a climbing bridge.

▶ Oxford

▲ New College

Oxford is both an inspiring (or perhaps, to some, an overwhelming) citywide temple of learning and a place with long associations with privilege and elitism. Some 26 UK prime ministers have studied at Oxford, including David Cameron. It looks like a film set, and there's an inescapable atmosphere of wizened oldness. It also gets really really busy with tourists, so judge the time of your visit carefully. If you plan on parking a car, think about whether you really need that second kidney.

Both Oxford's glories and its bad points make the handsome home of one of the world's best and oldest universities one of the most deeply *English* places in existence. The country's essence seeps from the walls. Heritage and pomp intermingle here with student Rag Weeks and the minutiae of daily life in a cosmopolitan setting. Oxford is simultaneously a mildly bizarre and eccentric anachronism and a modern city getting on with its business.

Lying just under 60 miles northwest of London, situated amid low hills at the meeting point of the River Thames and the River Cherwell, Oxford is in some ways a typical market town. What distinguishes it from the many others like it in England is of course its ancient university. Oxford consists of some 38 colleges and six private halls, which are spread throughout the city itself. Students from England and abroad compete fiercely for admission. While they may value the university's excellent contemporary academic reputation and the valuable connections they might make as Oxford students, many are also drawn by the sheer gravity of tradition. To attend Oxford is to follow famous footsteps along hallowed halls. The buildings themselves are ancient and beautiful. Many students feel that to study at Oxford is a privilege, a pleasure, and an affirmation.

Oxford's mellow ambience of well-aged gentility feeds on its blend of amazing architecture and an amazing setting. The architecture of the colleges ranges from Merton's early Gothic edifice to St Catherine's bracing modernism. The sprawl of riverside meadows and parkland attracts cyclists, punters, rowers, and less athletically minded visitors with an eye for scenery.

Although the city's origins are lost in time, Oxford has been an established town since the 9th century. It's life as a centre of education began in 1167, when students who had been expelled from Paris settled in the town under the patronage of Henry II. The university's colleges exert a palpable influence without entirely dominating city life. Beneath the mantle of Oxford the University,

Oxford the city still lives and breathes – although if you stay long enough, you gradually detect a frisson of tension between 'gown' and 'town'. Still, while today's students are noted for their boisterous post-exam antics, we can be thankful that things have calmed down over the years – in 1355, the St Scholastica's Day town/gown riot left 63 scholars and about 30 locals dead.

Beautiful, honey-coloured buildings populate the 'city of dreaming spires', among them the Museum of the History of Science, the Pitt Rivers Museum and the Ashmolean. The Ashmolean is England's oldest public museum. Founded in 1683, it houses a huge collection of art and antiquities. The famous and lovely Bodleian Library and Sheldonian Theatre nestle nearby in an enclave of mainly 17th-century buildings.

There's plenty to see in Oxford even if you're not an architecture buff. The lively covered market has been trading since 1773, making it one of Britain's oldest surviving markets. The town holds its main farmers' market at Gloucester Green every first and third Thursday of the month. Oxford was also the site of great automobile manufacturing. The Morris Oxford and the T-series MG sports car were created here.

The best way to explore the town is undoubtedly on foot, with serendipity as a guide and frequent stops at coffee shops for on-going refreshment. A range of organized tours, by bus or with a qualified guide, can deduct the aimless wandering from your free-range exploration. Do whatever floats your boat, as long as you nourish a healthy curiosity about and enthusiasm for one of the finest and most attractive cities in England.

SEE THE VIEWS OVER THE CITY

It's a good idea to get your bearings from the rooftops at the beginning of a visit to Oxford. You can climb the tower of the city's oldest building, St Michael's Church in Cornmarket Street. Alternatively, you could survey the city from Carfax Tower, a remnant of the 14th-century St Martin's Church. The tower is situated at the city's focal point, the busy crossroads known as Carfax. Another excellent vantage point can be found at the University Church of St Mary the Virgin on the High Street, which dates from 1280. Climb the 90ft tower to access the external viewing gallery. This parish church also serves the university, and for a time was also the university's reference library and the venue for its degree ceremonies. Less pleasantly, it also served as a courtroom for the trials of bishops Latimer, Ridley and Cranmer between 1555 and 1556. They were found guilty of heresy, and were burned at the stake in Broad Street A hundred metres away, you'll find the Martyrs' Memorial commemorating the event.

TAKE IN SOME HISTORY
St Edmund Hall
www.seh.ox.ac.uk
College of Oxford University,
OX1 4AR | 01865 279000
Open all year; closed 20–30 Mar,
23–26 Aug, 21 Dec–5 Jan
This college of Oxford University retains its distinctive ancient title of Hall. St Edmund dates back to the thirteenth century, before most of the other colleges had been founded, and its premises include the only surviving medieval academic hall in Oxford. By virtue of its longevity, St Edmund has an unusual array of buildings: a Norman crypt, a 17th-century dining hall, a chapel, a quadrangle and 18th- and 20th-century contributions.

Christ Church
www.chch.ox.ac.uk
St Aldate's, OX1 1DP | 01865 276492
Opening times are complicated – check ahead
Founded in 1524, this is Oxford's largest and most-visited college. It has both the biggest quadrangle and and England's smallest cathedral. Christ Church Cathedral, which predates the college, serves as its chapel. Within the great hall, you'll find features familiar from the *Alice in Wonderland* stories. That's because former Christ Church don Charles Dodgson (1832–98) is better known as Lewis Carroll. Christ Church's Ante Hall was the inspiration for Hogwarts' great hall in the Harry Potter movies.

Christ Church Picture Gallery is the only public gallery owned by a single college in either Oxford or Cambridge. Its collection of 300 paintings includes Italian Old Masters – among them Tintoretto, Leonardo da Vinci, Michelangelo and Carracci.

OTHER HISTORIC COLLEGES

Merton College (founded 1264) has peaceful gardens and the 14th-century Mob Quad, Oxford's oldest quadrangle. New College, which despite its name was founded in 1379, is famous for its hall, cloister and chapel, as well as its gardens, which are enclosed by the old city wall. Peep into St John's College, founded 1555, to see its arcaded Canterbury Quad. Queens College (founded 1341) features buildings by Sir Christopher Wren and Nicholas Hawksmoor. Farther out in Parks Road you'll find Keble College (1870), a relative newcomer whose elaborate red-brick buildings are a Victorian tour de force.

Radcliffe Square

These university buildings form an eye-catching architectural group. The Sheldonian Theatre (built between 1664 and 1668) was the first major architectural work by Sir Christopher Wren, who was Professor of Astronomy at the time. The interior assumes the shape of a Roman theatre, and its grand ceremonial hall is used for university functions and concerts. High above, the cupola provides an excellent viewpoint.

Close by, the Bodleian Library is one of six copyright libraries in the UK. As such it is entitled to receive a copy of every book published in the country. The circular domed

▲ Radcliffe Camera

Radcliffe Camera, designed by James Gibbs and built from 1737–49, is a reading room for the library.

Oxford Castle Unlocked

oxfordcastleunlocked.co.uk
44–46 Oxford Castle, OX1 1AY
01865 260666 | Open all year daily 10–5.30 (last tour 4.20)
For the first time in 1,000 years, the secrets of Oxford Castle will be 'Unlocked', revealing episodes of violence, executions, great escapes, betrayal and even romance. Walk through these ancient buildings and experience the stories that connect the real people of the past to these extraordinary events.

VISIT THE MUSEUMS AND GALLERIES

Oxford University Museum of Natural History

oum.ox.ac.uk
Parks Road, OX1 3PW
01865 272950 | Open daily 10–5; Times vary at Xmas & Easter

Oxford's Museum of Natural History was built between 1855 and 1860 to satisfy the growing, increasingly professionalized academic interest in biology, botany, archaeology, zoology, entomology and related fields. The museum reflects Oxford University's position as a 19th-century centre of learning, with displays of early dinosaur discoveries and Elias Ashmole's collection of preserved animals. Although visitors to the Pitt Rivers Museum must pass through the Museum of Natural History to enter it, the two should not be confused.

Ashmolean Museum of Art & Archaeology
See highlight panel opposite

Museum of the History of Science
mhs.ox.ac.uk
Broad Street, OX1 3AZ
01865 277280 | Open all year Tue–Fri 12–5, Sat 10–5, Sun 2–5
Got history overload yet? This special little place may get you reinvigorated. The first purpose-built museum in Britain, it contains the world's finest collection of early scientific instruments, including tools used in astronomy, navigation, surveying, physics and chemistry. The museum holds various events and exhibitions throughout the year.

Pitt Rivers Museum
See highlight panel overleaf

Museum of Oxford
museumofoxford.org.uk
Town Hall, St Aldate's, OX1 1BX
01865 252351 | Open Mon–Sat 10–5
This museum gives a succinct survey of the city's history from prehistoric times to the present, from woolly mammoths to Morris Motors. Its Oxford-area archaeological finds include a Roman pottery kiln, paintings and furniture, all of which are rather more interesting than they might sound. There's plenty of child-focused content as well.

Modern Art Oxford
modernartoxford.org.uk
30 Pembroke Street, OX1 1BP
01865 722733 | Open Tue–Sat 11–6, Sun 12–5
Founded in 1965 and currently funded by Arts Council England, this stylish gallery occupies a former brewery. It has changing exhibitions of contemporary art from Britain and beyond, as well as talks, live music and children's activities. There's also a shop and a cafe selling very good cakes.

GO BY RIVER
The Rivers Thames & Cherwell
These waterways slice through the remarkably verdant land close to central Oxford. The tree-lined Cherwell (pronounced charwell) is the place for punting, and provides almost rural views of Magdalen College (pronounced mordlin), one of Oxford's richest and most spacious colleges. Magdalen was founded in 1458,

▶ Ashmolean Museum of Art & Archaeology

ashmolean.org

Beaumont Street, OX1 2PH | 01865 278000 | Open all year Tue–Sun 10–5, BH Mon 10–5

Opened in 1683, the Ashmolean is the oldest museum in the country. It contains Oxford University's priceless collections and display many historically important art pieces and artefacts, including work from Ancient Greece through to the 20th century. The museum has undergone a massive redevelopment, including the building of 39 new galleries, an education centre, conservation studios and a walkway.

▶ Pitt Rivers Museum

www.prm.ox.ac.uk
South Parks Road, OX1 3PP | 01865 270927 | Open all year Tue–Sun
& BH Mon 10–4.30, Mon 12–4.30; contact museum for Xmas & Easter
opening times

The collections held at the museum (founded in 1884) are
internationally acclaimed, and somewhat unusually organized. The
museum contains objects from different cultures of the world and
various periods, all grouped by type or purpose. Highlights include
a striking 36-foot-high totem pole, a monkey-skull that boys from a
headhunting tribe used to imitate adults, like a modern child might
play with a toy kitchen, and a bottle that supposedly contains a
witch who would be released if said bottle ever broke.

and was set in its own deer park – walks through which are really stunning. University rowing crews train on the Thames (also known here as the Isis). Stroll through the Oxford Botanic Garden, founded in 1621, the oldest garden of its kind in Britain. Travelling thus, you can reach Christ Church Meadow and the confluence of the rivers on foot – or you could rent a punt or rowing boat from Magdalen Bridge or the Cherwell Boathouse in Bardwell Road and reach it by water.

SEE THE HISTORIC CHURCHES

The University Church of St Mary the Virgin

university-church.ox.ac.uk
High Street, OX1 4BJ
01865 279113 | Open daily 9–5,
Jul–Aug 9–6

St Mary the Virgin serves as both a parish church and the University Church. In the Middle Ages it was the centre of university life. The steeple, one of the finest in England, dates back to the early 13th century. Much of the exterior fabric of the church has been enriched with decoration from later centuries. One particularly notable example of such enrichment, the 1637 Baroque south porch, reflects the exuberance of its time.

The chancel retains its original oak stalls and misericords. Memorials to past worthies – clerical, academic and civic – abound throughout the church. Few are more

evocative than the slab recently erected on the north wall, close to the screen. It lists the martyrs of different religious persuasions who have been associated with the church over the centuries. The trials of Bishops Latimer, Ridley and Cranmer took place in the nave in 1554–5. In 1774, John Wesley preached his famous sermon attacking the sloth of the unreformed university here. Later, in 1833, John Keble and John Henry Newman began their Anglo-Catholic crusade from the same pulpit.

Oxford Oratory Church of St Aloysius Gonzaga

oxfordoratory.org.uk
25 Woodstock Road, OX2 6HA
01865 315800 | Open Mon–Fri
7am–7pm, Sat 8–7pm, Sun
7.45–12.30pm, 5–7.30

Jesuits built the Church of St Aloysius in 1873, and it became the principal Roman Catholic church in Oxford. Cardinal John Newman, the founder of the Oratory in England, had planned to establish an Oratory in Oxford in 1866, but his plans came to nothing, and the Oxford Oratory was finally established here in 1990. The building has a wide and spacious interior. Its equally wide apse has many Gothic features, fine lancet windows and a prominent rose window.

St Mary Magdalen

stmarymagdalenoxford.org.uk
c/o St Mary Magdalen Vicarage,
15 Beaumont Street, OX1 3AE

This 13th-century church is just outside the old city walls. It has two particular points of interest: it's as wide as it is long, and it's home to the city's largest Anglo-Catholic congregation. The church is also adjacent to a memorial to the Protestant martyrs. The Martyrs' Memorial was devised in 1841 by a Low Church group to commemorate the three martyrs, Bishops Latimer, Ridley and Cranmer.

St Michael at the North Gate
smng.org.uk
cnr Ship Street & Cornmarket Street, OX1 3EY | 01865 255776
Open daily 10.30–5 (10.30–4 in winter)

As its name implies, this church originally formed part of the town gate on the northern route out of the city, and was once connected to the ancient walls that protected the city and its inhabitants. Only a few traces of the northern wall remain, but the Saxon tower attached to St Michael's provides a vivid reminder of said tower's role in medieval times as a prison. At street level, a crudely blocked doorway indicates the exit used by Latimer, Ridley and Cranmer as they were taken to be burnt at the stake in the adjacent Broad Street. The site of the martyrdom is marked in the street there. Built in the first half of the 11th century, the tower is also significant as the oldest church tower in Oxfordshire. The church as it

stands today is mainly in the Perpendicular style, except for the fine Early English chancel with lancet windows at the east end. This is a church of town rather than gown, and it contains many memorials to non-academic Oxford worthies.

Wesley Memorial Church
wesleymem.org.uk
New Inn Hall Street, opposite St Michael's Street, OX1 2DH

Perhaps surprisingly, the Methodist Wesley Memorial Church gives Oxford one of its most elegant spires. Built in 1878 in a conventional Gothic style, Wesley Memorial has a spacious interior. The design of its aisles is typical of Methodist churches of the period, but overall the design is grounded in Church of England aesthetic principles. The first Oxford meeting house Wesley himself preached in was opposite the present church, now 32–34 New Inn Hall Street. Its importance is signified by a plaque on the wall.

GO TO THE MOVIES
Phoenix Picturehouse
picturehouses.co.uk
57 Walton Street, Oxford OX2 6AE
0871 9025747

Opened in 1913, the Phoenix shows independent and classic films. There's a small but well-formed bar offering wines, spirits and beers. It's ideal for those post-film debates. The cinema also screens live broadcasts by Stratford-upon-Avon's famous Royal

Shakespeare Company and hosts Q&A sessions with filmmakers of various kinds.

EXPLORE BY BIKE
Capital Sport
capital-sport.co.uk
01296 631671
'Luxury self-guided' cycling holidays in Oxford and the Cotswolds.

TAKE A BOAT TRIP
Blakes Holiday Boating
blakes.co.uk
0844 8567060
Take a narrowboat along the Oxford & Midlands Canal, or down the Thames to Lechlade.

GO SHOPPING
The Covered Market
oxford-coveredmarket.co.uk
Market St, OX1 3DZ | Open Mon–Sat 9–5.30, Sun 10–4
Oxford's legendary covered market has been developing since 1773. Today it houses a wide variety of stalls. You'll find jewellers, butchers and chocolatiers, as well as clothing and footwear dealers, delicatessens and giftshops.

Alice's Shop
aliceinwonderlandshop.co.uk
83 St Aldates, OX1 1RA
01865 723793 | Open Jul–Aug 9.30–6.30, Sep–Jun 10.30–5
This is the original Old Sheep Shop featured in Lewis Carroll's *Through the Looking-Glass*. The real-life Alice Liddell also used to buy her sweets here. Predictably, it stocks a wide

range of Alice-themed gifts. The shop is keen to promote Wonderlust generally, and happy to direct you to other Oxford sources of Alice-interest. The Alice's Day festival in July celebrates the birth of the *Alice in Wonderland* stories with city-wide events that actually last over two days. Local historian and guide Mark Davies conducts *Alice in Wonderland* tours; see website for details).

Blackwell's
bookshop.blackwell.co.uk
48–51 Broad Street, OX1 3BQ
01865 333555 | Open Mon 9–5, Tue 9.30–6, Wed–Sat 9–6
Blackwell's extensive Oxford empire spans seven shops. This incarnation is a renowned and well-stocked academic bookshop, but you can also check out the Art and Poster Shop at No. 27 and the Music Shop at Nos. 23–25.

▼ Covered Market

WALK THE RIDGEWAY NATIONAL TRAIL

nationaltrail.co.uk/ridgeway
The National Trails Office, Signal
Court, OX29 4TL | 01865 810224
The fantastic Ridgeway National
Trail is a chalk ridge used by
prehistoric man. As such it is
perhaps Britain's oldest road.
It's 136km (85 miles) long,
stretching from Overton Hill
near Avebury to Ivinghoe
Beacon in the Chilterns.

EAT AND DRINK

Gee's Restaurant ◎
gees-restaurant.co.uk
61 Banbury Road, OX2 6PE
01865 553540

Combine this impressive
Victorian conservatory with
an unpretentious, clear-
headed approach to culinary
matters that includes a
dedication to well-sourced
ingredients and it is easy to
see why Gee's has been
satiating the good people
of Oxford for three decades.
The restaurant's luminous,
handsome, Grade II listed
frame contains thriving
potted olive trees, garden-
style furniture, and a tiled
floor. Recent refurbishment
has resulted in a smart bar
with a vaulted roof and views
to the kitchen. The rustic and

▼ All Souls College

focused menu suits the relaxed mood, The food is based on excellent produce served up with style.

The Green Dragon Inn

green-dragon-inn.co.uk
Cockleford, Cowley, GL53 9NW
01242 870271

Tucked away in a small hamlet, this 17th-century stone inn offers peace and relaxation. One of the bars has furniture by Robert Thompson, with his trademark mice carved into the pieces. The menu here is extensive, and there are good wines to boot. Also, Tolkien hung around Oxford for decades, and the Middle Earth inn where hobbits meet for a half-pint is called The Green Dragon. Coincidence? Admittedly it's a popular name for public houses, but still.

Macdonald Randolph Hotel ◉◉

macdonaldhotels.co.uk
Beaumont Street, OX1 2LN
0844 8799132

The Randolph, opposite the Ashmolean, is an Oxford institution. Built in Victorian Gothic style and made famous by Colin Dexter's Inspector Morse novels, it has vaulted ceilings, ample oak panelling and a stiff air of formality. The restaurant's walls are decorated with college shields, and the service makes much use of trolleys. The cooking gently updates the great British tradition.

The Magdalen Arms

magdalenarms.com
243 Iffley Road, OX4 1SJ
01865 243159

Just a short stroll from Oxford city centre, this bustling pub is run by the team behind Waterloo's hugely influential Anchor & Hope gastro-boozer. There is a similar boho feel to the place. Its dark red walls, vintage furniture and the nose-to-tail menu will be familiar to anybody who knows the pub's London sibling. Real ales are complemented by a vibrant modern wine list.

Malmaison Oxford ◉

malmaison.com
Oxford Castle, 3 New Road,
OX1 1AY | 01865 268400

Who would have thought it? The city's former prison now has people turning up at its doors wanting to be let in. Reincarnated as a classy hotel by the boutique Malmaison chain, sybaritic bedrooms have been installed in the cells. Cast-iron staircases and arched doorways are an atmospheric reminder of its past, but Malmaison's mood is now pure 21st-century seduction, dressed up in shades of chocolate brown and aubergine. The moodily-lit brasserie in the old basement canteen eschews the traditional porridge, serving French classics as well as a please-all repertoire of simple modern dishes, all based on good-quality materials.

Mercure Oxford Eastgate Hotel ◉

thehightableoxford.co.uk
73 High Street, OX1 4BE
01865 248695

The 17th-century building with mullioned windows and a sandstone facade doesn't want for period charm, but the interior is contemporary and rather swanky, with well-designed fixtures and fittings and a decidedly cool restaurant called the High Table Brasserie & Bar. Old regulars such as C S Lewis and J R R Tolkien wouldn't recognise the place. The large, open-plan space's whitewashed walls, white-tiled flooring, bare wooden tables and grey banquette seating provide a perfect setting for its menu of British and Mediterranean-influenced food. The Mercure's also close to all the city-centre action.

Old Parsonage Hotel

oldparsonage-hotel.co.uk
1 Banbury Road, OX2 6NN
01865 310210

This beautiful town house hotel dates in part from the 16th century, and offers comfortable seating areas for day visitors. Afternoon tea is served in the cosy club-like restaurant, or, on warm summer days, on the terrace of one of the two small garden areas. A special menu offers a choice of Light Tea (scones with cream and preserves, various teas including Old Parsonage Blend, and coffees), or Very High Tea (sandwiches, home-baked cakes, and scones with cream and preserves, and tea or coffee); a Champagne Tea is also available. Other teatime offerings include toasted crumpets, homemade ice creams and sorbets, and hot chocolate or toddy to keep out the winter chill. Booking is recommended at weekends.

The Oxford Hotel ◉

pumahotels.co.uk
Godstow Road, Wolvercote
Roundabout, OX2 8AL
01865 489988

Within easy striking distance of the city centre, this modern hotel offers a number of options for unwinding. The Medio Bar's good for for a cocktail and a bar snack, while the Cappuccino Lounge dishes out light meals and afternoon teas. Up on the first floor, you'll find a smart and modish restaurant. With its breadth and depth, the menu satisfies customer expectations.

The Oxford Retreat

theoxfordretreat.com
1–2 Hythe Bridge Street, OX1 2EW
01865 250309

Smack beside the River Isis, the decked, tree-shaded waterside garden at this imposing gabled pub is best enjoyed after a day exploring the city of dreaming spires. Relax sipping cocktails or a pint of London Pride, then order from the eclectic pub menu. In winter, retreat inside and cosy up around the log fire.

The Punter

thepunteroxford.co.uk
7 South Street, Osney Island,
OX2 0BE | 01865 248832

Seek out this rustic-cool pub
on Osney Island, in the heart
of the city – it enjoys a
magnificent and very tranquil
spot beside the River Thames.
The decor is eclectic and
interesting, with mismatched
tables and chairs and bold
artwork on whitewashed walls.
Come for a relaxing pint of
Punter Ale by the river or refuel
on something tempting from
the daily menu.

The Turf Tavern

theturftavern.co.uk
4 Bath Place off Holywell Street,
OX1 3SU | 01865 243235

The Turf Tavern is a jewel
of a pub, and it's consequently
one of Oxford's most popular.
The Turf Tavern is certainly
one of the city's oldest pubs,
with some 13th-century
foundations and a 17th-century
low-beamed front bar. It's
not easy to find, but if anything
the tangled approach through
hidden alleyways adds to the
Turf's allure. Previously
called the Spotted Cow, it
became the Turf in 1842,
probably in deference to its
gambling clientele. It's also
had brushes with literature,
film and politics. Three
beer gardens help ease
overcrowding, but the 11
real ales and reasonably
priced pub grub keep the
students, locals and visitors
flowing in.

▶ PLACES NEARBY

The most obvious way to
head into the Cotswolds proper
from Oxford would be on the
A40 which soon calls in at
Witney (see page 242) then
Burford (see page 78), with
the Cotswold Wildlife Park
(see page 81) nearby. Though
heading northwest to
Woodstock and Blenheim
Palace (see page 246) is
another very attractive option.

St Mary the Virgin

iffley.co.uk
Church Way, Iffley, 2 miles south
of the centre of Oxford, off the
A4158, OX4 4EJ

St Mary's is a magnificent
building. It's rightly called
an almost perfect specimen
of a Norman church, with
unusually rich decoration both
inside and out. Built between
1170 and 1180, it was the gift
of the St Remy family, rich
patrons who held the manor
of Iffley in the second half of
the 12th century.

St Mary's consists of a
large, aisleless nave and a
chancel, with a massive
battlemented tower in the
centre. The west front
contains a superb doorway,
richly carved with chevron
and beakhead mouldings.
The south door is equally
splendid, with elaborately
carved capitals. Inside, the
principal features are the great
Norman arches supporting the
central tower, ornamented with
zigzag carving and shafts of
black marble.

▶ Painswick

Perched regally on the steep slopes of Painswick Valley, the 'Queen of the Cotswolds', as Painswick rather bumptiously calls itself, is a hive of activity. The village's energy and buildings collect in the network of lanes surrounding the church. Painswick is the most Dickensian of the Cotswold villages, and due to the character of the local stone, its overall colour is more likely to remind you of ivory than honey. Like other important towns around here, Painswick's prosperity reached its peak in the 17th and 18th centuries, when denizens harnessed the stream to work mills producing wool cloth. The purity of Painswick's water also meant that cloth dyeing became an important local industry. The fine houses built by the era's wealthy wool merchants give the village its character.

But Painswick's most striking feature is its church's graceful 17th-century spire. The church itself was mainly built in the 15th century, and contains some interesting monuments. But despite these attractions, the church*yard* is actually better-known. Clipped colonnades of yew have graced it since 1792. The colonnades are made up of 99 trees. Many attempts have been made to plant a final tree to bring the number to a round 100, but try as the gardeners might, that final tree simply will not take. Supposedly this is due to the intervention of the Devil

▼ The Cotswold Way, Painswick Beacon

himself, who always kills off the hundredth – perhaps out of a deep loathing for symmetrical landscape design? Rather like the Rollright Stones (see page 103), the trees are nigh-on impossible to count. Some have become intertwined with others, complicating the issue. The courtyard is also distinguished by its table tombs. These date from the 17th and 18th centuries. Many were carved by local mason Joseph Bryan and his two sons.

The Clipping Ceremony at Painswick church has nothing to do with pruning the famous yew trees. The name derives from the Old English word 'clyppan', meaning to embrace. The ceremony takes place on the nearest Sunday to 19 September, in association with the Feast of the Nativity of St Mary. In the afternoon, the children involved in the ceremony join hands to form a circle around the church. They approach the church and retreat from it three times, singing a traditional hymn. Painswick residents also bake a special cake. Known as 'puppy dog pie', it contains a small china dog – a reminder, perhaps, of the obscure pagan origins of the festivity.

A stroll around the heart of the town can be rewarding. Along Bisley Street, the original main street and the oldest part of Painswick, you'll find the Little Fleece. This National Trust bookshop is situated in a largely 17th-century house, which was itself built onto the 14th-century Fleece Inn.

The area around Painswick has strong associations with the Arts and Crafts Movement. Morris & Co designed the Congregational Church's window, while Sidney Barnsley designed both the Gyde Almshouses and the public baths. These traditions are carried on today by the Gloucestershire Guild of Craftsmen, the longest-established craft guild in Britain. They have a gallery in Painswick which displays high-quality contemporary work and which arranges events and exhibitions throughout the year.

Just outside the town on the Gloucester road, you'll find Painswick Rococo Garden. The landscaped 18th-century garden wraps around Painswick House and is utterly charming, particularly in early spring when snowdrops flower in abundance.

GO ROUND THE GARDENS

Painswick Rococo Garden
rococogarden.org.uk
GL6 6TH | 01452 813204
Open 10 Jan–Oct daily 11–5
This beautiful Rococo garden is the only one of its kind to survive intact. Ponds, woodland walks, a maze, a kitchen garden and herbaceous borders are all set in a Cotswold valley that's famous for its early spring snowdrops. Ring for details of special events.

SADDLE UP
Cotswold Trail Riding
cotswoldtrailriding.co.uk
Ongers Farm, Brookthorpe
01452 813344

EAT AND DRINK
Cotswolds88 Hotel ●●●
cotswolds88hotel.com
Kemps Lane, GL6 6YB
01452 813688

Cotswolds88 may have the achingly handsome stone exterior you might expect in this neck of the woods, but within lies a flourish of designer whimsy and boutique ambition. But there's substance to the playfulness, not least in the output of the hotel's Juniper restaurant. After canapés in the bar, the almost stage-set quality of the décor gives the restaurant a touch of theatricality. Beautifully slow-cooked venison comes accompanied with a bitter tonka bean jus, a tarte fine made of the haunch meat, watercress purée and red cabbage ketchup. A dessert of sticky toffee pudding with caramelised bananas and banana ice cream sounds relatively simple, but isn't. If you've any room left, British cheeses await. When the weather is up to snuff, take a stroll around the pretty gardens to admire the impressive house and the view.

The Falcon Inn
falconpainswick.co.uk
New Street, GL6 6UN
01452 814222

This small hotel, restaurant and pub in the heart of the town, opposite the church, dates from 1554 – but spent over 200 years as a courthouse. Expect a good choice of local real ales, including Hook Norton, and tasty, home-cooked food any time of day. An evening meal might offer pan-seared pigeon breast with pickled beetroot and parsnip purée; rack of lamb with garlic-roasted new potatoes and red wine jus to follow; and rhubarb and apple crumble for dessert. A blackboard offers daily specials, steaks and pies.

▷ **PLACES NEARBY**
Nearby Painswick Beacon is the site of both an Iron Age fort known as **Kimsbury Camp** and a golf course. From here you can catch massive views across the plain to Gloucester.

The neighbouring villages of **Sheepscombe** and **Slad** are noted for their associations with *Cider With Rosie* author Laurie Lee.

▷ Prinknash
Close to Painswick on the sheltered slopes beneath Cranham Woods, Benedictine Prinknash (pronounced 'Prinash') is one of Britain's few working abbeys. Despite looking like a huge cinema, the building just about succeeds in blending in with its surroundings. This is a testament to the use of good local

materials, in this case stone from the quarries around Guiting. The building has a16th-century foundation, and has been put to a variety of purposes over the centuries. It started as a hunting lodge for the abbots of Gloucester, and then became a manor house and chapel. Prince Rupert used it as his headquarters during the Siege of Gloucester. Horace Walpole celebrated its location in 1714, describing Prinknash as 'commanding Elysium'. The last private owner, a Catholic, invited the monks to leave their home on Caldey Island, off the Welsh coast, and relocate to Prinknash. Additional building work began in 1939.

The abbey is worth visiting for its gardens and the views it affords. The nearby Bird and Deer Park, set in 9 acres of parkland, is well stocked with birds, goats and deer.

ENTERTAIN THE FAMILY

The Bird and Deer Park
thebirdpark.com
Prinknash, GL4 8EX
01452 812727 | Open daily
Mar–Oct 10–5, Nov–Feb 10–4
The park is a sure-fire kid-pleaser, with peacocks, less-well-known (but equally attention-grabbing) birds, bats, donkeys and fallow deer. Visitors can feed the birds or take advantage of the beautiful riverside setting's great walking trails and picnic spots. The park is punctuated by follies like a Gypsy Caravan. They have special events on Christmas, Halloween and Easter, and a few less-seasonal events, including a Teddy Bears Picnic.

▶ **PLACES NEARBY**
Prinknash isn't far from Gloucester (see page 124). Appealing Painswick (see page 176) is to the south. The Great Witcombe Roman Villa, some lovely walkable woods and Cooper's Hill – of cheese rolling fame – are to the northeast.

Great Witcombe Roman Villa
english-heritage.org.uk
Off A46, 1.5 mile south of reservoir in Witcombe Park, GL3 4TW
0117 9750 700 | Access during reasonable daylight hours
The remains of this large villa, built around AD 250, include a bathhouse complex and the shrine of a water spirit.

▶ **The Rissingtons**
The three Rissingtons lie southeast of Bourton-on-the-Water. Around its attractive village green, **Great Rissington** has a handsome 17th-century manor house and a church with some interesting memorials. **Little Rissington**, on the slope of the Windrush Valley, has an RAF base. The church, set some way away from the village itself, has an RAF cemetery. The village overlooks former gravel pits, which have now been transformed into sanctuaries for birds.

Wyck Rissington is the loveliest of the three. Its 17th- and 18th-century cottages cluster around a wide green and village pond. From the 18th century, it formed part of the Wyck Hill estate. In the 1930s the depression forced landowners to sell off the village.

Like several near the Fosse Way, the church is dedicated to St Laurence, who was martyred in Rome in AD 257. The church contains some fine 14th-century stained glass, and Flemish wooden plaques dating from the 16th century. Cheltenham-born composer Gustav Holst was the organist here in 1892, when he was 17. Wyck Rissington is thus a stop on the Gustav Holst Way rambler's route.

▶ **PLACES NEARBY**

Bourton-on-the-Water (see page 70) and its myriad delights are close by. Stow-on-the-Wold (see page 195) lies to the north.

▶ Rousham House

rousham.org

OX25 4QU | 01869 347110 | Gardens open daily 10–dusk (last entry 4.30)

Since the 1630s, members of the same family have owned this imposing, almost fortress-like Jacobean mansion. Acquiring a nice bit of turf was all the rage (for rich people) on the eve of the English Civil War, and this plot on the curve on the River Cherwell hit the spot for staunch Royalist Sir Robert Dormer. The gardens, designed to complement the house and blend effortlessly into the Oxfordshire countryside, have changed little since landscape architect William Kent designed them a little more than a century later. As the only classical landscape gardens to have survived almost unaltered, they have acquired a unique place in the history of horticultural design.

Charles Bridgeman, a royal gardener, laid down the original plan for the gardens in the 1720s. It was Kent, however, who created an Augustan landscape, with features that evoke not only the glories of Renaissance Italy but also the splendor of ancient Rome. Kent was a Yorkshireman who'd studied art in London and then moved to Italy and painted frescoes for ten years. He envisaged this Oxfordshire garden as a landscape painting, and his design for it used shape, form, light and shade to maximum effect.

He used water from springs in the hill above to create cascades, rills and ornamental pools: simple features that formed romantic cameos within the classical framework. One curvaceous rill runs through a stone channel linking the Cold Bath and the so-called Venus's Vale. Other rills, sparkling and light-catching, feed into ornamental pools, and a white-water cascade tumbles into a grotto.

▶ PLACES NEARBY
To Rousham's northeast you'll find little **Lower Heyford**. The historic Holt Hotel, founded in 1475 as a coaching inn, sits at the crossroads between the A4260 Oxford Road and the B4030.

▶ Shipston-on-Stour

As the name might imply, Shipston (sheeps-town) was once an important centre of the wool trade. After the demand for local wool began to decline in the 19th century, Shipston continued to prosper thanks to its position. The strategic location that had enabled it to succeed as a market town made it an important stop for coaches. Many of the inns in the High Street date from that time. A branch line from the horse-drawn tramway linking Moreton-in–Marsh with Stratford-on-Avon opened in 1836. This line converted to steam power in 1889.

▶ PLACES NEARBY
A number of places around Shipston are worth a visit. To the northwest is Ilmington (see page 140), a delightful scattered village with has a fine manor house. Ilmington's church contains work by Robert Thompson, a celebrated early 20th-century furniture maker and craftsman whose signature was always a wooden mouse. The attractive village of **Honington**, to the north, can be approached via a minor road which leads over a pleasing five-arched bridge.

Just north of Honington you can find the well-manicured village of **Tredington**, complete with its parish church and fine 15th-century spire. Spot the curious fossilised remains of a creature like an ichthyosaurus (a fish lizard) in the porch floor. **Cherington**, to the south of Shipston, is home to a good selection of attractive 18th- and 19th-century houses made of local stone.

Church of St Lawrence
Church Lane, Oxhill, northeast of Shipston on Stour, CV37 0QR
Both the nave and chancel of St Lawrence's are 12th-century, and the north porch protects the original, beautifully-carved Norman north doorway. The porch and the sturdy little tower were built in the 15th century. On the south side of the church there's another beautiful Norman doorway. Above it, look for the row of strange carved heads. Inside, there is a 12th-century font with carvings of Adam and Eve in two of its 16 panels; the other 14 have trees, flowers and decorative patterns. A gravestone in the churchyard commemorates

Myrtilla, 'negro slave to Mr Thomas Beauchamp of Nevis. Buried Jan ye 6th 1705'.

Whatcote St Peter

Rectory Lane, east of the A429, south of the A422, CV36 5EB

Whatcote is a tiny hamlet located at the junction of two Roman roads, deep in rural Warwickshire. The village's small size and remote location make it all the more surprising that its church was hit by a bomb during World War II. It did a great deal of damage, but the church was restored in 1947. You can still see many features of the old church, including the 12th-century doorway on the north side of the nave. A tall medieval cross with an 18th-century sundial at its top stands in the churchyard. In the 17th century the church had the same rector, John Davenport, for more than 70 years. He died in 1668 at the age of 101.

The Red Lion ⊚

redlion-longcompton.co.uk
Main Street, Long Compton,
CV36 5JS | 01608 684221

The nearby Rollright Stones and their stories about kings and witches will give you plenty to ponder while you sip a pint of real ale at The Red Lion's bar. Built in 1748 as a coaching inn, the Grade II listed freehouse has a traditional interior of oak beams and inglenook fireplaces. More recent additions include some comfy leather armchairs to sink into. You can eat in the bar, or in the restaurant area that leads out onto a patio. Daily specials are chalked on the board to supplement the frequently-changing menu. There's a good children's menu, too.

▸ Shipton-under-Wychwood

Formerly neighbour to Bruern Abbey, and once located at the centre of the Wychwood Forest, Shipton was built in the Evenlode Valley around a large village green. At the lower end of the green you'll find St Mary's, a late 13th century church. A fine octagonal spire grows out of its tower. Within the church are a 14th-century effigy of a woman and a delightful Tudor monument of a family group at prayer.

The uniquely-named Shaven Crown Hotel, housed in a handsome stone building close to the green, can trace its history back to 1384. At one time the Cistercian monks of formerly nearby Bruern Abbey ran the hotel. Bruern was founded in the reign of King Stephen and dissolved in 1536. Nothing now remains of it. In contrast the Shaven Crown survived to have the dubious honor of once hosting English Fascist leader Sir Oswald Mosley during World War II. He was arrested during the course of his visit, though, so perhaps the Shaven Crown did have the last laugh.

On the green of Shipton-under-Wychwood, close to the Shaven Crown, stands a 1878 memorial for 17 parishioners. They died when a ship named the *Cospatrick* caught fire off Cape Town on its way to New Zealand in 1874. Tragically, of the 477 *Cospatrick* passengers presumably aiming to start a new life in the colonies, only three survived.

Although Wychwood Forest once covered a large area between Stanton Harcourt and Taynton, there is almost nothing left of it. A project to restore some of its original landscape and habitats is underway. Normans favoured Wychwood as a hunting ground, and the forest was well known for its deer. Most English kings prior to Charles I hunted here, and the citizens of Burford were entitled to do so as well. In later centuries, many of the vicinity's notable estate parks, such as Blenheim and Cornbury, were carved out of Wynchwood. A National Nature Reserve stands in the centre of what remains of the forest, just 2 miles east of Shipton.

SEE A LOCAL CHURCH
St Mary's church
Church Street, just east of the main road through Shipton, far side of the village green, OX7 6BP

The size and grandeur of St Mary's reflects the fact that Shipton parish used to include Ramsden and Leafield, villages that now have Victorian churches of their own. Shipton's largely 13th-century church stands between the Old Prebendal House and the village green. The tower and broach spire are typically Early English, and have some fine detailing.

Inside, the church is quite plain, with aisles on both sides of the nave and late Norman capitals in the chancel arch. Most of the windows are from the 13th and 14th centuries. Several of the monuments commemorate the Reade family, who were squires here

for 200 years. The 15th-century pulpit is carved from a single block of stone; the font is of the same period.

EAT AND DRINK
The Shaven Crown Hotel
theshavencrown.co.uk
High Street, OX7 6BA
01993 830500

▼ Shaven Crown Hotel

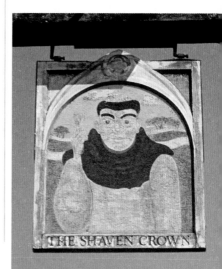

The monks of Bruern Abbey built this 14th-century coaching inn as a hospice for the poor. Following the Dissolution of the Monasteries, Elizabeth I used it as a hunting lodge. She gave it to the village in 1580, and it became the Crown Inn. Thus it stayed until 1930, when a brewery with a sense of humour changed the name in homage to the familiar monastic tonsure. The Inn is full of original architectural features, like the great hall. The bar serves light meals and real ales, while the restaurant offers Cotswold ham, beef, lamb and venison pie; beer-battered fish and chips; and a winter vegetable and bean hotpot. At the time of writing the hotel is closed for refurbishment, and will reopen Spring 2014.

▶ **PLACES NEARBY**

Shipton has Burford (see page 78) to its south, the Rissingtons (see page 179) due west, and popular Bourton-on-the-Water (see page 70) a short way beyond these.

▶ The Slaughters

Let's start with the names. Upper and Lower Slaughter have the reputation of being two of the prettiest Cotswolds villages, which is saying something in a region full of villages you'd happily retire to. Their repute is well justified, but it *is* rather at odds with their names, which suggest a rather different form of coming here to die. So when did the two mass slaughters the names allude to take place? They didn't. 'Slaughter' merely means muddy in Old English – and the villages are no longer even that muddy. If you were hoping for gore and feel a touch disappointed, perhaps take solace in the fact that Lower Slaughter especially has an unmistakable *Midsomer Murders* vibe.

Lower Slaughter is about a half-mile's walk from Upper Slaughter and a mile from Bourton-on-the-Water. A number of footbridges span the River Eye, and a 19th-century corn mill with a working waterwheel and steam chimney makes good use of it. Copse Hill Road, one of the most photographed streets in the Cotswolds, was voted Britain's Most Romantic Street in a Google Street View poll. After bringing Yet Another Photo of Copse Hill Road into the world, visitors can hit up the Victorian flourmill museum.

Upper Slaughter has less instant appeal and tourist infrastructure, but the village is arguably more appealing for that. It's the more pastoral of the two, partly clustered around its fine 17th-century manor (now a hotel) and 12th-century church. The church contains a monument to F E Witts, 19th-century rector, lord of the manor and writer of *Diary of a Cotswold Parson*. The scene beyond the church is absurdly picturesque – the forded River Eye bubbles below some wonderful stone cottages in the shade of an oak tree.

VISIT THE MUSEUM
Old Mill Museum
oldmill-lowerslaughter.com
Mill Lane, Lower Slaughter
01451 820052
This interesting museum demonstrates the mechanics of a Victorian flourmill with its working waterwheel and steam chimney. The collection includes one of only three unused millstones left in the country. There's also a gift and craft shop, and a riverside tea room that offers free tastings of their award-winning organic ice cream in summer.

EAT AND DRINK
Lower Slaughter Manor ⊛⊛⊛
lowerslaughter.co.uk
Lower Slaughter, GL54 2HP
01451 820456
This 17th-century manor house dates from the time of the Commonwealth, but despite the weight of centuries it's a superbly relaxing place to be. There are plenty of public rooms for lounging, and the rooms are colourful without being excessively cluttered.

Discerning local buying practices combine with a modernist approach to classical principles in the cuisine.

Lords of the Manor ⊛⊛⊛
lordsofthemanor.com
Upper Slaughter, GL54 2JD
01451 820243
This former rectory built in the 17th century. Standing in eight acres of lushly landscaped grounds, complete with lake, it's a wonderfully relaxed place. The staff are classically attired, and in the event of any dithering over wine there's a sommelier on hand, able to ride to the rescue. Chef Matt Weedon's dishes show novelty and daring.

▶ PLACES NEARBY
Bourton-on-the-Water (see page 70) is the natural itinerary-accompaniment to the Slaughters. Visit them all and you'll sample three classic Cotswolds villages, each with a very different flavour. Further west, **Naunton** is a handsome, quiet place, tucked into a valley and blessed with a friendly pub.

▶ Slimbridge
The Wildfowl and Wetlands Trust at Slimbridge is the brainchild of the late Sir Peter Scott, artist and naturalist. Established in 1946 as the Severn Wildfowl Trust, the salt marshes around the Gloucester and Sharpness Canal and the River Severn have now become home to one of the largest collections of

waterfowl in the world, ranging from swans and geese to flamingos and humming birds. Slimbridge is the winter home of Bewick's swans, which migrate every year from Siberia, and whooper swans, which come mainly from Iceland. Swans mate for life, and some pairs have been coming to Slimbridge for more than 21 years. The Trust operates an adoption scheme to help ensure their future. Excellent viewing facilities are available and in winter, towers and hides provide remarkable views of migrating birds. There are also displays of wildlife art and many other attractions.

The village of Slimbridge itself is well worth a visit. It boasts a 13th-century church, which is a very fine example of the Early English style. The Rectory, behind the church, stands on the site of the old Manor House. Maurice of Berkeley, a scion of the great Berkeley dynasty, left from here to fight at the Battle of Bannockburn in 1314. Slimbridge may have been the birthplace of William Tyndale, who first translated the Bible into English, but North Nibley (see page 254) also contends for the title – and they've gotten the jump on Slimbridge by putting up a monument to Tyndale, which is surely cheating. (Though we should point out that this monument manouvre also worked for Riverside, Iowa, which claimed the coveted 'birthplace of Captain Kirk' title over America's many potential Riversides with the aid of a strategic *Enterprise* statue and a very confident plaque in the public square.)

▼ Mute Swans, Slimbridge Wetlands Centre

MEET THE WILDLIFE

Slimbridge Wetland Centre

wwt.org.uk

GL2 7BT | 01453 891900

Open all year, daily from 9.30–5.30 (winter 5)

Slimbridge is home to perhaps the world's largest collection of swans, geese, ducks and flamingos. This internationally renowned reserve shows visitors an astounding array of wildlife, from water voles to waders, hares and dragonflies. Facilities include a tropical house, a wetland mammal exhibit, a discovery centre, a children's outdoor play area, a shop and a restaurant. You could also try a canoe safari.

▶ **PLACES NEARBY**

Frampton-on-Severn, which is two miles north of Slimbridge, is an extensive village, said to have the largest village green (22 acres) in England. The restored church contains a rare lead Norman font.

▶ Snowshill Manor & Garden

nationaltrust.org.uk

WR12 7JU | 01386 852410 | Open end Mar–early Nov Wed–Sun & BHs, House 12–4, Garden 11–5.30; Jul–Aug, Wed–Mon, House 11.30–3.30, Garden 11–5.30

Charles Wade was the sort of entertainingly eccentric and brilliantly left-field friend you'd be glad to have, but who you'd simultaneously rather didn't ever actually pop round to your house. Wade was a wealthy sugar plantation owner, and Snowshill Manor once belonged to him. His family motto was 'Let nothing perish', and Wade embodied it. He spent his life and his inheritance amassing a spectacular collection of everyday and extraordinary objects from across the globe, buying objects because of their colour, craftsmanship and design and restoring this golden-yellow Tudor-era manor house to display them. Laid out theatrically according to Wade's wishes, the Manor is literally packed to the rafters with 22,000 or so unusual objects – from bicycles to musical instruments, clocks, Chinese lacquer cabinets, farm implements, works of art, tiny toys, suits of Samurai armour and more. Having filled the manor house with his finds, Wade had to live without any comforts or conveniences in the old Priest's House out in the lovely terraced garden, and to sleep in an old Tudor bed.

The fame of Snowshill Manor rightly travelled far and wide. Eminent people – John Buchan, John Betjeman and J B Priestley among them – were frequent visitors. Queen Mary had a look around, and apparently said that the finest thing in the house was Wade himself.

Snowshill Manor is one of the most astonishing and absorbing museums it's possible to imagine. Its wildly diverse collection has something to interest all but the most hardened detractors of museums. But the interest of the place extends beyond the house itself. Wade was an architect, and a devotee of the Arts and Crafts ideals popularised by William Morris. In 1919 he commissioned another like-minded architect, M H Baillie Scott, to transform grounds he called 'a wilderness of chaos'. Chaos became a series of terraces, the Armillary Court, notable shrubbery, the Well Garden and the kitchen gardens. In short, the Manor is surrounded by an intriguing terraced hillside garden designed in the Arts and Crafts style.

Like the Hidcote Manor gardens (see page 135), the Snowshill Manor gardens were built as a series of interconnecting 'rooms'. Snowshill's rooms provide spectacular views over some of the most beautiful countryside in Gloucestershire. A beautiful double border to the left of the terrace garden combines bright red Oriental and yellow Welsh poppies. Artfully trained climbers conquer the other wall, while the bold lines of espaliered figs stand out in tempting fashion.

Charles Wade had a special love of the colour blue. The seats and woodwork throughout the gardens at Snowshill are painted with a particular shade now known as 'Wade' blue – a powdery dark blue with a touch of turquoise. This blue harmonises well with the Cotswold stone walls, and is a particularly attractive colour in a landscape setting. It also provides a sympathetic foil for the mauves and purples the gardens use to good effect. In adopting this 'signature' colour for the garden furniture, Wade acted in accordance with his feeling that no shade of green paint could possibly match the magnificent hues of nature.

A spring rising under the manor house feeds a garden fountain and several small basins and pools. As you climb the steps near the shrubbery, the path is overhung with weeping white mulberries. The atmosphere of the Victorian romantic garden is strong.

For almost two decades, the garden at Snowshill has been managed without the use of any chemicals. The gardeners rely on wildlife to maintain a perfect natural balance. They use natural feeds composed of seaweed extract, blood, fish and bone. Snowshill's home-grown compost has an added special ingredient: dove excrement from the dovecote. The judicious planting of nectar-rich species, including alliums, asters, echium, marigolds, mignonette and sedums, attracts bees and other beneficial insects into the garden. In turn, they earn their keep by feeding on aphids and other pests. Sloe, hawthorn, elderberry and spindleberry, guelder rose, wild roses, dogwood and field maple are planted along visitors' route to the manor. These British natural shrubs produce early blossoms, nuts or fruits, or provide habitat for birds and small mammals. Visitors to the garden who might be unaware of these specific planting plans are nonetheless almost certain to notice the joyous variety of bird songs and the friendly hum of the bees as they wander through the grounds.

Today, the National Trust owns and operates Snowshill. The trust displays Wade's eccentric collections and maintains the charming country gardens to its usual high standard.

▶ **PLACES NEARBY**

Pronounced, according to some, 'Snowzzle', or even 'Snozzle', charming and comparatively remote **Snowshill** village is gorgeous on a sunny day, when a temporary bookstall appears on the village green. Parts of *Bridget Jones' Diary* were shot here. A circuit of Stanway, Snowshill and Stanton makes for an excellent walk, allowing you to take in three handsome but different Cotswolds villages. Portions of the walk consist of a testing hill climb, so seek out or avoid it according to your level of fondness for that sort of thing.

▶ **The Sodburys**

What an Old Sodbury! There's something childishly pleasing about the names of the three Sodburys – Old, Little and Chipping. The three villages are all scattered around narrow lanes down the Cotswold escarpment, though their remote character has more in common with the vale than the nearby Edge.

Handsome **Chipping Sodbury** (Chipping means 'market') is the newest of the trio, established as a market town in 1227. J K Rowling, author of the Harry Potter books, was born here rather more recently. The main – market – street is extraordinary wide and the clock tower, the location of a twice-monthly farmers' market (second and fourth Saturdays of the month), is worth a glance. The houses on Hatters Lane are Tudor.

Old Sodbury, the original (as the 'Old' suggests), has an impressively elderly church and an atmospheric (if you can ignore the noisy A46) Bronze-to-Iron Age encampment above the town.

Little Sodbury is the most interesting of the three Sodburys. Small as it is, this village has a rich history. Gloucestershire-born scholar William Tyndale (c.1494–1536), the translator of the Bible into English, came to its manor house in 1521 as tutor and chaplain (you can see the Tyndale Monument near Wotton-under-Edge, page 252). A few years later, Henry VIII and Anne Boleyn stayed in the house, which has a wonderful 15th-century great hall. The church, the only one dedicated to St Adeline, an obscure saint who may have originated from Normandy, originally stood next to the manor house. Urgent repair work necessitated moving the church to its present site. It was built in Victorian times on the site of an earlier church, of which only the pulpit (where Tyndale would have preached) remains.

The Somerset, or Hawkesbury, Monument was erected near the Sodburys in 1846 to commemorate Lord Edward Somerset, one of the Badminton Beauforts. He served at the Battle of Waterloo with exceptional gallantry, and the government of his day gave him their thanks.

> **PLACES NEARBY**

Horton, to the north, was originally a Norman hall. It later became a manor house, and the National Trust owns its court, though it's currently closed to the public. **Hawkesbury Upton,** nearby on the Cotswold Edge, has the Somerset Monument. If you're going south along the A46, **Marshfield** is worth turning off for and looking about (especially if it's Boxing Day, see page 54). There's a broad, handsome high street, and if you could delete all the cars then just looking at it would probably take you back in time. Also look out for the Marshfield farm shop, which has excellent ice-cream.

▶ South Cerney

South Cerney, 3 miles southeast of Cirencester, is situated on the banks of the Churn. You'll find rows of attractive cottages here along Silver Street and Church Lane. The church has a Norman south doorway, above which are sculptures reflecting Heaven and Hell. Within, you'll find the remains of a 12th-century crucifix, one of the earliest surviving examples of wood carving in the country. The old Thames and Severn Canal passes just to the north of the village, and walks along the tow-path are possible. The village is best known nowadays for the series of flooded gravel pits that make up the Cotswold Water Park.

Broadly speaking these man-made lakes fall into two sections, one between Cricklade and Kemble (where South Cerney is situated), the other between Fairford and Lechlade. The park provides facilities for nature lovers, birders and sports people alike. The eight nature reserves and the wetlands collectively attract over 20,000 wildfowl, and birdlife gets particularly hopping in the winter. The various activities coexist happily on 150 lakes.

GET OUTDOORS

Cotswold Water Park
www.waterpark.org
GL7 5TL | 01793 752413
There are excellent birdwatching sites here, and visitors get a chance to see winter waterbirds, waders, nightingales, grebe, hobbies and more, as well as the chance to meet other locals – otters, water voles, dragonflies, fritillaries, orchids, birds, bats and even beavers. If you'd rather be active, the park gives you a choice of many activities, from angling to archery, cycling, climbing, sailing, snorkelling, walking and wakeboarding.

WALK THE HIGH ROPES

Head 4 Heights
head4heights.net
GL7 6DF | 01285 770007
A range of climbing, jumping and swinging and obstacle activities.

TAKE OFF

Ballooning In The Cotswolds
ballooninginthecotswolds.co.uk
Cotswold Water Park
GL5 3EX | 01453 753221
See page 72

EXPLORE BY BIKE

Go-By-Cycle
go-by-cycle.co.uk
Tall Trees Water Lane,
Somerford Keynes, GL7 6DS
07970 419208

This husband-and-wife operation offers all-terrain bikes, as well as with plenty of child–friendly options (including tricycles) and tandems.

SADDLE UP

South Cerney Riding School
southcerneyridingschool.co.uk
Cerney Wick Farm, Cerney Wick,
GL7 5QH | 01793 750151
The school provides tuition for students from two years old up, and caters for people with disabilities. The also offer 1–2 hour rides for riders of all ages and abilities on Cotswold Water Park bridleways.

10 quintessential Cotswolds names

▶ **Old Sodbury,** page 189

▶ **Little Sodbury,** page 189

▶ **Waterley Bottom**

▶ **Bishop's Itchington**

▶ **Ozleworth,** page 253

▶ **Stow-on-the-Wold,** page 195

▶ **Upper Slaughter,** page 184

▶ **Wotton-under-Edge,** page 252

▶ **Broughton Poggs**

▶ **Bourton-on-the-Water,** page 70

▶ **PLACES NEARBY**
Cirencester (see page 105) is to the north and **Cricklade** to the south. Little Cricklade's latin moto *in loco delicious* means 'a delightful place' and few would disagree. Dating back to the 12th century, the historical high street is still a treat today.

To the east are the Ampneys, villages set in flat countryside, with their historical churches. **Down Ampney** is also the birthplace of composer Ralph Vaughan Williams, who gave the village's name to one of his best-known hymns. There's a small exhibition about the composer inside the church.

▶ Stanton

Though its somewhat unpromising name means 'stony farm', little, attention-dodging Stanton is perhaps the fairest of all Cotswolds villages. It has a fine collection of farmhouses and cottages. Most of them were built during the 17th century, the golden period of Cotswold vernacular architecture. A village of quite ridiculous perfection, Stanton seems almost to have been preserved in aspic. As such it's regularly used as the backdrop for period films.

Stanton owes its peculiar 'frozen-in-time' quality to the man who bought much of the village before World War I, the architect Sir Philip Stott. Stott was originally from Oldham in Lancashire, but having moved to Stanton Court he was determined to restore the town. Stott's restoration introduced modern conveniences, but also ensured by covenant that the more unsightly features of the 20th century could never disfigure the village.

Stanton is a place to stroll around, after you've made use of the car park around the corner of Broadway road. The church, St Michael's, is delightful and well-worth a visit, particularly for its spectacular gargoyles. Elsewhere, look out for Stott lanterns and a medieval cross in the middle of the village. At the far end of the village is Shenberrow Hill, well worth investigating for its Iron Age earthworks and magnificent views.

SEE A LOCAL CHURCH
St Michael & All Angels
Church Lane, WR12 7NF
St Michael's has a handsomely slender spire, a number of 12th-century features in the north arcade and two pulpits – one 14th century, one Jacobean. It also has some 15th-century stained glass, which came from Hailes Abbey near Winchcombe.

GET CRAFTY
Stanton Guildhouse
Trust's Arts Events
stantonguildhouse.org.uk
WR12 7NE | 01386 584357

The Trust runs workshops in wood turning, pottery, furniture restoration, chair making, watercolouring, printmaking, stained and kiln-fired glass blowing and even mosaic making. It also holds literary readings, musical evenings, art exhibitions and motivational speaking sessions. Book early.

SADDLE UP
Cotswolds Riding
cotswoldsriding.co.uk
WR12 7NE | 01386 584250

Lessons for all levels of rider, including ponies for children.

▶ **PLACES NEARBY**
Stanway, and with it the arresting facade of Stanway House are only up the road (and only further down this page, by happy alphabetic coincidence), and should be combined with your Stanton visit. Both golden Broadway (see page 77) and Winchcombe (see page 233) are fairly nearby too.

▶ Stanway House

stanwayfountain.co.uk
Stanway, GL54 5PQ | 01386 584469 | Open Jun–Aug Tue & Thu 2–5

Not unlike nearby Snowshill Manor, Stanway's creatively named Stanway House has attracted and enchanted a surprising amount of famous people, especially writers. The nearby cricket pitch is the first clue. *Peter Pan* author J M Barrie (1860-1937) fell in love with Stanway and especially Stanway House. He holidayed at the house repeatedly, and donated the cricket pavilion. There Barrie entertained the likes of Sir Arthur Conan Doyle and H G Wells.

The Tracys, a family who'd owned land in the region since the Conquest, constructed the Jacobean building between 1590 and 1630. Two Mercian magnates gave the property to the Abbey of Tewkesbury as its first endowment. During the Dissolution of the Monasteries, Stanway changed hands for the only time in 1,270 years, when Richard Tracy obtained the lease of the property with the assistance of Thomas Cromwell. Current owner, Lord Neidpath, lives in the house, and although it contains many items of interest and value, a less fossilised atmosphere that Stanway's is hard to imagine.

Approaching the house, you pass the magnificent 14th-century tithe barn built by the Abbey. You also pass the charming, jewel-like gatehouse, which dates from around 1630. Splendid gables and magnificent tall windows give light to the Great Hall and dominate Stanway's facade. Beyond the screens passage, the hall still possesses an unmistakable Elizabethan atmosphere. There's a raised dais at one end, and at the other a minstrels' gallery above the screen – though it's now been

▲ Stanway House

made into a bedroom. The Audit Room has a rent table from 1780, where the estate still receives payment in person from its tenants.

The old water gardens have been superbly restored. Pride of place goes to the fountain, the tallest in Britain, which rises to over 300 feet. The old brewhouse has been revived. The coppers are built over log fires, making this one of the few log-fired breweries in the country. Stanway produces several beers. Stanney, the most popular, is available in local pubs.

For a long time the arresting 17th-century gatehouse, the only part of the house you can really see from the road, was thought to be the work of Inigo Jones. That theory's been superseded by the belief that it's the work of Timothy Strong, a mason from the Barringtons whose family worked with Sir Christopher Wren on St Paul's Cathedral. Either way the glow of the stone is breathtaking, particularly at sunset.

Visitors can reach Stanway House via the B4077 Stow road. Coming this way, they'll pass the striking *St George and Dragon* bronze war memorial by Alexander Fisher. It rests a plinth by Sir Philip Stott, 'saviour' of nearby Stanton. The local church, with its Jacobean pulpit, is next to the house. The name 'Stanway' is a reference to the old Salt Way trading route.

▶ **PLACES NEARBY**

Stanton (see page 192), the prettiest village in the Cotswolds, is just up the road, and should be combined with your Stanton visit. Happily both handsome Broadway (see page 77) and welcoming Winchcombe (see page 233) are fairly nearby too.

▶ Stow-on-the-Wold

There's something curiously satisfying about a place name that helps explain a town's geography, and the Cotswolds has a few of these. Stow is indeed up on the wolds, making it the highest town in the Cotswolds. It's also situated at the meeting point of eight roads and lies on the Roman Fosse Way, midway between Bourton and Moreton. Stow's an interesting, historical place, nowadays known for its horses and antiques. The amount of visitors it attracts is perhaps surprising, but as ever acerbic newspaper critic A A Gill took things too far when he called it 'catastrophically ghastly'.

Stow's heart is its old market square, for Stow's formative period was spent as a busy market town. The square, surrounded by attractive pubs, coaching inns, shops and restaurants, is not typical of the Cotswolds – its even, rectangular shape is more reminiscent of an Italian piazza, sans arcades. Perhaps Stow's exposed position on the wolds dictated its shape, to protect market traders from the wind? A number of walled alleys or 'tures' lead into the square. It's thought these once directed sheep towards the market place. Gloriously, old stocks remain in a corner of the square, while in the centre stands the Victorian St Edward's Hall. Its bombastic situation and massive presence tend to overpower the more modest lines of the other buildings. The medieval market cross, just to the south of the Hall, was placed in its prominent location that it might appeal to the religious conscience of traders as they engaged in their dealings.

The imposing Norman church of St Edward overlooks the square is. In 1646 it played host to 1,000 Royalist prisoners after the final bloody battle of the Civil War, which was fought near neighbouring Donnington. The church's north door is picturesquely framed by a pair of tree trunks, while just outside the churchyard, on Church Street, you'll find Stow's 17th-century school (now a Masonic hall). Visitors will find a fine private collection of Victorian, Edwardian and later toys, as well as other childhood memorabilia in the Toy and Collectors Museum, located in Park Street's Park House. The Royalist pub, at the junction of Park Street and Digbeth Street (which runs southeast from the square), claims to be the oldest pub in the county. It might not be all talk: unlike the many other claimants for this title, remains of wooden beams have been discovered in the Royalist, and tests prove these beams were in place a thousand years ago.

There are a number of villages in the vicinity of Stow that are worth visiting. Broadwell is a 45-minute walk (or a short drive) to the north. It's built around a large green with a ford, and overlooked by a fine pub, The Fox. The Swells, Lower and Upper, are to the west. In Lower Swell, beside the River Dikler, the unusual design of Spa Cottages persists as a reminder of the chalybeate spring – that's water containing iron salts to the rest of us – that was discovered here in 1807. Investors hoped that this discovery would encourage visitors to come and take the waters, according to the fashion of the time, but the project foundered. At the tiny rural hamlet of Upper Swell, the road crosses a narrow 18th-century bridge near a mill, complete with a 19th-century wheel.

If you are looking to keep children entertained, the Cotswold Farm Park (see page 133) to the west of Stow, near Temple Guiting, is a must. Created by Cotswold farmer Joe Henson, the farm has a fascinating collection of rare British breeds, which it aims to help protect.

GO SHOPPING
Stow-on-the-Wold Farmers' Market
fresh-n-local.co.uk
The Square, GL54 1BL
Second Thu of each month, 9–1

EAT AND DRINK
Fosse Manor
fossemanor.co.uk
GL54 1JX | 01451 830354
You'll find Fosse Manor on the fringes of Stow-on-the-Wold. The creeper-clad exterior of this former rectory looks like it conceals a scene of country-house chintz, but inside the Fosse brings a pared-back, neutral-hued contemporary style. Five acres of idyllic grounds and gardens provide the backdrop to dining in the smart restaurant. The kitchen too, has stayed in touch with current trends, serving up appealing menus of uncomplicated modern British ideas built on top-grade local produce.

Number Four at Stow Hotel & Restaurant @@
hotelnumberfour.co.uk
Fosseway, GL54 1JX | 01451 830297
This stylish boutique hotel operates in a building dating from the 17th century. Number Four is one of those places that gets everything pitch perfect, from the opulent contemporary look to the sort of prescient service that anticipates guests' needs. In the oldest part of the house, light and modern cooking is served in characterful, beamed and painted-wood-panelled Cutler's Restaurant. Head chef Brian Cutler uses local, seasonal produce from a well-chosen network of suppliers to good effect in well-executed dishes.

The Unicorn
birchhotels.co.uk
Sheep Street, GL54 1HQ
01451 830257
This eye-catching 17th-century property in Stow-on-the-Wold's main square is built from

honey-coloured limestone and bedecked with flowering window boxes. The interior is stylishly presented, with Jacobean pieces, antique artefacts and open log fires. Food is served in the oak-beamed bar, in the stylish restaurant or, if the weather is fine, in the secluded garden. Freshly made sandwiches are also available.

White Hart Inn

thewhitehartstow.com
The Square, GL54 1AF
01451 830674

Some of Stow's mellow stone buildings date from the 12th century, including parts of the White Hart. The Hart's two cosy bars benefit from open fires. An atmospheric dining room serves lunchtime snacks such as a Lincolnshire poacher and piccalilli sandwich. For dinner you could start with Cornish scallops with chorizo, follow with local pheasant cooked with cloves and cinnamon and round off with chocolate marquise. There's a spacious car park.

Wyck Hill House Hotel & Spa ◉◉

wyckhillhousehotel.co.uk
Burford Road, GL54 1HY
01451 831936

Visitors' first sight of this old Cotswolds property with lovely views of the Windrush Valley gives them some high expectations. These are met by Wyck Hill's antique-furnished lounges, its oak-panelled bar and its smartly kitted-out dining room with neutral-shaded walls, comfortable upholstered chairs and French windows looking over the estate.

▶ PLACES NEARBY

Little **Adlestrop**, known as Tedestrop in the Domesday Book, is comparatively remote. You'll find it off the A436, between Stow-on-the-Wold and The Greedy Goose pub, near Salford. It's a one-shop village, best known for a poem of the same name by war poet Edward Thomas:

'Yes, I remember Adlestrop –
The name, because
        one afternoon
Of heat the express-train drew
        up there
Unwontedly. It was late June.
The steam hissed. Someone
        cleared his throat.
No one left and no one came
On the bare platform. What I saw
Was Adlestrop – only the name
And willows, willow-herb,
        and grass,
And meadowsweet, and
        haycocks dry,
No whit less still and lonely fair
Than the high cloudlets
        in the sky.
And for that minute a
        blackbird sang
Close by, and round him, mistier,
Farther and farther,
        all the birds
Of Oxfordshire and
        Gloucestershire.'

▲ The Shakespeare

▶ Stratford-upon-Avon

'I am a stranger here in Gloucestershire: These high wild hills and rough uneven ways draws out our miles, and makes them wearisome.'
Richard II

If William's Shakespeare's only reference to the Cotswolds in his world-famous plays is anything much to go on, Shakespeare was not an enthusiastic hill-walker. Shakespeare may be from the Cotswolds, but the historic market town that bore him that reveals little about Billy's early career. His birth and baptism are recorded, but other than the fact that 'he had been in his younger years a schoolmaster in the country' (John Aubrey, 1681), he remains a vague personage until he materialises in London, virtually a fully-fledged poet and playwright. He spent much of his life in Stratford – perhaps innagurating the now-mightly tradition of retiring to the

Cotswolds – providing Stratford with more than enough justification to celebrate his association with the town tastefully, authoritatively and lucratively. Well, and why not? There is no better place to start exploring Stratford than the fine 16th-century building where Shakespeare was born. It's located on what was then and is now a busy thoroughfare. Just on the edge of the town centre you'll find the Church of the Holy Trinity. It's worth visiting in its own right for its delightful architecture, but most visitors come to pay their respects to Shakespeare, who lies buried here. Not far away sits the thatched farmhouse cottage where Shakespeare's wife Anne Hathaway grew up. The cottage is at Shottery, on the town's outskirts. It remained in the possession of Hathaway descendants until the late 19th century, and still contains numerous items belonging to the family.

It's likely that Stratford would have made an enticing destination even in an alternate universe where there never was a Shakespeare. It's quite a delight to stroll along the streets, inescapably imbued with Shakespeariana, taking in the splendours of medieval craftsmanship and the aura of 16th-

and 17th-century England. Among the town's finest buildings are the aforementioned house in which Shakespeare was born, Thomas Nash's House on Chapel Street (owned by the first husband of Shakespeare's grand-daughter), and Hall's Croft in the Old Town (named after Dr John Hall, who married one of Shakespeare's daughters). Stratford's most ornate home, Harvard House, is a splendid example of an Elizabethan town house. Rebuilt in 1596, Harvard House is the home of the Museum of British Pewter. At Wilmcote, 5 miles north of Stratford, you'll find Mary Arden's House, the site of the Shakespeare Countryside Museum. Mary Arden, Shakespeare's mother, lived in this timbered farmhouse before marrying John Shakespeare and moving to Stratford.

Stratford is internationally renowned as the home of the Royal Shakespeare Company, long recognised as Europe's – and indeed the world's – leading classical theatre corporation. Its annual repertoire of superb theatre productions features a mix of classical plays by Shakespeare, his contemporaries, and other classical playwrights, modern drama and musicals. The RSC also specially commissions many new plays. Some of the most distinguished actors and directors in the world perform with the company.

A successful campaign to bring theatre to Stratford began in 1875, with a donation of land from Charles Flower. Little did Flower know that Stratford would one day be a titan in the field. The world-famous company was founded in Stratford in 1879, with the opening of the Shakespeare Memorial Theatre. That theatre was destroyed by fire, and a replacement was built in 1932. The art deco building, by Elisabeth Scott, was Britain's first important public structure to be designed by a female architect. In later decades, the RSC spread its wings far and wide, occupying London's Aldwych theatre in 1960 and a studio theatre (the Warehouse) in 1977. Between 1982 and 2002, it took space in the Barbican and, more recently, the Roundhouse in Camden.

The company expanded its Stratford home as well. In 1974 the RSC opened a studio theatre, The Other Place, and in 1986 it opened the Swan. The company has recently opened the new 1,000-seat Royal Shakespeare Theatre.

Even with all this on the go (not to mention the falderal involved in filming performances for distribution and sending companies touring around the world), the RSC still resists sliding into any kind of complacency. The company consistently manages to present not simply performances that set the industry standard, but also productions that redefine their texts and advance the field of theatre. Sir Anthony Quayle,

Sir Peter Hall and Sir Trevor Nunn have been among the RSC's artistic directors.

You might be fooled into thinking otherwise at times, but there is more to Stratford than Shakespeare. Famous for its literary associations, Stratford bustles with culture and history. But there are also superb shops and restaurants, as well as a vibrant Friday market. You could try your luck at the horses at the exciting Stratford Races, take a tour of the city on an open-top bus, make a visit to a butterfly farm or spend the afternoon on a boat trip on the River Avon. The medieval bridge that spans the Avon greatly contributed to the town's early economic prosperity. It still provides a link between the town and the surrounding countryside.

▼ The River Avon

TAKE IN SOME HISTORY

Shakespeare's Birthplace
See highlight panel opposite

Anne Hathaway's Cottage
See highlight panel overleaf

Harvard House
stratford-upon-avon.co.uk
High Street, CV37 6HB
01789 204507
This ornate timbered house was once the home of Katherine Rogers, mother of clergyman John Harvard (1607–38), who emigrated to Massachusetts in the US shortly before his death. His generous bequests to the newly founded US college at Cambridge led to its being named after him. Harvard University now own the house, which also contains the Neish Collection of Pewter. It's not currently open to the public, but still worth a look from the outside.

Hall's Croft
shakespeare.org.uk
Old Town, CV37 6EP
01789 292107 | Open all year daily, Apr–Oct 10–5, Nov–Mar 11–4
This elegant 17th-century house belonged to Shakespeare's eldest daughter, Susanna, and her husband, the wealthy physician John Hall. It is an impressive building, with many exquisite furnishing and paintings from the period and an exhibition on early medicine. The gardens are pretty and relaxing, and there's also a cafe.

Nash's House & New Place
shakespeare.org.uk
Chapel Street, CV37 6EP
01789 292325 | Open all year daily, Apr–May & Sep–Oct 9–5, Jun–Aug 9–6, Nov–Mar 10–4
Nash's House is the elegant home that Shakespeare's granddaughter lived in with her first husband. It's been preserved and restored in keeping with the period: the ground floor is furnished as it would have been in the late 15th century.

New Place is the site of the house Shakespeare retired to and where he subsequently died in (1616).

10 Famous Cotswolders

- ▶ WWII British Prime Minister Winston Churchill
- ▶ World-famous playwright William Shakespeare
- ▶ *Cider With Rosie* author Laurie Lee
- ▶ Polar explorer Edward Wilson
- ▶ Harry Potter author J K Rowling
- ▶ King Alfred the Great (born in Oxfordshire)
- ▶ Influential poet John Betjeman
- ▶ Prince Charles (lives near Tetbury)
- ▶ Princess Anne (lives near Minchinhampton)
- ▶ Composer Gustav Holst

▶ Shakespeare's Birthplace

shakespeare.org.uk
Henley Street, CV37 6QW | 01789 201 845 | Open all year daily, Jun–Aug
9–6, Apr–May & Sep–Oct 9–5, Nov–Mar 10–4

This is the house where the world's most famous playwright was
born and grew up. Here, you can discover the fascinating story of
Shakespeare's life, and see it brought to life by the costumed
guides. Enjoy the state of the art *Life, Love and Legacy* exhibition,
and see Shakespeare Aloud!'s live performances in the garden.

▶ Anne Hathaway's Cottage

houses.shakespeare.org.uk

Cottage Lane, Shottery, CV37 9HH | 01789 204016 | Open all year daily, Apr–Oct 9–5, Nov–Mar 10–4

Shakespeare's wife once lived in this pretty thatched cottage, and it stayed in the Hathaway family until the 19th century. Much of the original family furniture remains. You can get here by walking along the country lane from Hall's Croft, which might help you avoid the traffic.

VISIT THE MUSEUM
Mary Arden's Farm and the Shakespeare Countryside Museum
houses.shakespeare.org.uk
Wilmcote, CV37 9UN
01789 204016 | Open mid-Mar–early Nov 10–5

The childhood home of Shakespeare's mother is 3 miles north of town. The Shakespeare Countryside Museum surrounds the cottage. It has displays about life and work on a Tudor farm, a working blacksmith's and falconers. Walk here along the towpath of the Stratford-upon-Avon Canal, or take the train one stop beyond Stratford.

MEET THE BUTTERFLIES
Stratford Butterfly Farm
butterflyfarm.co.uk
Tramway Walk, Swan's Nest Lane, CV37 7LS | 01789 299288
Open daily 10–6 (winter 10–dusk)

Hundreds of the world's most spectacular and colourful butterflies populate the lush tropical landscape of the UK's largest live butterfly and insect exhibit, flitting above splashing waterfalls and fish-filled pools. See the strange and fascinating Insect City: a bustling metropolis of ants, stick insects, beetles and other insects. Arachnoland features big spiders, scorpions and other troublesome terrors.

CATCH A PERFORMANCE
Royal Shakespeare Company
See highlight panel overleaf

SEE A LOCAL CHURCH
Holy Trinity Church
stratford-upon-avon.org
Avonside, beside the River Avon, CV37 6BG | 01789 266316
Open Mar–Oct Mon–Sat 9–5, Sun 12.30–5, Apr–Sep Mon–Sat 8.30–6, Sun 12.30–5, Nov–Feb Mon–Sat 9–4, Sun 12.30–5

There's no escaping the Shakespeare industry in Stratford. Yet the church escapes the heaviest crowds of tourists, saved by the fact that it's a short walk away from the town centre. Shakespeare is buried in the chancel. His memorial, commissioned by his widow in 1616, was said to have been his best likeness.

The church itself is outstanding, and would be celebrated even without the Shakespeare connection. Its origins are pre-Norman, but the present building dates from the 13th century and after. It is a large building, full of light, with a central tower crowned by a tall and beautiful spire erected in 1763. The architect G F Bodley deftly restored the church in the 19th century. The organ case he designed sits splendidly above the crossing arch in the centre of the church. The church contains many memorials and other items of interest, and Clopton Chapel is particularly full of these. The early 17th-century tomb of George Carew and his wife Joyce Clopton is one of the chapel's finest monuments. In the chancel, look out for 26 misericords. These date from about 1450, and include some famous examples.

CELEBRATE SHAKESPEARE'S BIRTHDAY

shakespearesbirthday.org.uk
Nearest weekend to April 23
Shakespeare was not born on 23 April. That was, however, the date of his baptism, and therefore the date on which his birthday is celebrated with a weekend of events around the town.

GO TO THE MOVIES

Stratford Picturehouse
picturehouses.co.uk
Windsor Street CV37 6NL
0871 9025741
This modern two-screen cinema shows the latest releases.

BOOK BEAUTY TREATMENTS

Wildmoor Spa & Health Club
wildmoorspa.com
Alcester Road, CV37 9RJ
01789 299666
After a cultural session in Shakespeare's home town, you may feel the need for a bit of pampering. Individual treatments and day sessions are available at this sleek, modern spa and health club, based around an old farmhouse on the edge of town.

PLAY A ROUND

Stratford-on-Avon Golf Club
stratfordgolf.co.uk

Tiddington Road, CV37 7BA
01789 205749

EXPLORE BY BIKE

Capital Sport
capital-sport.co.uk
01296 631671
'Luxury self-guided' cycling holidays in Stratford and the Cotswolds.

EAT AND DRINK

The Arden Hotel ◉◉
theardenhotelstratford.com
Waterside, CV37 6BA
01789 298682
The Arden, just over the road from the Bardolatry going on at the RSC Theatre, has had a megabucks redecoration, which has replaced the hotel's rather dated air with some seriously stylish grand hotel ambience. Portrait photographs of thesps in character line the walls. There's a champagne bar for after-show schmoozing. The elegantly spacious Waterside Brasserie, with its big windows and comfortable bucket chairs, is the hotel's best feature. The cooking draws a graceful arc through the brave new world of the modern British repertoire.

Billesley Manor Hotel ◉◉
pumahotels.co.uk
Billesley, Alcester, B49 6NF
01789 279955
Billesley Manor is a charming mellow-stone Elizabethan mansion, sitting in eleven acres of preened grounds, which also contain a century-

▶ Royal Shakespeare Company

www.rsc.org.uk

Waterside, CV37 6BB | 0844 8001110

The Royal Shakespeare Company (RSC) maintains Stratford's theatrical traditions, presenting both Shakespeare's plays and other works. The principal theatre, the Royal Shakespeare, was designed in cinema-style in the 1930s. Both the Royal Shakespeare and its smaller sister theatre, the Swan, re-opened in early 2011 after being comprehensively redesigned. Venues built to house the company during these works, such as the hexagonal Courtyard Theatre, have now become permanent fixtures. Visit the website to see what's on and when. You can also take a guided tour behind the scenes. To rub shoulders with thespians, visit The Dirty Duck. This 16th-century watering hole near the theatre complex is a favourite with RSC actors.

old topiary garden and fountain. It's the quintessential English country-house setting – all plushly-upholstered comfort, classic oak-panelling in the Stuart Restaurant – and the kitchen sticks to the script, sending out classically-inspired dishes with a nod to modern trends and presentation and a keen eye on seasonal ingredients.

The Legacy Falcon Hotel ◉
legacy-hotels.co.uk
Chapel Street, CV37 6HA
0844 411 9005

The Falcon is a stunning 16th-century property, with a black-and-white timber facade and some good-and-proper lean action going on. It's just not historic if it doesn't look like a lawsuit waiting to happen. The Falcon looks pretty dapper inside these days, with plenty of period detailing, smart fixtures and fittings, and a contemporary finish. The updated old-world charm has been carried through successfully into the restaurant, a richly carpeted room with beams and some exposed-stone walls. The kitchen keeps things unfussy and focused. The Falcon's relative proximity to the RSC theatre makes its pre- and post-theatre menus particularly useful features, so you can fit a meal in around a performance.

Macdonald Alveston Manor ◉
macdonald-hotels.co.uk
Clopton Bridge, CV37 7HP
01789 205478

Happily, historic Alveston Manor – set in primped grounds rich with the scent of closely-mown lawns – hasn't lost all its Tudor-house charm in its hotel makeover. The story that its cedar tree was the backdrop for the debut performance of *A Midsummer Night's Dream* will excite those drawn to the area in pursuit of things Shakespearean. The Manor Restaurant's traditional charms – original oak beams and timbers, mullioned windows and candlelight – don't let the side down. Granted it's an old-school conventional setting, but the kitchen's smartly executed British cooking has a decidedly modern spin.

Mercure Stratford-upon-Avon Shakespeare Hotel ◉
Chapel Street, CV37 6ER
01789 294997

From the outside, this link in the Mercure chain is all you'd hope for given the location. The historic, black-and-white timbered building is a real looker. It's no slouch inside either. A contemporary finish blends nicely with the original features. That goes for Othello's Bar Brasserie, too, with its darkwood furniture, fireplace, smart table settings and splashes of colour from upholstered chairs. Modern British sums up the menu's aspirations, with help from some preparations from farther afield.

Menzies Welcombe Hotel Spa & Golf Club ❀❀

menzieshotels.co.uk
Warwick Road, CV37 0NR
01789 295252

The mid-Victorian Welcombe Hotel is a gabled, quasi-Jacobean confection, with a magnificent oak-panelled lounge and an open fireplace. The corporate-beige dining room's swagged brown drapes frame a view over the hotel's 150-acre grounds. The kitchen pilots a course through the busy waters of modern European cuisine. A bells-and-whistles main course sees a loin of local venison teamed with a vanilla-poached pear, puréed celeriac, baby leeks and chocolate oil. Pear and vanilla having been dispensed with at main-course stage, dessert must mean time for... parsnips? Somewhat bizarrely, the root vegetables turn up in the form of ice cream and crisps to accompany a chocolate tart.

The One Elm

1 Guild Street, CV37 6QZ
01789 404919

Named after the elm tree marking the boundary of Stratford-on-Avon, the One Elm occupies a prime location in the town centre conveniently near the theatre. Opening at 9.30am for coffee and breakfast, there's an informal, almost continental feel about the place, especially in the stylish front lounge area with its wood floor, brightly painted walls, squashy leather sofas and low tables displaying the day's newspapers. Beyond the central, open-to-view kitchen is the more formal dining area. The upstairs seating area has an even grander feel. The menu consists of eclectic modern pub food, while the secluded terrace gives you a feeling of being abroad.

▶ PLACES NEARBY

From Stratford you'll need to head south or risk leaving the Cotswolds. Why would you want to do that? The most obvious things to head for are Bredon Hill (see page 76) – especially if you fancy stretching your legs – and uber-elegant Chipping Campden (see page 96). You could also call in at Hidcote Gardens (see page 135) to see some serious flower power.

▼ Statue of the Jester in Henley Street

St Nicholas' Church, Loxley

Wellesbourne Road, CV35 9JP

Loxley's church is a study in contrasts. It sits on a sloping site in a wildflower-speckled churchyard, but it also has less than pastoral a battlemented tower from the 13th century. The church's origins are far earlier than that. Parts of the building are Saxon, and date from about AD 950. Much of the church was rebuilt in the 18th century. The large windows in the nave, with their clear glass, and many of the internal fixtures and fittings date from this restoration. There are many excellent monuments to the rich wool merchants who poured their wealth into the creation of the building.

St James the Great

Church Road, Snitterfield, CV37 0LG

William Shakespeare's family came from Snitterfield, and his grandfather Richard was a churchwarden. His Uncle Henry had a farm in the village, but had a poor reputation with regard to the church. He was fined for 'dressing inappropriately' and was eventually excommunicated for non-payment of his church tithes.

Much of the church of St James the Great was built during the 13th and 14th centuries. The tower was built in at least two phases, its construction having been interrupted by England's first wave of the bothersome Black Death (1348–9). One of the most interesting features of the church is its 14th-century font. Like others in Warwickshire, the font has carved heads round the base of the bowl. Time has weathered and chipped at these faces, giving their expressions an enigmatic quality. Centuries after they were first carved, they are nevertheless still commanding.

The church has several literary connections. Poet Richard Jago was a curate here in the 18th century, and was buried in a vault in the church in 1781. His poems have perhaps not weathered as well as the faces on the font. They include a long account of the Battle of Edgehill, which took place nearby.

The Old Quaker Meeting House, Ettington

Halford Road (the approach path is hard to find from the road – look for a modest notice board), several hundred yards south of the parish church, CV37 7TH | Usually only open on Sundays, but can be opened on request.

Built between 1681 and 1684, this tiny meeting house – in common with most Quaker meeting houses – is anything but ostentatious. It's a very simple, single-storey building, with an exterior of local stone and a plain slate roof. It's just as modest inside. It stands in a peaceful garden that also serves as a Quaker burial ground.

▶ Stroud & the Five Valleys

Stroud is the sort of place where rainbow trousers don't get a second glance, and people just assume that you can probably juggle – or failing that, at least ride a unicycle across a wire while playing Bach on the violin. Really? Just a backwards somersault then. Stroud, partly because of its size and industrial heritage, doesn't have the instant visual appeal of Painswick or Tetbury. But get to know it, and you'll find a place full of individualism, traditionalism, wholesomeness and resurgent folk culture. It's the sort of place where words like 'organic' are the norm rather than the exception. It's full of independent shops, cafes and galleries, and has the largest farmers' market in the country. It's been only half-jokingly nicknamed the Covent Garden of the Cotswolds. More places should be like Stroud.

The Cotswold Edge runs north–south for around 90 miles, unbroken expect for one large, convoluted dent. The landscape here is the natural place for a settlement, sitting as it does at

▼ Stroud from Selsley Common

the head of five valleys. Stroud became the centre of the wool industry from the 15th century, as cloth supplanted fleece in importance. During the 18th century the valleys bristled with mills, powered by the rivers on the bottoms of the valleys. This is perhaps the one place in the Cotswolds where you can really see Industrialisation of sorts. There were once 150 mills running simultaneously in the Five Valleys, before decline set in as the industry moved away to Yorkshire.

Today Stroud spreads over the Cotswold slopes like a cloth. It has no great beauty, but it is nonetheless a place of independent spirits – and independent shops. This bustling town of considerable interest is centred in the area around the High Street. Close by, you will find the Shambles, the former meat market, and the Tudor Town Hall. The handsome 19th-century Subscription Rooms on nearby George Street are now home to the Tourist Information Centre. The Museum in the Park, situated next to the Stratford Park Leisure Centre, offers an excellent insight into the history of the area. Among other items, it displays a collection of early lawnmowers – Mr Budding, the inventor of the lawnmower, was from this valley.

Southwest of Stroud lie **Selsley Common** and Selsley. Selsley's church is of particular interest – it has stained glass by William Morris, Philip Webb, Dante Gabriel Rossetti, Edward Burne-Jones and Ford Madox Brown. A little farther west, near Stonehouse, you'll find one of the area's pre-industrial legacies. The 13th-century **Frocester Tithe Barn** is one of the finest of its type in England.

To the east of Stroud is hill-hugging **Chalford**. Its houses cling to its steep lanes and line the terraces and shelves of the north slope of the valley. The Chalford Community Store maintains the tradition of door-to-door deliveries from the local shop. Some of the paths are too steep and narrow for any form of modern transport to be practical, and so a woman named Anna and two donkeys, Chester and Teddy, do the rounds. A legacy of the Industrial Revolution, Chalford's houses were built by the clothiers and merchants who made their fortune during the 18th and 19th centuries, and by weavers working first from home and later in the mills that still line the Thames and Severn Canal. Chalford's two churches contain work produced by members of the Arts and Crafts Movement.

There are some good walks to be had along the **Stroudwater Canal**. Once the more successful part of the Thames and Severn Canal system, Stroudwater functioned until 1941, and is now being restored. The Thames and Severn Canal system was one of those great Georgian enterprises that were magnificent in conception but almost redundant by the time of their realisation. The canal system, completed in 1789, was intended to facilitate trade between two rivers that were important commercial waterways. The project was plagued by problems related to the number of locks, the size of the 2.17-mile Sapperton Tunnel, and even a shortage of water – which you'd have thought would be the one thing they'd have plenty of. Other, better canals and the arrival of the railways put paid to it, and the last recorded journey was made in 1911. The two temple-like tunnel portals are visible at Coates and Daneway, where the pubs, built for the boatmen, still function. A stroll along the old canal is recommended, as is a visit to the village of **Sapperton**, the home of Ernest Gimson and the Barnsley brothers, of Arts and Crafts Movement fame.

Just to the north of Chalford is gorgeous little **Bisley** village, with pubs and a church with a dramatic spire. The church-yard contains a unique 'Poor Soul's Light' – a 13th-century structure that contained candles lit during masses for the poor.

Woodchester, south of Stroud, is the site of a Roman villa with a magnificent Orpheus mosaic buried in the churchyard – which, frustratingly, can't be viewed. Woodchester Mansion lies south of Woodchester, on the road to Dursley. The house, abandoned by its builders in the mid 1870s before it could be completed, is a fascinating place to visit. It is preserved in the state of construction at which it was abandoned.

Rodborough Common, just to the southwest of Stroud, links to Minchinhampton Common (see page 148). A good place for walking, the common is also the site of Rodborough Fort, which local dyer George Hawker built as a pleasure-house in 1764. It was rebuilt in Victorian style in 1870.

VISIT THE MUSEUM
Museum in the Park
museuminthepark.org.uk
Stratford Park, Stroud, GL5 4AF
01453 763394 | Open Apr–Sep
Tue–Fri 10–5, Sat–Sun and BH
11–5, Oct–Mar Tue–Fri 10–4,
Sat–Sun 11–4; closed Mon (except
Aug, BH & Good Friday; Aug Mon
10–5)

In his 1897 will, William Cowle included a bequest of £4000 to provide a museum for Stroud. This likeable museum exists thanks to him. Housed on two floors of a Grade II 17th century wool merchant's mansion, it celebrates the rich history of the Stroud area. There are also a small gift shop and a cafe.

LOOK FOR GHOSTS
Woodchester Mansion
woodchestermansion.org.uk
Nympsfield GL10 3TS | 01453
861541 | Opening days are erratic
so check ahead – usually 11–5 (last
entry 4)

Do you spook easily? Woodchester Mansion is a 19th-century Victorian-Gothic masterpiece, mysteriously abandoned mid-construction in 1873 – the most popular theory is simply that the site was so haunted that the workers dropped tools (which can still be seen) and legged it. Hidden in a secluded valley, this Grade I listed building has been saved from dereliction – frozen in time, but never to be completed. The carvings in Woodchester Mansion are among the finest of their kind in the world.

Entrance to the car park is on the B4066 (Stroud–Dursley road) five miles south of Stroud, at a junction with a minor road leading to Nympsfield. Beware – putting the postcode in your satnav won't take you here.

GO TO THE THEATRE
Cotswold Playhouse
cotswoldplayhouse.co.uk
Parliament Street, Stroud, GL5 1LW
01453 760960

TAKE OFF
Cotswold Gliding Club
cotswoldgliding.co.uk
Aston Down Airfield, Cowcombe
Lane, Chalford, GL6 8HR
01285 760415

The Gliding Club offers day courses and trial lessons in motorless glider planes.

SADDLE UP
Bownhill Equestrian Centre
Woodchester | 01453 872144

Set in 300 acres, Bownhill offers lessons, courses and hacking for riders at least one year old. Disabled visitors are welcome.

GO SHOPPING
Stroud Farmer's Market
fresh-n-local.co.uk
Cornhill Market Place, GL5 2HH
Open Sat 9–2

GO WALKING
There's excellent walking to be had around here, with five valleys to chose from, atmospheric woodlands and big views from the hilltops. Laurie Lee's Slad Valley, Sapperton

and the Golden Valley are all great destinations, as are the Jurassic grasslands of Selsley, Minchinhampton Common (see page 148) and Rodborough Common (see page 213). The two commons are close enough to be enjoyed in one walk and offer endless big views into the valleys, though you needn't bother with climbing hills if you don't fancy it.

EAT AND DRINK

Bear of Rodborough Hotel
cotswold-inns-hotels.co.uk
Rodborough Common, GL5 5DE
01453 878522
This 17th-century former alehouse takes its name from the bear-baiting that used to take place near by. It's located amidst the rolling, windswept grassland of Rodborough Common where cattle roam free in the summer months. The area offers far-reaching views of the Stroud Valley and Severn Vale. Head to the bar for a pint of Wickwar before seeking a seat on the York stone terrace or in the gardens, with their walled croquet lawn.

The Bell at Sapperton
bellsapperton.co.uk
GL7 6LE | 01285 760298
Built of mellow Cotswold stone and set in an idyllic village close to Cirencester Park, the 300-year-old Bell attracts local walkers, families, drinkers, diners and even horse riders. On warmer days, the secluded rear courtyard and landscaped front garden are lovely venues for alfresco dining. The Bell attracts discerning folk for its Hook Norton and Stroud ales, and its innovative, homemade pub food, served throughout four cosy dining areas, each with their own individual character.

The Cafe Above, Walkers the Bakers
1 Threadneedle Street, Stroud, GL5 1AF | 01453 762441
Just a few steps from the High Street, the Cafe Above is a typical Stroud establishment – independent, family-run and offering very tasty products. The cafe serves drinks all day. As well as light snacks, homemade meals are available.

The Ram Inn
theraminn.com
South Woodchester, GL5 5EL
01453 873329
Originally a farm, this 17th-century Cotswold-stone inn became an alehouse in 1811 and is still full of historic little gems. In winter seek the warmth of the huge fireplace, but in other seasons head for the terrace and admire the splendid views. Children have their own choices, and gluten-free diets are catered for.

Stroud Brewery
stroudbrewery.co.uk
Unit 11, Pheonix Works (off Hope Mill Lane), London Road, Thrupp, GL5 2BU | 01453 887122
The popular Stroud Brewery's distinctive, award-winning beverages are excellent value,

and the process of their manufacture is diligently ethical and eco-minded. The beer-making waste gets eaten by lucky local pigs and cows. Very much in accordance with the Stroud ethos, the Brewery also hosts workshops on wild brewing, willow basket weaving and the like. They're developing a cult following.

Woodruffs Organic Cafe

woodruffsorganiccafe.co.uk
High Street, Stroud, GL5 1AJ
01453 759195

Organic, locally sourced and seasonal food makes up the menu at this friendly cafe. Their fare is mainly vegetarian (and they'll cater for more specific diets, too), but with several fish dishes on offer, the selection of meals is very enticing indeed – and it all looks so healthy. Ruddy delicious cakes, too.

The Woolpack Inn

thewoolpackinn-slad.com
Slad Road, Slad, GL6 7QA
01452 813429

Close to the Cotswold Way in beautiful Slad Valley, this friendly local is a favourite with walkers (muddy boots are not frowned upon). Laurie Lee fame used to be a regular at The Woolpack, too. Although ale aficionados make a detour here to sample the Uley Pigs Ear, the food is of equal importance. Meat is sourced from within a 14-mile radius, while fruit and vegetables come from Cirencester or locals' gardens.

▶ **PLACES NEARBY**

Bisley

Perched at the top of a wooded valley, delightful Bisley is an undiscovered Cotswold secret, despite the fact trash-novel writer Jilly Cooper lives here. Queen Elizabeth I once owned a house here too. As with most of these sorts of places there's not much to actually do, other than amble about the historic village, go 'ooh' a bit then visit the pub for lunch. But there aren't many better places to do that than here.

Slad

Made famous by Laurie Lee, there's little more to Slad than his much loved Woolshed pub and perhaps an over-the-wall look at the houses Lee was brought up in and the one he lived in as an adult. As the area seems to be under constant threat from developers it's best to visit it now while it's still strikingly similar to the way Lee lovingly described it in *Cider With Rosie*.

Sheepscombe

No name could be more Cotswolds than Sheepscombe, alluding to the region's famous industry and landscape in one go. On the edge of the Slad Valley hidden amongst beach woods you won't see a single tourist here. Again it's pretty enough for a short visit without there being a great deal to do.

▶ Sudeley Castle

Sudeleycastle.co.uk

Near Winchcombe, GL54 5JD | 01242 602308

Open 17 Mar–3 Nov, daily 10.30–5

Despite a castle not being a very Cotswolds type of thing – the region's not really a place of grand gestures and aggressive buildings, tending more towards the cosy and twee – you may find this to be one of highlights of the Cotswolds. Set in deeply wooded countryside and beautifully sited beneath the Cotswold escarpment, Sudeley Castle incorporates the remains of a magnificent medieval mansion. It also has some spectacularly colourful ornamental gardens.

During its Tudor and Elizabethan heyday, Sudeley was a place of eminence. Henry VIII is believed to have visited with Anne Boleyn in 1532. His last wife, Catherine Parr, eventually married the ambitious Sir Thomas Seymour, Lord High Admiral of England, in 1547 and moved to Sudeley. She died here after childbirth, and was buried in the chapel. Strangely this then seemed to be forgotten about, as her coffin was 'discovered' there again in 1782, and opened – souvenirs including locks of her hair and a tooth are still on display today.

The ill-fated Lady Jane Grey was among the large retinue that the Queen Dowager brought to Sudeley. Jane was later imprisoned in the Tower of London and beheaded, and still later portrayed by Helena Bonham-Carter in the inevitable biopic, opposite that fetching chap who played Westley in *The Princess Bride*. Win some, lose some. Queen Elizabeth I was to visit the castle on three occasions.

King Charles I found refuge here during the Civil War, when his nephew Prince Rupert established his headquarters at the Castle. It was damaged during a battle, and on Cromwell's post-war orders was left neglected and derelict for nearly 200 years. King George III was among those sightseers who came to admire the castle's romantic ruins.

After this long period of neglect, brothers William and John Dent, from a rich family of Worcester glovers, bought Sudeley in 1830. After their deaths their cousin, John Coucher Dent inherited the castle. His wife Emma devoted her life to the enrichment of Sudeley. The original mellow stone of the banqueting hall, the tithe barn and the dungeon tower remained; the rest of the house was restored with the help of architect Sir George Gilbert Scott, who designed the beautiful tomb of Catherine Parr – over three hundred years after her death – in the church.

Conducted tours of the still privately-owned castle reveal a remarkable collection of furniture and paintings. All are displayed with a delightful studied nonchalance. Visitors enter the castle apartments through the Rent Room, where an agent would have once collected the tenants' payments, or the North Hall, formerly the guardroom. This room displays a fine portrait of Charles I by Van Dyck. *Allegory of the Tudor Succession*, a remarkable painting by Lucas de Heere, hangs in the Queen's Bedroom. Blatantly political, it shows Queen Elizabeth I surrounded by the goddesses of peace and plenty. In marked contrast, her predecessor Queen Mary is depicted with her husband, Philip II of Spain, and Mars, the Roman god of war.

Among Sudeley's relics of Queen Catherine Parr are her prayer book and a love letter to Seymour, accepting his proposal of marriage. Civil War armour discovered during excavations and a fascinating letter from Charles I to the freeholders of Cornwall are also displayed.

Sudeley Castle's gardens were laid out during the 19th-century restoration. The Queen's Garden is famous for its rose collection; and the fine terraces offer spectacular views over the ancient trees in the Home Park. There are exhibitions, a gift shop and a plant centre.

▶ PLACES NEARBY

Inviting Winchcombe (see page 233) is the perfect place to base yourself if your visit is any kind of hiking holiday. Even if it's not, consider a hike up Cleeve Common (see page 236) and/or Belas Knap (see page 239).

▶ **Sudeley Castle**
See highlight panel on page 217

▶ **Tetbury**

Tetbury should be more famous, but it's still not really on the tourist buses' radars. It's an unreasonably handsome, small, tranquil, charming market town set among the broader slopes of the southern Cotswolds. By the 18th century, Tetbury was one of the most important cloth market towns of south Gloucestershire. Its main streets radiate from the still-impressive market square. The square is dominated by the 17th-century Town Hall or Market House which rests on three rows of tubby Etruscan pillars – though it was reduced by one storey in 1817. The excellently named Snooty Fox Hotel (the artist formerly known as the White Hart), also on the square, was rebuilt by the designer of Westonbirt House with the aim of providing for attendees of the Beaufort Hunt.

The road next to the Snooty Fox leads to Chipping Steps and the site of the old livestock market. The old market is surrounded by some handsome 18th- and 19th-century houses, and near the Old Priory. The road continues down to Millennium Green – the scene of the annual Woolsack Races on Spring Bank Holiday Monday – at the foot of Gumstock Hill.

South from the square, along Church Street, you'll find the magnificent St Mary the Virgin Church, which was rebuilt in Gothic style in the late 18th century. The spire is 186 feet tall. The interior, lit by Perpendicular-style windows, is coolly elegant, with rows of box pews presided over by panelled galleries and two splendid chandeliers. The church is the home of the Tetbury Heritage Display.

At the western end of Long Street, which runs west out of Market Square, Tetbury has an unusual museum. The Tetbury Heritage Centre is housed in the cells of the Old Court House. It displays police memorabilia, such as uniforms on loan from Gloucestershire Constabulary.

GET OUTDOORS
Westonbirt Arboretum
See highlight panel overleaf

TAKE OFF
Ballooning In The Cotswolds
ballooninginthecotswolds.co.uk
Tetbury | 01453 753221
See page 72

EAT AND DRINK
Calcot Manor ◉◉
calcotmanor.co.uk
Calcot, GL8 8YJ | 01666 890391
Set in 220 acres of prime Cotswolds countryside, Calcot Manor left behind its seven-centuries-old origins as a lowly farmhouse long ago. Nowadays

Westonbirt Arboretum

forestry.gov.uk

Westonbirt, GL8 8QS | 01666 880220 | Open all year daily, Apr–Aug Mon–Fri 9–8, Sat–Sun 8–8, Sep–Mar Mon–Fri 9–6, Sat–Sun 8–6; park will always close at dusk if earlier than published closing time

The Victorian-era National Arboretum boasts more than 16,000 trees (of around 2,500 species) from Britain, China, North America, Japan, Chile and other temperate climates. Thriving specimens populate the Arboretum's 600 acres and line much of its 17 miles of footpaths. The Arboretum dates to 1829, and was designed by Lewis Vulliamy. Vulliamy also designed the Snooty Fox in Tetbury and Dorchester House (demolished to make way for the hotel of the same name) in London. It's especially special in autumn of course, a season innagurated by the late-summer Treefest in August, but it's wondrous at any time of year. The magical Enchanted Christmas illuminated trails enliven the lead up to Christmas.

it's a boutique-style country hotel, offering luxurious rooms and state-of-the-art spa for style-conscious sybarites. The Conservatory Restaurant looks to Mediterranean for inspiration, while local suppliers furnish the building blocks for its skilfully-wrought modern output. The wide-ranging menu has all bases covered.

Gumstool Inn

calcotmanor.co.uk

Calcot Manor, near Tetbury, GL8 8YJ | 01666 890391

This stylish country inn, a stone farmhouse built by Cistercian monks in the 14th century, is now a popular free house. Part of Calcot Manor Hotel, the buzzy and comfortable Gumstool Inn has a real country-pub atmosphere. It stocks a good selection of ales, such as Butcombe Bitter, and local ciders, including Ashton Press. Gumstool offers an excellent choice of wines by the glass or bottle. The food here is top-notch gastro-pub fare, and there is a pronounced use of local suppliers. Winter evenings are warmed with cosy log fires. Booking is recommended.

Hare & Hounds Hotel ◎◎

cotswold-inns-hotels.co.uk

Westonbirt, GL8 8QL

01666 881000

The handsome Cotswold-stone house cuts quite a dash as a country-house hotel, and the Beaufort Restaurant really puts it on the map. The vaulted hammer-beamed ceiling and stone mullioned windows strike an elegant pose, while the well-designed chairs and smartly laid tables suggest this place is not stuck in the past. The modern British dishes show adroit technical skills and impressive flavours.

The Priory Inn

theprioryinn.co.uk

London Road, Tetbury, GL8 8JJ

01666 502251

Parts of this thriving gastro-pub and hotel date from the 16th century, when it was a stable block and grooms' cottages for the neighbouring priory. The beers are from microbreweries such as Wickwar. White wine and sparkling rosé spring from a vineyard at Malmesbury, while fresh ingredients come from sources based strictly within 30 miles of the inn. A happy coincidence of extraordinary suppliers ensures that visitors can confidently settle into the traditional, bare-boarded, beamed bar or the more contemporary lounge and restaurant in anticipation of starters like smoked Bibury trout fishcake and mains like seared West Country venison haunch with blackberry and sage jus. Children have the opportunity to create personalised wood-fired pizzas. The May Day Bank Holiday beer and cider festival is rightly popular.

Snooty Fox Hotel

snooty-fox.co.uk
Market Place, Tetbury, GL8 8DD
01666 502436

Occupying a prime spot in the heart of Tetbury, this 16th-century coaching inn and hotel retains many of its original features. Sit in a leather armchair in front of the log fire with a pint of Wadworth 6X and order from the extensive bar menu – eggs Benedict, or a bowl of mussels, perhaps. Alternatively, head for the restaurant.

The Trouble House

troublehousetetbury.co.uk
Cirencester Road, Tetbury, GL8 8SG
01666 502206

Named after a series of unfortunate events at the pub – namely agricultural riots, two suicides and a disastrous fire – this historic inn stands beside the stretch of the A433 linking Tetbury and Cirencester. It's a destination dining pub, with a rustic-chic interior that includes scrubbed tables, wooden floors, pastel-painted walls and three warming log fires. Modern British cooking draws restaurant tourists from across the Cotswolds – so booking is advisable. Nowadays, the house is largely trouble-free.

10 places to sleep

- ▶ **Barnsley House,**
  Barnsley,
  barnsleyhouse.com
- ▶ **Bibury Court Hotel,**
  Bibury,
  biburycourt.com
- ▶ **Calcot Manor Hotel,**
  near Tetbury,
  calcotmanor.co.uk
- ▶ **Cowley Manor Hotel,**
  near Cheltenham,
  cowleymanor.com
- ▶ **Hare And Hounds Hotel,**
  Westonbirt,
  cotswold-inns-hotels.co.uk
- ▶ **The Lords of the Manor,**
  Upper Slaughter,
  lordsofthemanor.com
- ▶ **The Lygon Arms,**
  Broadway,
  thelygonarms.co.uk
- ▶ **St Anne's B&B,**
  Painswick,
  st-annes-painswick.co.uk
- ▶ **The Wild Thyme,**
  Chipping Norton,
  wildthymerestaurant.co.uk
- ▶ **Wyck Hill House Hotel,**
  Stow-on-the-Wold,
  wyckhillhousehotel.co.uk

▶ PLACES NEARBY

Chavenage (see page 86), just over a mile to the northwest of Tetbury, is a delightful and possibly very haunted manor with a fine collection of 17th-century tapestries. The chapel, with its early Norman font, is close by. **Rodborough Manor**, about 4 miles to the northeast, is an impressive example of the Arts and Crafts style. Three miles southwest of Tetbury is the magnificent Westonbirt Arboretum (see page 220), managed by the Forestry Commission.

▶ Tewkesbury

Tewkesbury is one of those Cotswolds names that just rolls pleasurably off the tongue, allowing the mouth a full but enjoyable workout as it collects the full gamut of enunciations. Go on, treat yourself, say it slowly a few times...

And we're back. Considering the musicality of its name, it's unsurprising that Tewkesbury has inspired more than its fair share of writers. But its larger historical significance is largely governed by its location on the banks of the rivers Severn and Avon, which were instrumental in the 16th-century cloth and mustard trades, and the later flour trade. Its importance depended, too, on its medieval Benedictine monastery, of which only the magnificent church remains. Robert Fitzhamon, one of William the Conqueror's most powerful barons, built the monastery between 1102 and 1121. He used the Severn to import stone from Normandy for its construction. After his death, the 'Honour of Tewkesbury', as the patronage came to be known, passed to an illegitimate son of Henry I, and then to the de Clare family. The abbey became one of the most powerful in the kingdom, building many fine tithe barns in the process – some of these survive, for example at Stanway (see page 193). The abbey used these to store the fluffy booty from its large ranges of sheep grazing land.

▼ Cottages in Mill Street

Other Norman lords and their dynasties were connected with the abbey, and many of those lords are buried here. The 14th century brought two major changes to the Norman structure. First, first vaulted roofs were inserted. Second, Lady Eleanor le Despenser, widow of one of England's most influential lords, transformed sections of the building. In part she worked to create a shrine to her husband and her family – like a really expensive and permanent Late Medieval scrapbook. Her ancestor Robert Fitzhamon, her husband Hugh le Despenser and her son and his wife are buried in the chapels around the choir. Many other hugely important participants in the wars, feuds and general politics of the Middle Ages are buried here. Among these is Edward of Westminster, Prince of Wales. He was the only son of Henry VI, and only heir apparent to the English throne to ever die in battle (right here in Tewkesbury). Some of the finest medieval stained glass in England glitters down on all this. Much of it dates from Eleanor's time.

The abbey was dissolved in 1539, but Tewkesbury's citizens bought the church for a total of £483. Because of its location – close to two rivers that tend to flood, and with the abbey lands at its back – the town, unable to expand, folded in on itself. Throughout the 17th and 18th centuries the townspeople built densley around narrow alleyways off the main streets. Surviving alleys such as Machine Court, Fish Alley and Fryzier Alley run off main streets like Barton Street, Church Street and High Street. Tewkesbury's collection of half-timbered and brick houses presents one of the finest historical ensembles in the country.

The heritage and tourist information centre, Out of the Hat, is an ideal place to start a visit to the city. The Abbey Church of St Mary dominates the town with its great 148-foot-square Norman tower. One of the most striking interior features is the set of 14 Norman pillars that support the 14th-century roof. The choir is illuminated by 14th-century stained-glass windows, while six chapels containing monuments to the wealthy families that have influenced both the church and the town radiate around it. The west front exterior is notable for its dramatic Norman arch.

There is a lot to enjoy in the town. In dry weather a circular walk should include a stroll across the Ham to the river. The Ham is not a vast porky plane, but an enormous meadow that separates the Mill Avon from the Severn. Perhaps skip it if you're visiting in winter – the Ham invariably floods. The handsome Bell Hotel is opposite the church. From here Mill Street leads you down to the abbey mill. It's called Abel

Fletcher's Mill because it is thought to have played a role in Dinah Craik's 1856 novel, *John Halifax, Gentleman*. Much of the novel is set in the fictional town of Norton Bury, which is modelled on Tewkesbury. From here you can either walk along St Mary's Road, with its attractive timbered cottages, or cross the Avon and strike out across the Severn Ham. Every year the grass of the Ham, which is owned by the town, is cut and auctioned off according to a centuries-old tradition.

At the Severn, turn right to walk along the weir, and then return across the meadow this side of the flour mills. You can cross the old mill bridge and then walk along the Avon. At King John's Bridge, recross the river. Then turn right into the High Street and walk to St Michael's Tower. The tower is built on the site of the medieval High Cross that the Puritans razed in 1650. On your left, Barton Street will take you to the fascinating Tewkesbury Museum. Located in a 17th-century building, the museum features a model of the 1417 Battle of Tewkesbury (see page 39, *The Cotswolds at War*). Many of the Lancastrian troops defeated in the battle sought sanctuary in the church, but they were slain nonetheless. That happens so often you almost wonder why they bothered trying it. 'Bloody Meadow', as the battlefield came to be known, is south of the church, off Lincoln Green Lane. The 'Battlefield Trail' will get you there and show you around.

▼ River Avon

Church Street, to your right, takes you past the distinctive Royal Hop Pole Hotel, which famously featured in Charles Dickens' picaresque *Pickwick Papers*. Beyond the hotel is a row of restored 15th-century cottages. These were built by medieval merchants. One, known as the Merchant's House, is presented as it would have looked in its heyday. Another, the John Moore Countryside Museum, takes its name from the local writer. Moore's stories were based on Tewkesbury and the countryside and villages to the northeast, around nearby Bredon.

On the right, an alleyway leads down to the Old Baptist Chapel and Court. Although the building dates back to the 15th century, it became a chapel only in the 17th century.

Tewkesbury has a number of old and interesting inns. The previously-mentioned Royal Hop; the Tudor House in the High Street, built in 1540 by the Pilgrim Fathers; Ye Olde Black Bear, near the junction with Mythe Road and High Street, which possibly dates back to 1308; and The Ancient Grudge, which takes its name from the Wars of the Roses.

Tewkesbury has yet more literary associations. Barbara Cartland (1901–2000) had links with the town, and the family monument is to be found in the churchyard. The poet John Milton played the organ that now sits in the abbey church when it was located at Hampton Court. Daniel Defoe's observations on the town are recorded in his *A Tour Through the Whole Island of Great Britain*, published 1724–26. He called Tewkesbury 'a large and very populous town situated upon the River Avon', famous 'for a great manufacture of stockings'. Seventy years later the essayist William Hazlitt, walking from Shropshire to Somerset, recorded how he spent a night in a Tewkesbury inn reading Saint Pierre's *Paul and Virginia*.

▼ Tewkesbury Abbey

TAKE IN SOME HISTORY
Tewkesbury Abbey
tewkesburyabbey.org.uk
Church Street, the A38
Gloucester road, GL20 5RZ
01684 850959 | Open Mon–Tue,
Thu, Sat 8.30–5.30, Wed, Fri
7.30–5.30, Sun 7.30–6
With its enormous and imposing central tower, Tewkesbury Abbey is a Norman church built on a cathedral scale. The sheer size of the building is further emphasised by the huge

arch that entirely makes up the west end, which rises to the full height of the nave. The look and feel of grandeur is continued inside, where giant pillars soar up to the roof.

VISIT THE MUSEUMS

The John Moore Countryside Museum

johnmooremuseum.org
41 Church Street, GL20 5SN
01684 297174 | Open Apr–Oct Tue–Sat 10–1 and 2–5; open most Sat rest of year

Established in 1980 in memory of writer and naturalist John Moore, the Countryside Museum is located in a cottage in a row of historic timber-framed buildings. It's home to an extensive Natural History collection that features specimens of the mammals and birds native to the surrounding countryside, woodlands and wetlands of the Cotswolds.

The Merchant's House

johnmooremuseum.org
45 Church Street | 01684 297174
Open Apr–Oct Tue–Sat 10–1 and 2–5; open most Sat rest of year

Just a few doors down from the John Moore Countryside Museum is the Merchant's House, a two storey building which has been beautifully restored by the same owners and furnished to show the construction of a 15th century shop and dwelling. Insightful stuff.

Out of the Hat

Church Street, GL20 5AB
01684 855040 | Open Apr–end Oct, Mon, Wed, Sat 10–4, Nov–end Mar Mon, Tue, Fri, Sat 10–4

This meticulously restored 17th century building was once a hat shop. Nowadays it's a heritage centre. A wander through this charming building with interactive and portable guides moves though Tewkesbury's history, from its initial settlement to the Wars of the Roses, the Civil War, the Industrial Revolution and the present day.

Tewkesbury Museum

tewkesburymuseum.org
64 Barton Street, GL20 5PX
01684 292901 | Open Apr–end Aug Tue–Fri 1–4, Sat 11–4, Sep–Dec Tue–Fri 12–3, Sat 11–3, Jan–Mar Sat 11–3

Owned by a charitable trust, the Museum displays historical objects that illustrate the history of Tewkesbury and surrounding villages from pre-history to the present day. There are examples of stone, metalwork, pottery and coins from the Neolithic, Medieval and Roman Periods, and exhibits on the 1471 Battle of Tewkesbury, a unique model fairground (with over 100 figures) and on Tewkesbury's very own Polar explorer, Raymond Priestly, who travelled to the Antarctic with both Ernest Shackleton and Robert Scott.

GET ON THE WATER
Croft Farm Waterpark
croftfarmleisure.co.uk
Bredons Hardwick, Tewkesbury,
GL20 7EE | 01684 772321
Croft Farm is a windsurfing and
sailing centre. Kayaking,
canoeing and even husky sled
rides are also available.

GO TO THE THEATRE
Roses Theatre
rosestheatre.org
Sun Street, GL20 5NX
01684 295074

GO SHOPPING
Toff Milway
toffmilway.co.uk
Conderton, near Tewkesbury, GL20
7PP | 01386 725387
A wide range of homemade
functional and artistic pottery,
all made by the curiously-
named, but obviously prolific
and hard-working, Toff.

PLAY A ROUND
Hilton Puckrup Hall
hilton.com
Puckrup, GL20 6EL | 01684 271591
Open all week
Set in 140 acres of undulating
parkland, Puckrup Hall is one
of the county's finest courses.
Strong and testing with
relatively modest yardage, it
demands excellent course
management and accurate
striking, with a layout that

manages to entertain golfers
of all abilities.

EAT AND DRINK
The Beckford Inn
thebeckford.com
Cheltenham Road, Beckford,
GL20 7AN | 01386 881532
This traditional coaching inn
provides a real family welcome.
Smartly refurbished, it has a
roaring fire in the cosy bar on
colder days. On warmer days,
check out its delightful gardens.
The food is top-quality made
from fresh local and home-
grown produce.

The Fleet At Twyning
thefleetattwyning.co.uk
Twyning, near Tewkesbury,
GL20 6FL | 01684 274020
With a highly enviable setting
on the banks of the River Avon,
this popular pub offers a range
of food from light snacks to
good-value three-course meals,
as well as a wide selection of
cheeses. The inside has a cosy
atmosphere with a fireplace.
There's also a large, inviting,
south-facing patio.

▶ **PLACES NEARBY**
Deerhurst (see page 115), to
the south, has a fine Saxon
parish church. Classy
Cheltenham (see page 88)
would be the other obvious next
port of call.

▶ Thornbury
Thornbury, an attractive market town just north of Bristol, is
known for its Tudor castle. The castle was built in 1510 by the
extravagantly titled Edward Stafford, 3rd Duke of Buckingham

and Lord High Constable of England. After the Duke was executed on charges of treason, Henry VIII appropriated Thornbury Castle. In 1535 he stayed here with Anne Boleyn here. Queen Mary I also spent time here during her teens. She returned the castle to the Staffords, but after the Civil War it fell to ruin. It remained disused until 1824, when it became the residence of the Howard family. Now a luxury hotel, it is particularly noted for its handsome brick double chimney and the fine tracery of its oriel windows.

The Church of St Mary the Virgin has a fine medieval tower, which apparently sways six inches when the peal of eight bells inside it rings. Inside the church is an unusual medieval stone pulpit. A cottage on Chapel Street houses the Thornbury and District Museum, which has exhibits on local life and heritage. The museum hosts events and organises guided walks. A way-marked heritage trail starts at the town hall in the High Street.

PLAY A ROUND
Thornbury Golf Centre
thornburygc.co.uk
Bristol Road, BS35 3XL
01454 281144
These two 18-hole pay-and-play courses, designed by Hawtree, are set in undulating terrain with views towards the Severn estuary. The Low 18 is a par 3 with holes ranging from 80 to 207 yards, and is ideal for beginners. The High course puts the more experienced golfer to to test. There's also an excellent 25-bay floodlit driving range.

EAT AND DRINK
Thornbury Castle ◉◉
thornburycastle.co.uk
Castle Street, BS35 1HH
01454 281182
This is the only English Tudor castle now run as a hotel. Once inside, everything is predictably and pleasingly castley. There are arrow-slit windows, roaring log fires, oak panelled walls, suits of armour and tapestries – but medieval hog-roast banquets are no longer on the menu. The kitchen takes a rather more contemporary, country-house view of things, deploying well-sourced local ingredients – including herbs and vegetables from the garden and wines from the castle's own vineyard – in creative combinations. Foie gras parfait with apple crumble, cider reduction and wild sorrel opens things on a luxurious footing; next comes a three-way serving of Middle White pork, comprising shoulder, belly and loin served with baby vegetables, creamed potato and rich braising juices. Finally, apple tarte Tatin is matched with blackberry bubbles and decadent clotted cream ice cream.

Ronnie's of Thornbury ⊛⊛

ronnies-restaurant.co.uk
11 St Mary Street, BS35 2AB
01454 411137

Hidden away in an unlikely location in the town's shopping precinct, Ronnie's is popular with locals. The vibe is easygoing whether you pop in for brunch or dinner. The modern European cooking style keeps things local, seasonal and to the point. The 17th-century building wears its contemporary look well. Paintings and photos by West Country artists perk up the classic stone walls, beamed ceilings, wooden floors and neutral hues. Kick start the day with coffee and eggs Benedict, or round it off with an intelligent, precisely cooked dinner such as cassoulet with confit duck and a fashionable quail's Scotch egg, followed by roasted pork loin matched with a pork and apricot pie, butternut squash, caramelised apple and pork crackling. For pudding, there may be almond sponge with ginger and rhubarb pannacotta, or go for a savoury finish with the splendid array of English artisanal cheeses.

The Anchor Inn

anchor-inn-oldbury.co.uk
Church Road, Oldbury-on-Severn,
BS35 1QA | 01454 413331

Originally a mill house, parts of this stone pub date back to 1540. The Good Pub Guide awarded it Value Pub of the Year. Plenty of traditional English dishes are served in a friendly atmosphere. The lounge has cushioned window seats. Outside, a pretty stream flows by the large garden.

▶ PLACES NEARBY

Thornbury finds itself a bit cut off from its Cotswolds play–friends by the pesky M5, but the Sodburys (see page 189), to the southeast, aren't really all that far off. Bristol's to the south.

▶ Uley

Uley is a large and pretty village that became prosperous due to the wool dyeing trade. There is still a functioning brewery, and a fine pub – the Old Crown. Uley's 18th-century houses scuttle down the hillside into a deep valley. The long, flat-topped hill of Uley Bury overlooks the town. This flat 32-acre plateau, surrounded by steep drop-offs of nearly 330-foot (100m), made a spectacular site for a hill-fort, and Iron Age Cotswoldians took advantage of it. The bury is worth a visit. It offers magnificent views down the escarpment, out across the Severn Vale and over the perky outlier hills of Cam Long Down (which local legend has it were built by the Devil) and Downham Hill (known locally as 'Smallpox Hill', because it was once the site of an isolation facility for disease victims). The boundaries of Uley Bury's 30-acre, multi-vallate fort are easy to detect, and date from around 300 BC. The site has never been excavated, though visitors have found Roman coins here.

North of Uley, towards Frocester Hill, you'll find Hetty Pegler's Tump. The unusual name comes from the 17th-century landowner's wife. This 180-foot Neolithic barrow, surrounded by a stone wall, has a long central chamber. This can be entered, albeit with some discomfort; it may be wise to take a torch.

Nearby, slightly to the north, is Coaley Peak. This ideal picnic site has more cracking views across the Vale and down the escarpment. The Nympsfield Long Barrow is also on Coaley Peak. This chambered tomb dates to the Neolithic period, around 2500 BC. An excavation here in 1862 uncovered the remains of at least 13 bodies, including the skeleton of a child in a stone cist or coffin, as well as flint arrowheads and pottery. The internal chambers were constructed out of oolitic limestone that was probably quarried nearby. The long barrow has long been associated with legends and stories, including a rumor that it once served as a refuge for lepers.

East of Uley, within striking distance by foot, is Owlpen Manor. This beautifully situated and very picturesque 15th-century manor house was restored in the 1920s, and now displays a good collection of Arts and Crafts furniture. Close by are a 19th-century church and an 18th-century mill. About a mile east of Owlpen is Matara, a tranquil garden at Kingscote. Eastern and Western ideas of garden design blend here, producing a very restful result.

▼ Hetty Pegler's Tump

TAKE IN SOME HISTORY
Owlpen Manor
owlpen.com
Uley, Gloucestershire, GL11 5BZ
01453 860261

This Tudor manor house
(1450–1616) stands in a formal
garden of magnificent yews. It
feels deliciously hidden-away in
Owlpen, a hamlet of Cotswold
cottages surrounded by and
secluded in a dramatic, curvy
landscape. The house itself,
which was left relatively
undisturbed for hundreds of
years until the Arts and Crafts
Movements started careful
restoration, is strikingly
handsome. Some of Owlpen's
cottages are holiday homes,
available for rent.

GO ROUND THE GARDENS
Matara Gardens of Wellbeing
matara.co.uk
Kingscote Park, Kingscote, GL8 8YA
01453 861050 | Open May–Sep,
Sun–Thu 1–5 (may be closed for
private events)

In 28 acres of glorious
Cotswolds parkland, Matara
Gardens of Wellbeing is built on
earth-friendly principles. There
are hundreds of trees, including
oaks, beeches, apple trees,
rowans and groves of
magnolias. Land is set aside for
wildlife, and the planting
choices encourage butterflies
and bees. The cafe's food is
fresh, seasonal, local, organic,
from sustainable sources and
free from animal cruelty
whenever possible.

GO BACK IN TIME
Uley Long Barrow
(Hetty Pegler's Tump)
english-heritage.org.uk
0870 3331181 | Open at any
reasonable time (torch required
for interior)

This 180-foot long Neolithic
long barrow is popularly known
as Hetty Pegler's Tump, which
sounds very *Carry On*. The
mound, surrounded by a wall, is
about 85 feet wide. It contains a
stone central passage and three
burial chambers. The tump
recently re-opened after being
closed for the duration of a
two-year programme of
structural repairs. Take a torch.

▶ Whittington Court
hha.org.uk
Whittington, GL54 4HF | 01242 820556 | Contact for opening times

Whittington Court stands on the western edge of the
Cotswolds, east of Cheltenham. The moat that surrounded the
property still runs along two sides of the south garden.
Whittington Church, probably once the court's private chapel,
stands close by. It contains family memorials, including a brass
to Richard Cotton (d.1556), for whom the house was built.

The original plan was E-shaped, but during the court's
history the porch was moved to the eastern end of the great
hall. The present cross wing was rebuilt in the 17th century.

Although Whittington Court seems to be a house built in the 16th and 17th centuries, its origins are much earlier. Probably named Witetune in Anglo-Saxon times, the manor of Whittington belonged to the de Crupe family in the Middle Ages. The tombs of three members of the family lie in the 12th-century church. Later the Despenser family, who were Earls of Gloucester, owned Whittington. After the death of the great Earl of Warwick, his widow, Anne, was persuaded to transfer Whittington to King Henry VII.

In 1545 the manor came into the hands of the Cotton family. It was John Cotton who had the privilege of entertaining Queen Elizabeth at Whittington during a progress she made through Gloucestershire in 1592. Records state that she 'dyned at Mr Coton's at Whytinton'. The manor later passed to Ann Cotton, who was married to Sir John Denham, a courtier, poet and dilettante architect who, at the Restoration, was given the post of Surveyor-General of the King's Works. It is likely that Denham brought his taste to bear in that period, adding some of the classical features to the house. The Grand Staircase has an original 17th-century dog gate on the first half-landing. This prevented dogs from going into the bedrooms.

▶ **PLACES NEARBY**
Cheltenham (see page 88), is to the west. Little **Andoversford** is to the east.

▶ Winchcombe

Winchcombe was once the capital of the Anglo-Saxon kingdom of Mercia, but nowadays it has an equally prestigious, if unofficial, title: capital of walking in the Cotswolds. The Cotswold, Warden's, Windrush and Gloucestershire Ways all call into town, as does the newer, 42-mile Winchcombe Way. Needless to say there are lots of excellent short walks available in the hills and valleys nearby.

Winchcombe is a town with a whole lot of history. As well as being a Saxon capital, it's near an ancient Salt Way trading route. Nearby Salter's Lane and Salter's Hill reflect this. Winchcombe was also home to an important abbey during the Middle Ages. The abbey was popular with pilgrims, who came to worship at the burial place of the martyred Prince Kenelm. Dissolved in 1539, all that remains of the complex is one side of the wall of the abbey terrace and the abbey church, now Winchcombe parish church. The handsome church, built between 1465 and 1468, owes its present form to wealthy local woolmen. The 40 or so gargoyles on the exterior, the Winchcombe Worthies, are said to represent really unpopular monks. They served as a contemporary sign of dissatisfaction with the abbey, and many are still very amusing today. The stone coffin inside the church is said to have once contained St Kenelm's body. The church also possesses a piece of embroidery that is attributed, in part, to Catherine of Aragon.

Around the west end of the church, towards the west tower door, you'll see what look like pockmarks in the north aisle wall. These holes were made by Parliamentary musket ballls during the Civil War. Nearby Sudeley was held by Royalist sympathisers, and when Roundhead troops took the town in 1643, they brought the Royalist soldiers here and executed them by firing squad.

The main street has an assortment of interesting buildings, including the fine Jacobean old school on Abbey Terrace, as well as two small museums. The Railway Museum is essentially a collection of memorabilia. The Winchcombe Folk & Police Museum in the town hall, next to the Tourist Information Centre, features finds from the Belas Knap neolithic barrow (see page 239). Outside the Museum, you'll see the old village stocks.

▼ Winchcombe, distantly

Gloucestershire has relatively few castles, but Sudeley Castle (see page 217) is superb, as are its spectacular gardens. Visitors can enter the Castle via Vineyard Street.

A number of places worth visiting are close to Winchcombe. These include Sudeley, Belas Knap, Cleeve Common and Toddington. At Toddington, you can board a restored steam train and ride a scenic stretch of the Gloucestershire Warwickshire Railway. You can also take the railway to Cheltenham Racecourse. The remains of Hailes Abbey, just off the Stow road, evoke the romance of the Middle Ages. Nearby Hailes parish church is also of great interest, with its medieval wall paintings, stained glass, 15th-century rood screen and attractive woodwork.

The slopes around Winchcombe were put to a number of uses apart from their obvious role nourishing sheep. The monks from the abbey made wine here. Tobacco was an important crop here for some decades after the Dissolution of the Monasteries, until the government decided that the competition hampered the new colony of Virginia and proscribed the domestic cultivation of tobacco.

TAKE IN SOME HISTORY
Hailes Abbey
english-heritage.org.uk
Near Winchcombe, GL54 5PB
01242 602398 | Usually open 10–5, but check website

Richard, Earl of Cornwall, brother of King Henry III, founded Hailes Abbey in 1246 in thanks for surviving a shipwreck. It housed the Holy Blood of Hailes, claimed to be a phial of Christ's blood, and became a pilgrimage site. After the Dissolution in 1539, when many religious institutions in England were closed or destroyed, the abbey declined precipitiously. King Henry VIII's commissioners even claimed that the Holy Blood of Hailes was actually just duck's blood, and it's difficult to venerate the holy martyrdom of a duck. Now only a few of the cloister arches and foundations remain, though one Cistercian drain still works, 750 years after its installation. They just don't make 'em like that anymore.

VISIT THE MUSEUMS
Winchcombe Folk & Police Museum
sunloch.me.uk/museum
Town Hall, GL54 5LJ | 01242 609151 | Open Apr–Oct Mon–Sat 10–1, 2–4.30 (4 on BH)

This fun folk and local history collection concerns itself with the history of Winchcombe. The police collection includes British and international uniforms and equipment from down the years. There are activity sheets for children and a small shop.

Winchcombe Railway Museum & Gardens

winchcomberailwaymuseum.co.uk
Gloucester Street, GL54 5LX
01242 609305 | Currently closed

Opened in 1968, this is a unique collection of railway artefacts housed in a charming Cotswold garden. Visitors are encouraged to get involved – to operate signals and ring the bells. There's also an ambulance carriage from World War I. Light refreshments and icecreams are available. There's a gift shop, and you can even buy free-range eggs and plants from the garden in season. It's currently closed for refurbishment, but will reopen in 2015.

▼ Cleeve Common

GO BACK IN TIME
Cleeve Common

cleevecommon.org.uk

Neolithic man first cleared the trees from Cleeve Common, the highest point in the Cotswolds, around 6,000 years ago. There's evidence of prehistoric and Roman settlement here. Along with nearby Leckhampton Hill, Cleeve Common has the thickest sections of exposed Jurassic rocks in the country, and is a Site of Special Scientific Interest. The remains of an Iron Age hill-fort, dating from around 500 BC, take up three acres of the common. These remains are arranged in a rough quarter-circle in the northwestern corner of the Common, above the settlement of Nutterswood. There's a cross dyke too, which probably served as a territorial boundary in the Bronze Age.

You may find examples of five species of orchids, including musk orchids, on the common. You might also see glow-worms, roe and muntjac deers, stoats, weasels and hares. Birds including meadow pipits, finches, linnets, yellowhammers, fieldfares, jackdaws, buzzards, kestrels, ring ouzels, stonechats, wheatears and great grey shrikes all call the common home. Cleeve Common is also one of the few locations where the Duke of Burgundy butterfly can still be found in abundance. The views, which extend all the way to the Malverns, can be pretty sensational.

SEE SOME LOCAL CHURCHES

Hailes Church

Off Salter's Lane, opposite Hailes Abbey, GL54 5PB

This tiny church is just down the road from its well-known neighbour, Hailes Abbey. It dates from the 12th century, but was given a thorough overhaul in the 13th century because of its close relationship with the then-new abbey. It remained relatively unaltered until the 17th century, when the church was reorganised to reflect changes in religious thinking; those physical alterations have been swept away in their turn. The stained glass in the east window is 15th-century, and originally came from the nearby abbey. During the 13th century the interior of the church was covered with wall paintings. Many of these survive, albeit in a somewhat faded and fragmentary state. They include a rendition of the popular *St Christopher Carrying the Christ Child* theme, as well as mythical creatures.

St Peter's Church, Winchcombe

Gloucester Street, GL54 5LU

This beautiful town church was built in the first half of the 15th century. It is the only church of its era in Gloucestershire to have a nave arcade of eight bays, and the only church of its era in the county without a chancel arch. These features give the church a wonderful light and airy feeling. They also draw the eye straight down to the east window and the bright masterpiece in stained glass therein. The window depicts Jesus walking on the water, with a faltering St Peter, who is beginning to sink. John Hardman Powell made the window in the late 1800s. A gallery of gurning stone figures array the church exterior, each one different from its fellows.

TAKE A TRAIN RIDE

Gloucestershire Warwickshire Railway

gwsr.com
Toddington Station, GL54 5DT
01242 621405

This line was built between 1900 and 1906 to improve through-services from Birmingham to Bristol and the West Country. It also carried fruit from the farming areas in the Cotswolds and Vale of Evesham to the rest of the nation. It closed in 1960, reopening as a heritage line in 1984. Nowadays visitors can enjoy views of classic Cotswolds countryside and the novelty of a steam train while taking a 25-mile round trip between Laverton and Cheltenham Racecourse.

SADDLE UP

Woodlands Riding Stables

Glebe Farm, Wood Stanway, GL54 5PG | 01386 584 404

Woodlands offers escorted hourly/daily rides for visitors of all ages and abilities, as well as pub and picnic rides and riding holidays. Its all-weather arena is available for hire or lessons.

WATCH THE HILL CLIMB
Prescott Speed Hill Climb
www.prescott-hillclimb.com
GL52 9RD | 01242 673136
Prescott, 2 miles west of
Winchcombe, hosts classic car
and bike weekends on their
steep, hilly course.

GO WALKING
Take a walk from Winchcombe
up to the Jurassic grasslands of
Cleeve Common, the highest
point in the Cotswolds. The
common offers suitably vast
views. Moving on from there to
enigmatic long barrow of Belas
Knap makes for perhaps the
best half-day walk in the whole
region. Hailes Abbey is also
within walking distance.

EAT AND DRINK
Wesley House ◉◉
wesleyhouse.co.uk
High Street, GL54 5LJ
01242 602366
This 15th century merchant's
house gets its name from the
famous Methodist preacher,
who stayed here in the 18th
century. Period features like
beamed ceilings, an inglenook
fireplace and bare stone walls
in the traditional main dining
room have been brought up to
date with contemporary flair.
Expect colour-changing
lighting and big flower displays.
There's also a stylish
conservatory with big views of
the surrounding countryside.
The food is rooted in the 21st
century, bringing together
interesting combinations of
ingredients with aplomb.

Wesley House Wine
Bar & Grill ◉
wesleyhouse.co.uk
High Street, GL54 5LJ
01242 602366
Historic Wesley House – built
for a merchant back in the 15th
century – has a few tricks up its
sleeve these days. Not the least
of these is its Wine Bar & Grill,
which is a delightful 21st-
century interloper amid all this
antiquity. Sip on a cocktail and
tuck into some sparky
brasserie-style food. With
mirror-balls, purple lighting,
and zebra-skin barstools,
there's no lack of contemporary
swagger about the place.

The White Hart Inn
and Restaurant
whitehartwinchcombe.co.uk
High Street, GL54 5LJ
01242 602359
Popular with walkers, this
16th-century inn is an
appealing place to unwind.
There's a wine shop, as well as
a cosy bar and an intimate
restaurant. Though the Hart
prides itself on its amazing
selection of wines, there are
also plenty of real ales. Enjoy
simple and unpretentious
British food, made from locally
sourced ingredients.

Juri's Tearoom
juris-tearoom.co.uk
High Street, GL54 5LJ
01242 602469
This award-winning tea room
is run by a Japanese family
dedicated to maintaining high
standards. The traditional

stone building is Grade II-listed and located on the High Street. The food is hand-made on premises, using local, free-range or organic ingredients whenever possible. Juri's freshly made cakes and other treats are first class.

> **PLACES NEARBY**

Nowhere nearby has as many attractions as Winchcombe. Sudeley Castle (see page 217) is practically part of Winchcombe, and then there's Cleeve Common and Belas Knap. The Guitings (see page 133), to the southeast, aren't that far off. Cheltenham (see page 88) is to the west.

Belas Knap Long Barrow
english-heritage.org.uk
Cleeve Hill | 0117 9750 700
Open any reasonable time

Dating from approximately 3800 BC, the remains of 31 bodies were found in Belas Knap Long Barrow when it was excavated in the 19th century, along with some Roman pottery – we may not have been the first visitors here. Particularly notable for its elaborate 'false entrance', the four-chambered burial cairn has been restored several times.

> The Windrush Valley

The Windrush rises near Taddington, south of Snowshill. It wanders through several villages, widening beyond Bourton and continuing north to join the Thames. The Windrush Way, a pleasant walking path, goes from Winchcombe to Bourton-on-the-Water.

Sherborne, on a tributary of the Windrush, has been part of the Sherborne estate for centuries. Before that, the Abbots of Winchcombe owned the land, and their sheep were sheared on the banks of the river every summer. A cottage at the eastern end of the village of Sherborne boasts a complete Norman doorway, which was presumably removed from an earlier incarnation of the local church. John 'Crump' Dutton, Royalist hunchback and former owner of Sherborne House, allegedly still haunts the local manor. The house was rebuilt in the 19th century. Occupied by the military during World War II, it then became a boarding school. It now belongs to the National Trust. Although it is not open to the public, there are waymarked walks through the nearby woods and parkland. Lodge Park, an elaborate grandstand built in the 17th century for deer-coursing, is open to the public.

The next village to the east of Sherborne is **Windrush**. Windrush's church is topped with a fine Perpendicular tower. Its magnificent Norman south doorway is surrounded by beakheads, bird-like grotesques with mysterious origins. Then come the Barringtons, first Little, then Great. The Barringtons

▲ Naunton

were once renowned for their stone quarries, and for the Kempsters and the Strongs, the local families of masons who worked them. No evidence remains of these old subterranean quarries. **Little Barrington** is a quiet village, with cottages prettily clustered about its village green. The nearby Fox Inn is next to a bridge that crosses the river. It was built by local master mason Thomas Strong, the principal contractor of St Paul's. Christopher Wren regarded Strong as the leading builder of his day. **Great Barrington**, to the north, has a Norman church with some fine monuments by 18th-century sculptor Joseph Nollekens. To the east of the church you'll find the country house and landscaped gardens of Barrington Park.

East of Great Barrington lies **Taynton**, another village that once supplied London and Oxford with its famous prime building stone. Taken from open-cast quarries, the stone was transported overland to Lechlade, and thence by barge to London. Beyond Taynton is **Burford**, and then **Widford church**. The 13th-century church is all that remains of a once-thriving village that simply disappeared, probably as a result of the plague. Built on the site of a Roman villa, the church stands small and solitary on a raised mound overlooking the river. Its box pews and wall paintings, which date from the 14th century, are worth a look.

A short way from Widford, you'll find **Swinbrook**. The village is associated with the Mitford family, and the Mitford family's share in the public consciousness now pretty much begins and ends with Lord Redesdale's five daughters: Nancy, Diana, Unity, Jessica and Deborah. Unity became a close friend of Adolf Hitler; Diana married Sir Oswald Moseley, leader of the British Union of Fascists; Deborah became the Duchess of Devonshire; and Nancy and Jessica (the communist) became well-known writers. There was also a sixth daughter, who the Times called 'Pamela the unobtrusive poultry connoisseur', but for some reason people tend to forget about poor Pamela. Nancy, Pamela, Diana and Unity are buried in the graveyard of the church, which also contains the wonderful triple–Decker monument to the Fettiplace family, who once owned a mansion here. Across the river to the southeast is **Asthall**, a charming village with a fine Elizabethan manor. Exhibitions of stone sculpture are held in the gardens for a short period every other summer.

TAKE IN SOME HISTORY
Asthall Manor
asthallmanor.com
Burford, OX18 4HW
01993 824319
The Mitford sisters, brother Tom and parents Lord and Lady Redesdale lived here between 1919 and 1926. and Asthall Manor turns up as Alconleigh in Nancy's *The Pursuit of Love*.
The manor house is private, 'but the people who live here like to share parts of it from time to time,' says the website, via specific entertainments such as the sculpture displays. Check their website for events and open days.

GET OUTDOORS
Lodge Park and Sherborne Park Estate
nationaltrust.org.uk
Lodge Park, Aldsworth, GL54 3PP

01451 844130 | Open Mar–end Oct, Fri–Sun, 11–4, but occasionally closed for weddings; Sherborne Estate open dawn till dusk
National Trust-owned Sherborne Park is a working estate. It has an abundance of wildlife, from fallow and roe deer to badgers and foxes. The 18th-century water meadows are home to otters and water voles. Around the Pleasure Ground, there are child–friendly orienteering and sculpture trails, which start at Ewe Pen Barn. Parking is available at Northfield Barn. If you and yours enjoyed the sculpture trail, there's another children's quiz/trail at nearby Lodge Park, a 17th-century grandstand also owned by the National Trust. Lodge Park also offers picnic facilities and refreshments.

SEE A LOCAL CHURCH
St Mary's Church
Pebble Court, west side of
Swinbrook village, Windrush
Valley, OX18 4DY

Land mines, eh? Pesky things. St Mary's church has a curious 19th-century tower and an enormous east window, which was blown out by an exploding land mine in 1940. St Mary's is set in an attractive landscape, but nothing about the church's unassuming exterior hints at the extraordinary richness of the 17th-century monuments inside. These monuments depict six members of the Fettiplace family, which was one of the great families of Oxfordshire until they died out in the late 18th century. The highly stylised marble effigies are laid out on shelves. Each reclines rather raffishly on one elbow. There are also brasses commemorating other Fettiplaces. The only Mitford son, Tom, who was killed in Burma in 1945, has a memorial inside the church.

▶ Witney

Another Windrush town, Witney remains famous for its blankets. This mini-industry somehow managed to survive the collapse of the Cotswold woollen industry after the Industrial Revolution. The Market Square is the centre of the town. It contains an unusual Butter Cross, refurbished in the 19th century, and a 17th-century Town Hall. Beyond, near a green, you'll find the 13th-century church, complete with its massive tower. The green is also near a fine collection of houses that date from the 17th and 18th centuries. The town's museum is in Gloucester Court Mews, on the High Street. On the High Street you'll also see the Blanket Hall. The Witney Blanket Weavers Company, a group of prosperous weavers who were granted their charter in 1711, built it in 1721.

The Cogges Manor Farm Museum is just southeast of Witney, and is well-signposted from the A40. The museum reflects farming life in Victorian times. Among the machinery and livestock, you will find a working kitchen and dairy.

VISIT THE MUSEUM
Witney and District Museum
witney.net
Gloucester Court Mews, High Street,
Witney, OX28 6JF | 01993 775915
Open Apr–Oct, Wed–Sat 10–4
Sun (phone for information)

This large ground-floor gallery details the history of Witney over the last 1000 years, including the history of local industries such as Witney blanket manufacture, glove making and brewing. Exhibits include the town's old stocks. The Museum is housed in a traditional Cotswold stone building.

It was once the home of Malachi Bartlett, the proprietor of a well-known local building firm. The west end of the building was once used as a smithy, while the upper floor was a 'laths store'.

ENTERTAIN THE FAMILY
Cogges
cogges.org.uk
Church Lane, Cogges, OX28 3LA
01993 772602 | Open Apr–Oct,
Tue–Sun & BH Mon 10.30–5
(Manor house only open wknds & BH)

Cogges is a manor house dating from the 13th century. Today it has a walled garden, a moat and islands to explore, a castle-style adventure playground, a zip wire, and a cafe. There are also farmyard animals, including a Shetland pony, pygmy goats, pigs, rabbits, quails and Cotswold sheep. The manor house itself is only open on weekends and bank holidays.

PLAY A ROUND
Witney Lakes Golf Course
witney-lakes.co.uk
Downs Road, OX29 0SY
01993 893011
Five large lakes come into play on eight holes. This excellent test of golf will have you using every club in the bag.

EAT AND DRINK
The Fleece
fleecewitney.co.uk
11 Church Green, Witney,
OX28 4AZ | 01993 892270

Overlooking the village's beautiful church green in the heart of picturesque Witney, this fine Georgian building was once the home of Clinch's brewery. Nowadays, it serves food and drink from lunch through to dinner. Its well-kept ales are a big draw.

The Horseshoes
horseshoeswitney.co.uk
78 Corn Street, Witney, OX28 6BS
01993 703086
Built of Cotswold stone, this Grade II listed building sits on Witney's original main street. A traditional family-run pub,

▼ The Blanket Hall clock

it has a charming and stylish interior, with stone walls, low ceilings, wood and flagstone floors, and blazing log fires in winter. Its impressive selection of ales includes Ringwood Fortyniner and Wychwood Hobgoblin.

The Restaurant at Witney Lakes Resort ◉

witney-lakes.co.uk
Downs Road, Witney, OX29 0SY
01993 893012

This expansive resort venue in David Cameron's constituency has all eventualities nailed. It caters for business conferences and weddings, looks after golfers and fitness fanatics, and has a thoroughly modern restaurant, replete with bare oak tables, tea-lights, floral decorations and a large central bar. There are wine evenings, sponsored by champagne houses, and Thursday is Foodie Night, when all the culinary stops are pulled out. The cooking is mostly modern brasserie fare, and highly reliable.

▶ PLACES NEARBY

Witney's halfway between Oxford (see page 161) and Burford (see page 78), which likes to call itself the 'gateway to the Cotswolds'. Cute Minster Lovell (see page 149) is also in between these two. There's a church just on its outskirts that's worth visiting. The village of **North Leigh** is about 3 miles northeast and has a fine Roman villa and church.

North Leigh Roman Villa

english-heritage.org.uk
2 miles north of North Leigh,
off A4095 | 0870 3331181
Check website for opening hours

The remains of this Roman villa are located by a loop of the River Evenlode. This was a courtyard-style villa, with a range of buildings on the three sides of a rectangle and a corridor and gatehouse on the fourth side. The villa dates to the early 4th century, but finds of Iron Age pottery suggest earlier occupation on the site. Historians think that the majority of homes like this were built for leading members of the strata of the native population that had been co-opted into the empire, rather than having been constructed as residences for Roman officials. Nothing says 'I side with Rome rather than my own people, and also keep up with the Marcus Aurelius Joneses' quite like this impressive mosaic floor. The villa was abandoned when the Romans withdrew from Britain in the 5th century.

St Mary's Church

Church Road, North Leigh,
OX29 6TX

The tall Saxon tower of St Mary's was not always at the west end of the church. The original nave, to the west of a central tower, was dismantled in the late Norman period. The Norman chancel became the nave, and a new chancel was added in the late 13th century.

The interior of the church has many fascinating features. A dramatic, highly coloured Doom painting over the chancel arch has survived from the 15th century. Below it is an unusual and rather heavy Victorian stone screen. The Perrott aisle, on the north wall, is an Italianate memorial chapel from about 1700. Don't overlook the tiny Wilcote chantry chapel, a superb example of mid-15th-century Perpendicular Gothic design, with fan vaulting, a beautiful east window with original glass, and fine alabaster effigies. It is among the treasures of Oxfordshire.

St Kenelm
Old Minster, OX29 0RR
Beautifully sited on the River Windrush, St Kenelm's stands next to the dramatic ruined manor house of the Lovells, who rebuilt the original priory church (or minster) in the mid-15th century. Soon afterwards, this great family made its exit from history, Francis Lovell, the ninth Baron, henchman and lifelong friend of Richard III, disappeared in 1487. The crown seized the Lovell lands, and he was never heard of again.

The cruciform church has scarcely been altered since it was built. The central tower rests on four great pillars. A fan vault spans the crossing. A well-preserved Lovell tomb with a fine alabaster effigy and colourful heraldic symbols occupies the south transept.

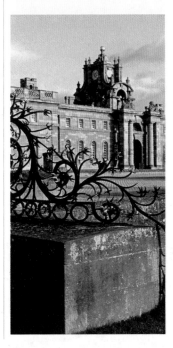

▶ Woodstock & Blenheim Palace

Woodstock is a small town of some charm just to the north of Oxford, not to be confused with the town in upstate New York that hosted the legendary 1969 music festival. Oxfordshire's Woodstock is home to one of the greatest palaces in England, World Heritage-listed Blenheim, which is most famous as the ancestral home of the Churchill family.

Woodstock has enjoyed royal patronage since Henry I built a park and hunting lodge here in the 12th century. His grandson, Henry II, preferred to use it to entertain his mistress, the fair Rosamund. The lodge became a palace, and the town grew around it. Geoffrey Chaucer, the medieval author of *The Canterbury Tales* and *Troilus And Criseyde* (which, be honest, you haven't read), may have lived in Woodstock for some years. In later centuries the town was noted for its glove-making.

▼ Blenheim Palace seen across the lake

The story of Blenheim Palace began when John Churchill married the future Queen Anne's lady-in-waiting and confidante, Sarah Jennings. As soon as Anne became queen in 1702, she gave Churchill the title of Duke of Marlborough. His career was a triumph, with a string of spectacular victories in the War of Spanish Succession. The first victory saw England defeat France and Bavaria in the Battle of Blenheim in 1704. In recognition of the nation's gratitude, Anne gave him the manor of Woodstock and the money to build a grand house there.

John Vanbrugh, the architect, designed a main block surmounted by four towers. Two wings projected off the main block, which earned it the nickname 'Blenheim Castle.' Its Baroque extravagance was brilliantly humanised by the beauty of the 2,000-acre park, which was landscaped by the ubiquitous 'Capability' Brown.

Blenheim's facade is a magnificent sight. From the central block, curved walls lead to the east and west wings. As you enter through the east gateway, look out for the carvings of the English lion strangling the French cockerel. Inside, there is another reference to the Battle of Blenheim on the 67 foot-high ceiling of the marbled Great Hall, in the oval painting by Sir James Thornhill. In 1874, in a small, plain bedroom, American expat Jennie Churchill gave birth to a son, Winston. Winston's father, Lord Randolph Spencer-Churchill, briefly became Chancellor of the Exchequer, but his son was to achieve far greater fame through his dogged leadership of Britain during World War II. A nearby exhibition about Winston includes a set of his young curls and a maroon velvet boiler suit that he wore during the war, together with some of his oil paintings. Winston Churchill was premature (which may well be Tactful for 'born less than eight months after his parents' marriage'), and born at Blenheim by chance. He nevertheless maintained a great affection for the place, and is buried at nearby Bladon churchyard.

A prodigious display of ill feeling, in keeping with the magnitude of the undertaking, sadly accompanied the construction of Blenheim Palace. The design is the work of Sir John Vanbrugh, who also built Castle Howard in Yorkshire. With Sarah Jennings, the wife of the Duke of Marlborough, Vanbrugh found himself in the hands of a demanding employer. Her capricious nature finally led him to resign the commission in 1716, fortunately after most of the work had been accomplished. Although Nicholas Hawksmoor oversaw the final stages of construction, it was largely the Duchess' tenacity that ensured the completion of the building after the death of her husband. Not only did she find the money when Queen

▶ Blenheim Palace

Anne's government failed to stump up all the promised funds, she was also responsible for much of the interior design.

Today the palace is full of gilt and grandeur, with carvings by Grinling Gibbons, Flemish tapestries illustrating the martial valour of the duke, and a fine collection of paintings. In the Great Hall you'll find a magnificent ceiling painted by Sir James Thornhill, while the Long Library is one of the longest single rooms in Britain. The first duke and duchess are buried in the chapel, which was built by Hawksmoor in 1731. The room where Sir Winston Churchill was born is the focal point of an exhibition devoted to his life.

The beauty of the relationship between the palace and its grounds can best be appreciated by walking from the town and entering the park through Nicholas Hawksmoor's Triumphal Arch. The arch surmounts what is also known as the Woodstock Gate, just off Park Street. Walk around the palace, cross the Grand Bridge and explore the views as you walk to the Column of Victory, then enjoy the rose garden and the world's largest symbolic hedge maze, designed to mimic the architecture of the palace itself. There's also a butterfly house and a children's playground. The park also serves as a venue for events such as craft fairs, horse trials and even jousting throughout the year.

The town of Woodstock itself is worthy of exploration, too. The streets that cluster around the 18th-century Town Hall are lined with a fine assortment of houses and inns from the 17th and 18th centuries. The most famous is the ivy-clad Bear Hotel, which dates back to the 13th century. St Mary Magdalen Church is set in a charming churchyard, and is surmounted by a classical tower from 1785. The original Norman south doorway is particularly fine. Opposite the church, in Park Street, is Fletcher's House. Originally built for a 17th-century merchant, it now houses the Oxfordshire Museum. Its galleries and exhibitions about the history and traditions of Oxfordshire cover three floors. The museum has a convenient small cafe and bookshop, and if you're looking for something to do with fussy children, the town stocks are preserved at the museum entrance. This elegant townhouse also has pleasant gardens.

TAKE IN SOME HISTORY
Blenheim Palace
See highlight panel overleaf

VISIT THE MUSEUM
Oxfordshire Museum
oxfordshire.gov.uk
Fletcher's House, Park Street,
OX20 1SN | 01993 814110
Open all year, Tue–Sat 10–5,
Sun 2–5, open BH Mon,
please check for opening hours
Situated in the heart of
Woodstock and set in attractive
gardens, Fletcher's House
provides a home for the county
museum. The museum is the
product of an award-winning
redevelopment. It celebrates
Oxfordshire, and features
collections on local history, art,
archaeology, landscape and
wildlife, as well as a gallery
exploring the county's
innovative industries, from
nuclear power to
nanotechnology. Interactive
exhibits offer new learning
experiences for visitors of all
ages. The museum's purpose-
built Garden Gallery houses
a variety of touring
exhibitions of regional and
national interest. A display
of dinosaur footprints from
Ardley Quarry and a replica
megalosaurus are located in
the walled garden.

EAT AND DRINK
The King's Arms Hotel
kings-hotel-woodstock.co.uk
19 Market Street, OX20 1SU
01993 813636
The white-painted, Georgian
Kings' Arms fits in perfectly in
well-to-do Woodstock, with its
air of distinction and its
handsome country décor. It's
only a short stroll from the
splendour of Blenheim Palace,
after all. For all its period
charm, there's a good deal of
contemporary polish to the
place. This is not least
noticeable in the Atrium
Restaurant, with its sharp,
modern good looks: think
chunky wooden tables and
black high-backed chairs on a

▶ Blenheim Palace

blenheimpalace.com

Woodstock, OX20 1PP | 0800 849 6500 | Open daily; Palace, Park & Gardens mid-Feb–mid-Dec (ex Mon–Tue in Nov & Dec) 10.30–5.30 (last admission 4.45); Park daily all year 9–6 (last admission 4.45 or dusk)

Home of the Dukes of Marlborough and birthplace of Sir Winston Churchill, Blenheim Palace is an English Baroque masterpiece. Fine furniture, sculpture, paintings and tapestries are set in magnificent gilded staterooms that overlook sweeping lawns and formal gardens. 'Capability' Brown landscaped the 2,100-acre park, which is open to visitors and offers pleasant walks and beautiful views. A permanent exhibit called 'Blenheim Palace: The Untold Story' explores the lives of those who have lived here through the eyes of the servants. Check ahead for details of the full event programme throughout the year. It might include a Jousting Tournament and the Battle Proms.

black-and-white chequerboard floor, plus original artworks and huge antique mirrors with rococo frames. The menu is a happy mix of old and new, too, with lots of gently modish things to choose from.

The Feathers Hotel ◎◎
feathers.co.uk
Market Street, OX20 1SX
01993 812291

A feature in Woodstock since the 17th century, The Feathers carries itself in a thoroughly modish manner these days. This is boutique hotel territory, and The Feathers blends the indisputable traditional charms of the old building it occupies with a stylish contemporary sheen. The dining room, which is split into two on quiet nights, has crisp white linen-clad tables, with silver cutlery and sparkling glassware. It's a suitable setting for the refined modern British cooking produced by the team in the kitchen. Much is made of seasonality and locality. If you're up to it, there's the 'gin experience' tasting menu, where a different gin is paired with, or appears in, each of the seven courses.

Macdonald Bear Hotel ◎◎
thebearwoodstock.co.uk
Park Street, OX20 1SZ
01993 811124

Woodstock is certainly not without attractive old buildings, and this creeper-covered hotel is one of them. Inside, the great age of the property can be seen in the beams, stone walls and fireplaces of the traditional-looking dining rooms. Unlike that other McDonald, this Macdonald's beef is naturally reared in Scotland and aged for a minimum of 21 days.

Harriet's Cake Shop and Tea Rooms
20 High Street, OX20 1TF
01993 811231

Charm oozes from this quaint tea room. Its interior of wood panelling and exposed stone, complete with original fireplaces, is complemented by a vintage bread oven. Waitresses dressed in traditional black and white uniforms serve the tea. Wherever possible, the ingredients used in Harriet's various foodstuffs have a Cotswold origin. The shop offers, for example, special cream teas that make use of Cotswold clotted cream and honey sourced from a local farmer. The shop itself sells a fascinating range of teapots, homemade preserves, cakes and confectionery.

▶ PLACES NEARBY

As far as the Cotswolds are concerned, Woodstock is stuck out on a bit of a limb. But Witney's (see page 242) keeping a friendly eye on it from the southwest, and if Woodstock really gets lonely, Oxford (see page 161) is only eight miles to the south.

▶ Wotton-under-Edge

Wotton-under-Edge is one of the most interesting small towns in the Cotswolds. Tucked comfortably under the escarpment (there's a clue in the name), it feels pleasingly unblemished by the passage of time. However the old market town was very much blemished in the 13th century, when King John, enemy of the Berkeley family, burnt it to the ground. Rude.

In the Middle Ages, Wotton was an important wool town. After being rebuilt, it did well in cloth trade of the 17th and 18th centuries. Because transportation to other textile industry centres, such as Stroud and Dursley, was easier, Wotton didn't become over-industrialised. This means that its town centre has gone more or less untouched since the early Victorian period. A number of Wotton's late medieval, Jacobean and Regency houses are still in use today. Much-loved 20th-and-21st-century poet Ursula Askham Fanthorpe lived in the town, and wrote such poems as 'Wotton Walks' and 'Tyndale in Darkness'.

In the Middle Ages, markets and fairs were held at the Chipping, part of which is now a car park. The old fire station in the Chipping is now an interesting heritage centre, which shows the history of the town and the surrounding area. From the Chipping, Market Street leads to a junction with High Street and Long Street, past the Star Inn and the Town Hall.

On the corner of Market Street and High Street you'll find the smart, red-brick Tolsey House. It was granted to the town in 1595 by the Countess of Warwick to serve as a market court. The old police station overlooks the High Street from the other side of Haw Street.

Long Street, the main shopping thoroughfare, is lined with buildings in an array of architectural styles. A stroll along Orchard Street on the right will bring you to the school where Isaac Pitman, inventor of shorthand, taught. At the end of Long Street, turn left into Church Street, opposite the 17th-century Falcon Inn. On the right you'll see a row of delightful almshouses, which were built in 1638. If you like, go into the courtyard and visit the little chapel, lit by a pair of depictive stained-glass windows.

Church Street then crosses over Old Town to Culverhay. This brings you to the 18th-century Church Hall, former home to the Blue Coat Church of England School. The Church Hall is also the entrance to the parish church, which was consecrated in 1283. Most of the church, however, dates from the 15th century. Beyond the churchyard is Potters Pond. There you'll find the Ram Inn. Dating from before 1350, the Ram is thought to be both the oldest surviving building in the area and *very* haunted.

The surrounding area is excellent for walking in. The Cotswold Edge, especially the Tyndale Monument (see page 118), provide epic views. Just over a mile to the east at Ozleworth stands Newark Park. This unusual 16th-century house was built as a hunting lodge, and offers magnificent views across the countryside.

TAKE IN SOME HISTORY
Newark Park
nationaltrust.org.uk
Ozleworth, Wotton-under-Edge,
GL12 7PZ | 01793 817666
Open Mar–end Oct, 11–5; closed
Mon–Tue and Jan; very limited
opening Nov–Dec

This corner of south Gloucestershire can feel surprisingly remote. Sometimes barely a sign of modern life is visible amid the overgrown valleys and tumbling combes. Newark Park looks down into the Ozleworth valley and out onto Somerset's Mendips. Founded by an influential courtier to Henry VIII, Newark Park is a place of architectural intrigue, quaint gardens and sprawling parkland. The estate's prosperity wasn't permanent, and some time later it almost collapsed into financial ruin. Fortunately, it was dramatically rescued by a Texan architect who became the Trust's first tenant in 1970.

VISIT THE HERITAGE CENTRE
Wotton-under-Edge Heritage Centre
wottonheritage.com
The Chipping, Wotton-under-Edge,
GL12 7AD | 01453 521541
Open Tue, Thu–Fri 11–1 and 2–4,
Sat 10–1, Apr–end Oct Sun 2.30–5

The Centre holds three to four exhibitions a year, which display interesting items from local and sometimes national history. In addition, there's a small library and archive. The centre also arranges nine lectures a year.

PLAY A ROUND
Cotswold Edge Golf Club
cotswoldedgegolfclub.org.uk
Upper Rushmire, GL12 7PT
01453 844167

This meadowland course is situated in a quiet Cotswold valley, which offers magnificent views. The course's first half is flat and open, while its second half is more varied.

EAT AND DRINK
Tortworth Court Four Pillars Hotel ⊛
four-pillars.co.uk
Tortworth, GL12 8HH
01454 263000

This impressive, listed Victorian house was built in the middle of the 19th century for the 2nd Earl of Ducie. It's a cracking example of Victorian architecture, with vast gables and soaring chimneys: ideal material, then, for the country-house hotel treatment. With 30 acres of lovely gardens, including its own arboretum, spa facilities and a range of restaurants and bars, there's plenty to admire here. The house is magnificent inside, too, and splendidly proportioned. Moreton's, the main dining room, with its ornately carved panels and huge mullioned windows, was originally the library. The brasserie-style menu might see you start with a tartlet of red onion and Jerusalem artichoke with a pesto dressing, or fresh mussels and bacon cooked in Stowford Press cider. Main courses are in a similar vein. Thai vegetable curry sits alongside braised duck leg with blackberry and red wine sauce.

▶ **PLACES NEARBY**

North Nibley

Notable for the 111-foot Tyndale Monument up on the limestone edge above the village and some big views across the vale from the same spot. Local man William Tyndale translated the Bible into English, which challenged the hegemony of the Roman Catholic Church and English Laws. Predictably, in retrospect, he was convicted of heresy, executed, then burnt at the stake in 1536. More cheerily, North Nibley means *the clearing near the peak*.

Kingswood is to the south and intriguing Newark Park (see page 253) is to the east.

▶ North Nibley

A49

wens
Cross

Ross-on-Wye

Hartpury

HEREFORDSHIRE

A4131

Pencraig

A40

Huntley

Whitchurch

A40

Mitcheldean

Symonds
Yat

Upper Lydbrook

A4136

260

A48

Monmouth

Cinderford

A4151

Newnham

Hardwicke

Coleford

FOREST

Redbrook

OF

St Augustine's
Farm

A466

DEAN

Whitminster

M5

Trellech

St
Briavels

Blakeney

A48

Frampton
on Severn

Lydney

**Slimbridge
Wetland Centre**

Stonehouse

Tintern
Parva

Sharpness

Slimbridge

Frocester

St
Arvans

River Severn

A38

Woodch
Ma

Coaley Peak

Chepstow

A48

Berkeley

Dr Jenner's
House

Cam

Uley Long Barrow

Uley
Bury

Ov

M48

Stinchcombe
Hill

Ul

**Berkeley
Castle**

Dursley

M4

Woodford

North
Nibley

Matara Gar
of Wellb

Falfield

**Wotton-
under-Edge**

Corswold Way

Ne
Par

Thornbury

Kingswood

Alveston

Wickwar

Hawkesbury
Upton

Almondsbury

Horton
Court

M49

M5

A39

**Little
Sodbury**

Badm

Avonmouth

A4174

**Chipping
Sodbury**

**Old
Sodbury**

A4

M32

M4

A369

**Dyrham
Park**

Pucklechurch

A46

Marshfield

BRISTOL

Cold
Ashton

Long
Ashton

River Avon

Bitton

A370

A38

Keynsham

Swainswick

A4

A431

A36

BATH

Holt Heath

A4133 Droit

A449

Clifton upon Teme

Fernhill Heath

A443

Bredenbury

Knightwick

WORCESTER

Bromyard

A44

A4440

Leigh Sinton

Powick

Stoul

Stoke Lacy

Bishop's Frome

A449

WORCESTERSH

A465

A4103

Newtown

West Malvern

Great Malvern

HEREFORDSHIRE

Malvern Wells

Upton upon Severn

A4104

A438

Ledbury

Ripple

A4172

A438

Much Marcle

Pendock

Tewkesbury ★

A449

Dymock

M50

★ Deer

Newent

Coombe Hill

GLOUCESTE

A417

A38

Hartpury

Ross-on-Wye

● Nature in Art

A40

Longford

A40

Mitcheldean

Huntley

★ GLOUCESTER

Upper Lydbrook

Brockworth

Cooper's Hill

A4136

A48

Cinderford

A4151

256

Hardwicke

Prinknash ★

Wit R.

Newnham

● St Augustine's Farm

Painswick Beacon

A4173

Sheeps

FOREST

Whitminster

★ Painswick

OF

Frampton on Severn

● Slad

DEAN

M5

Blakeney

A48

Slimbridge Wetland Centre ★

Stonehouse

Stroud

Bis

Lydney

Selsley

Rodborough Common

River Severn

Index, themed

Page numbers in **bold** refer to main text entries

Index, places

Page numbers in **bold** refer to main entries; page numbers in *italics* refer to maps

The Automobile Association wishes to thank the following photographers and organisations for their assistance in the preparation of this book.

Abbreviations for the picture credits are as follows – (t) top; (m) middle; (b) bottom; (l) left; (r) right; (c) centre; (AA) AA World Travel Library.

Trade Cover: Steve Vidler/Alamy
SS Cover: AA/D Hall

4tl AA/S Day; 4tr AA/H Palmer; 4b AA/J Tims; 5r AA/D Hall; 5bl AA/J Tims; 8–9 AA/S Day; 11 AA/H Palmer; 12t AA/H Palmer; 12b Matthew Barnes/Alamy; 13bl Courtesy of Pitt Rivers Museum, University of Oxford; 13tl The National Trust Photolibrary/Alamy; 13mr Courtesy of Cotswold Wildlife Park; 14t AA/C Jones; 14m Courtesy of Birdland; 14b AA/J Tims; 15t AA/M Moody; 15m Courtesy of Cotswold Motoring Museum & Toy Collection; 15b AA/K Doran; 16 AA/D Hall; 18 AA/S Day; 19 AA/H Palmer; 20 AA/S Day; 21 AA/C Jones; 22 AA/D Hall; 23 AA/D Hall; 24 AA/S Day; 24–5 AA/T Souter; 27 AA/S Day; 29 AA/S Day; 31 AA/F Stephenson; 32 AA/P Baker; 35 AA/K Doran; 36 Martin Beddall/Alamy; 36–7 Colin Underhill/Alamy; 39 AA/R Rainford; 40 Tim Gainey/Alamy; 41 AA/K Doran; 42 AA/D Hall; 43 AA/S Day; 44 Simon Reddy/Alamy; 45 Stephen Shepherd/Alamy; 47 AA/J Tims; 50 AA/S Day; 53 AA/F Stephenson; 54 AA/S Day; 56 AA/A Burton; 58–9 AA/M Moody; 61 Homer Sykes/Alamy; 64 AA/D Hall; 66 AA/D Hall; 69 AA/D Hall; 70 AA/D Hall; 73 Courtesy of Cotswold Motoring Museum & Toy Collection; 74 Courtesy of Birdland; 79 AA/S Day; 81 Courtesy of Cotswold Wildlife Park; 86 dk/Alamy; 91 AA/R Duke; 92 AA/R Duke; 98 AA/S Day; 104 AA/T Souter; 107 AA/R Duke; 112 AA/S Day; 116 AA/S Day; 119 AA/S Day; 126 AA/H Palmer; 131 AA/H Palmer; 134 AA/C Sawyer; 135 AA/S Day; 136 AA/S Day; 139 AA/D Hall; 141 AA/D Hall; 145 AA/K Doran; 149 AA/S Day; 155 AA/S Day; 161 AA/J Tims; 165 AA/J Tims; 167 AA/J Tims; 168 Courtesy of Pitt Rivers Museum, University of Oxford; 171 AA/J Tims; 172 AA/J Tims; 176 AA/S Day; 183 AA/K Doran; 186 AA/R Duke; 194 AA/A Lawson; 198 AA/M Moody; 201 AA/H Palmer; 203 AA/H Palmer; 204 AA/J Wyand; 207 Matthew Barnes/Alamy; 209 AA/M Moody; 211 AA/D Hall; 212 AA/K Doran; 217 AA/F Stephenson; 220 AA/M Moody; 223 AA/D Hall; 225 AA/F Stephenson; 226 AA/D Hall; 231 AA/S Day; 234 AA/D Hall; 236 AA/D Hall; 240 AA/S Day; 243 AA/S Day; 245 AA/M Birkitt; 246 AA/C Jones; 249 AA/H Palmer; 250 AA/C Jones; 254–5 Cotswolds Photo Library/Alamy

Every effort has been made to trace the copyright holders, and we apologise in advance for any unintentional omissions or errors. We would be pleased to apply any corrections in any following edition of this publication.

Series editor: Rebecca Needes   Indexer: Marie Lorimer
Author: Damian Hall   Designer: Tracey Freestone
Copy editor: Erin Horak   Digital imaging & repro: Ian Little
Proofreader: Jackie Bates   Art director: James Tims

Additional writing by other AA contributors. *Lore of the Land* feature by Ruth Binney. Some content may appear in other AA books and publications.

Has something changed? Email us at travelguides@theaa.com.

'WE KNOW BRITAIN'

The AA was founded in 1905 as a body initially intended to help motorists avoid police speed traps. As motoring became more popular, so did we, and our activities have continued to expand into a great variety of areas.

The first edition of the AA Members' Handbook appeared in 1908. Due to the difficulty many motorists were having finding reasonable meals and accommodation while on the road, the AA introduced a new scheme to include listings for 'about one thousand of the leading hotels' in the second edition in 1909. As a result the AA has been recommending and assessing establishments for over a century, and each year our professional inspectors anonymously visit and rate thousands of hotels, restaurants, guest accommodations and campsites. We are relied upon for our trustworthy and objective star, Rosette and Pennant ratings systems, which you will see used in this guide to denote AA-inspected restaurants and campsites.

In 1912 we published our first handwritten routes and our atlas of town plans, and in 1925 our classic touring guide, *The AA Road Book of England and Wales* appeared. Together, our accurate mapping and in-depth knowledge of places to visit were to set the benchmark for British travel publishing.

Since the 1990s we have dramatically expanded our publishing activities, producing high quality atlases, maps, walking and travel guides for the UK and the rest of the world. In this new series of regional travel guides we are drawing on over a hundred years of experience to bring you the very best of Britain.